Skardon changed his aim to cover White's withdrawal, but it was already too late. He caught the words: "Geoff, Geoff, I'm hit!"

Oblivious of his own safety, Skardon ran to White, diving beside him and pulling him behind the big tree, which afforded protection though fire still poured in from the flanks. Skardon saw blood spurting from White's upper thigh and knew that a tourniquet must be applied within seconds.

Expecting a hand-grenade at any moment, he grabbed White's collar and with all his strength dragged him a full ten yards to a shallow depression. As the firing continued to break down branches and thud into the earth around them, Skardon said:

"I think we've had it, Chalky."

"I know, skipper, thanks for trying."

SAS

Secret War in South-East Asia

22 Special Air Service Regiment in the Borneo Campaign, 1963–1966

Peter Dickens

IVY BOOKS • NEW YORK

Ivy Books
Published by Ballantine Books
Copyright © 1983 by Peter Dickens and Lionel Leventhal Ltd.

SAS: Secret War in South-East Asia was first published in 1983 (Arms & Armour Press) as SAS: The Jungle Frontier and is reproduced now exactly as the original edition, complete and unabridged.

ISBN 0-8041-0833-1

This edition published by arrangement with Greenhill Books.

Manufactured in the United States of America

First Ballantine Books Edition: September 1992

*"We are the pilgrims, Master; we shall go
Always a little further. . . ."*

(J. E. Flecker)

(Inscription on The Clock, Bradbury Lines, Hereford)

CONTENTS

PREFACE

It was the SAS who suggested that I, a sailor, might like to write this book. They presumably had a reason because they are a cool, calculating lot who never do anything without one. In this case it might have been that they were increasingly vexed at being thought of as thugs, which their habitual tight-lipped security tended to encourage, and calculated that, being predisposed to admire and sympathize, I might do something to buff up their image. I could, of course, have given no understanding as to that, having a code of sorts and knowing nothing whatever about them—which is the common lot of humanity unless they decide to talk; but I was immediately heartened to find that what they wanted was the story as I saw it, warts and all if I were to discover any, and that the high gloss finish with which they were often presented by the media nauseated them anyway. I realized then that this approach reflected their whole way of life; necessarily, for on the frontier of achievement, with life itself at stake, only truth mattered.

This attitude was so interesting that I accepted the challenge, with elation at the honour and the prospect of telling what used to be called rattling good yarns with a fascinating environment. But there was also sombre foreboding at the daunting labour needed to master the complex facts as though I were a soldier; to relate them comprehensibly without over-simplification; and achieve what I conceived to be my overriding aim of getting even a little way under the skin of these men who assiduously claim to be just like the rest of us but are not.

And so, for years, absorbed, wondering, and with unbounded gratitude for their unrestrained help and warm hospitality, I listened to Malcolm "Yank" Allen (in the Borneo jungle), his wife Glenys, Tony "Lofty" Allen (in Worcester Police Station),

Paddy Baker (with awe in his RSM's office), Roger Blackman, Steve Callan, Bill Condie, Bob Creighton (in his pub the "Pippin Inn"), Peter de la Billière (who set me going and kept me up to the mark in his irresistible style), Bridget his wife, John and Terry Edwardes, Ken Elgenia (in the horse cavalry lines of the Blues and Royals), Ray and Dorothy England, Keith Farnes, John Foley, Alf Gerry, Terry Hardy, Norman Hartill, Nick Haynes, Bob Heslop, Pete Hogg, Jerry Hopkins, Don Large, Richard Lea, Eddie Lillico, Colin "Old Joe" Lock, Malcolm and Bridget McGillivray, Fred Marafono, Willy Mundell, Dare Newell, John Partridge, Jim Penny, Pete Scholey, Mike Seale, George Shipley (who with unflagging interest arranged for me to meet many of his comrades), John Simpson (who introduced me to the SAS in the first place), Geoff Skardon, "Rover" Slater, John Slim, Ian "Tanky" Smith, Lawrence Smith, Philip "Gipsy" Smith (with difficulty, he being engaged in an escape and evasion exercise from the VAT-man), Alf and Margaret Tasker, Ian Thomson, Maurice Tudor, Kevin Walsh, Johnny Watts, John White, Mike Wilkes, Frank Williams (in the Ulu Bar of the "David Garrick" in Hereford, and through him "Gipsy" Smith and several others), Mike Wingate-Gray, John Woodhouse, Roger Woodiwiss, and some who were not Borneo veterans but whose assistance has still been invaluable. Their styles and titles are omitted because those matter little to themselves, judging each other as they do by their quality as men, which is also what interests me most. Only Lieutenant-General Sir George Lea, KCB, DSO, MBE, must be accorded that respect since, as well as commanding 22 SAS in Malaya, he was Director of Operations in Borneo when the war there was won; Lady Lea also helped me considerably.

The book being my own and not commissioned, its imperfections are mine too. One of these is my arbitrary decision to discard many good stories so that we can get to know a comparatively few men in a book of reasonable length which cannot therefore be a definitive Regimental history, and I humbly offer my apologies to both SAS and other readers who think I have strayed too far one way or the other. I hope that what I have written is true; I have certainly tried hard to ensure that it is, being uneasily aware that, for all their deadly (meaning deadly) earnestness, my informants were often possessed of a bubbling and irreverent sense of humour which might well have engendered a massive leg-pull. Therefore, I cross-checked every story, but it never happened—I think; and my only deliberate mistake is to change the names of the jungle tribesmen who played a noble part in defending their country and freedom but whose efforts might not be appreciated by those in authority across the border.

I am enormously indebted to many not in the SAS for helping me to understand the campaign at every level up to the highest, the jungle environment, and the SAS themselves as viewed from outside. They are The Right Honourable Denis Henley, CH, MBE, MP, Secretary of State for Defence during the second half of this brilliantly successful campaign; Lieutenant-General Sir Anthony Farrar-Hockley, KCB, DSO, MBE, MC, Principal Staff Officer to General Lea; Colonel D. F. "Nick" Neill, OBE, MC, of the 2nd King Edward VII's Own Goorkha Rifles with whom the SAS worked closely in the decisive cross-border phase of the campaign; Group Captain P. H. Champniss, AFC, Royal Air Force, who commanded 43 Squadron (Hunters) in South Arabia and largely helped to save 3 Troop SAS from annihilation; Major Charles M. McCausland of the 7th Duke of Edinburgh's Own Gurkha Rifles, who introduced me to the jungle with the enthusiastic thoroughness of a professional naturalist; Jennie, his wife; Gillian Standring of the London Zoo, who instructed me expertly in the private lives of orang-utans, king cobras and other denizens of the forest; and Major Pengiran Abidin of the Royal Brunei Malay Regiment, who flew me to the highest peak in his country to survey the breathtaking grandeur that is Borneo.

Others to whom I owe much in various ways are Major General Martin Farndale, Colonel Norman Roberts and Mary Roberts, Bob Gaunt, Lieutenant-Colonel Douglas Johnson, Nigel and Diana Mossop, and Tony Geraghty, the author of *Who Dares Wins* and *This is the SAS*, who gave me the run of his SAS photographs which I thought exceedingly kind. Finally, I am greatly blessed with a family whose enthusiasm for the book has equalled my own; Debbie, who typed it beautifully on a machine selflessly borrowed by John from his father's office, whose staff also allowed it to be duplicated to their great inconvenience; Jonathan and Marion, who guided me through the tracks and ambushes of the publishing "ulu"; and, most of all, Mary my wife, who has lived alongside the SAS for longer than she or I care to remember and supported me with a constancy nothing short of crucial. To all these people, strangers and intimates, who have gone to such lengths of help and encouragement, my gratitude is profound.

And now to the nitty (always) and gritty (often) of the SAS in the jungle; no high gloss there.

Peter Dickens, Withyham, 1983.

ACKNOWLEDGMENTS

I am grateful to copyright holders not mentioned in the Preface for permission to reproduce the following photographs: The Special Air Service Regiment, *The Soldier*, John Edwardes, George Shipley, Philip Smith, and Malcolm McGillivray.

Peter Dickens

CHAPTER 1

INCIDENT ON MELANCHOLY MOUNTAIN

28 February 1965

Ian Thomson from the Fifeshire coalmines, trooper in the Special Air Service and lead scout of a patrol across the enemy frontier into Indonesian Borneo, crouched motionless behind a bamboo curtain, watching, listening, sniffing. Behind him at five-yard intervals, Sergeant Eddie Lillico and the two rear men blended with the jungle, awaiting his findings.

No leaf stirred, although leaves and the stems that bore them were the whole environment. If just one had done so the effect on the men would have been galvanic, for no breeze penetrated from the tree-tops to the jungle floor and no animal would have been so foolish as to advertise its presence, knowing man to be nearby and wanting none of him. A hornbill shrieked indeed, but from a safe distance. Even further away, a family of long-armed gibbons, high in the trees, hooted with wild intensity and volume enough to echo eerily from the mountain behind, which marked the border with Sarawak in Malaysia. Thus do gibbons proclaim their territory and menace intruders; but when man plays the territory game, he does not hoot, he shoots, and since Lillico and his men were purposely intruding into Indonesia, they were very, very quiet.

Their vigilance was occasioned by an old camp that they had found the evening before, when a cursory survey, which was all the gathering darkness permitted, had revealed much of interest. There were bamboo lean-tos, which the Army calls "bashas" though the term can be applied to anything from a makeshift tent to a sizeable hut. Significantly, these had no roofs, which natives would have made from palm leaves but which soldiers could more readily improvise with their ponchos; and the camp's military nature was confirmed by labels on rusted tins stating the equivalent of "Indonesian Army, rations for the

1

use of.'' The time since last occupation, six months or so, was given by the length of new shoots from cut saplings, an inch a fortnight give or take allowances for such factors as species, altitude and recent rainfall, together with other signs which to Lillico, after four years in Malaya and two in Borneo, were as informative as another printed label. But he realized that there was more to be gleaned which might be important, especially as the area had not been visited before by the British. He had accordingly withdrawn, and the full patrol of eight men basha'd up for the night on the slopes of Gunong Rawan, which Thomson translated as Melancholy Mountain.

A commander's job is to decide priorities, and Lillico reviewed the orders given him by his Squadron commander, Major Roger Woodiwiss, in the light of this unexpected discovery. His main task was to watch the River Sekayan, three miles over the border, which was known to be the enemy's main line of communication. Absolute secrecy was the essence of such missions. If the enemy were to detect the least sign of the patrol's presence, they could be expected both to harry it, forcing it to divert its energies from reconnaissance to its own survival, and to suspend any activity worth watching anyway.

Yet another reason for avoiding contact with the enemy was that this was, in part, a training patrol, planned by Woodiwiss for the benefit of several recruits to ''D'' Squadron, whose third tour in Borneo was only just beginning. The habitat of the SAS being beyond the frontier, whether that takes them into jungle, desert, mountains, the sectarian ghettos of West Belfast, the Iranian Embassy in London, or Pebble Island, the newcomer must end his apprenticeship by crossing it for the first time; and that is no less testing an experience for the NCO whom he follows than it is for him, and is best taken gently.

Should the camp therefore be fully explored? Surely, yes. There was no urgency in reaching the river, and facts concerning the enemy were always useful in building up the jig-saw of Intelligence upon which active operations depend for their success, and which it is one of the tasks of the SAS, and others, to provide. Lillico's only uncertainty lay in having to visit the same place twice, for that would contravene Standard Operating Procedures (SOPs) which had evolved after long experience, and incidents such as when poor ''Buddha'' Bexton had been killed last June (Chapter 6). On that occasion, however, the enemy was known to have been present, so circumstances were not really comparable. In any case, SOPs were not rigid rules but guides for the isolated patrol commander, who had to be free to act as he saw fit in circumstances known only to him if anything of value was to be accomplished.

Lillico therefore made his dispositions for checking out the camp. If there was nothing to indicate that the enemy might be there, neither was there any proof that he was not; beyond the frontier he must be assumed present every second of the time or the soldier's life will be short and his purpose unachieved, and each move, however apparently routine, must be planned as a tactical operation. He designated the night stopping place as the Emergency Rendezvous, to which anyone becoming separated should return, and left half his force there. For the task in hand, the smaller the team the less likely it was to give itself away. Four men was the optimum number so as to include all specialist skills between them. Lillico selected Thomson and two others, rejecting a promising youngster called Kevin Walsh who had an uncontrollable cough that debarred him absolutely, as far more serious disorders need not have done.

Leaving behind their heavy packs (called bergens) for greater mobility, they set off with only their belts, which contained everything needed for a short period, and, of course, their weapons. A soldier can be as effective in the jungle as the creatures who are born to it, but only when he has learnt to treat his weapon, like theirs, as an integral part of himself. Without it he might endanger his friends as well as himself so that retaining it to the end transcends necessity and becomes a matter of honour. Thomson carried a 5.56mm Armalite light automatic rifle. It is the lead scout's unenviable role to be first into danger, to which, happily surviving the first onslaught, he must respond instantly and furiously with a volume of fire that can sometimes nullify the enemy's advantage of surprise. The rest had 7.62mm self-loading rifles (SLRs), the British Army's standard infantry weapon with a hefty punch and great accuracy, which fired single shots as fast as the trigger could be pulled.

They contoured round the mountain at first until they reached the spur leading down to the camp. To be lead scout of a jungle patrol in enemy territory is an art made up of many skills, and Lillico had no doubt that Thomson was the right man; a short, compact lump of gristle with a vivid imagination, quick perception and reaction, and a gift of Scottish gab when circumstances permitted, which now they did not. To move in the jungle was to be vulnerable because the enemy could hide so easily, and only the slightest clues could be hoped for to warn of his presence in time; far slighter for instance than a fag-end, which would stand out like a motorway sign to a trained jungle soldier and was not to be expected. Thomson pressed all his senses into service; his eyes to look through the first green wall of foliage to the next for as small an abnormality as a single leaf hanging awkwardly; his ears to detect the least sound not made by nature, and his nose to catch the faintest whiff of, perhaps, hair cream, which could hang for hours in the lifeless air, saying it with perfume. The SAS did not use the stuff, of course; enthusiastic to a degree for anything that would enhance operational effectiveness, they scorned irrelevances such as sartorial elegance, and looked like the ruffians they were not.

All this was routine, the forest was virginal for the whole 1,500 yards to the camp. When Thomson reached the outskirts he stopped, motioned discreetly with his Armalite, and the others stopped too without bunching. SOPs then required a longer wait with even greater alertness, and for ten full minutes Thomson peered round the left side of a massive bamboo clump at the clearing, unchanged since yesterday. The bashas were interspersed between many similar clumps, and tall trees acted as screens against prying eyes from aircraft or mountain-top. To his left was a massive rock and beyond that trickled one of many small streams in a gully; this was "ulu," headwaters country, as far as you could get from anywhere.

Nothing was remotely suspicious, and their only tension was the self-imposed one of always expecting the unexpected. Thomson turned his head slowly to query Lillico with his eyes and, receiving a barely perceptible nod, he lifted the bamboo frond behind which he had hidden and stepped out into the open.

"The place er-r-r-rupted. Oh God, it's hard to describe." The ground at his feet spurted into his face as though propelled by a subterranean force, and where there had been absolute stillness he was engulfed by roaring, rattling, reverberating, tearing, throbbing, jarring noise.

"How I got away with it I'll never know. There was this guy with a light automatic laid down beside a tree no more than twelve yards to my right front. He must have known I was there all along yet he couldn't hit me, must have been even more scared than me." That was indeed likely, the common if surprising experience being that the man waiting in ambush with all his advantages becomes even more tense at the prospect of inevitable action than his opponent, whose mind is uncluttered, ready to receive impressions and to react instinctively.

Thomson's response could not have been faster, but the odds were too one-sided. The Indonesian soldier raised his point of aim and, "I was picked up and thrown to my left behind this rock; that was lucky because the guy couldn't see me, but when I tried to get up my leg wasn't there and blood was gushing into my face from my left thigh. I thought, Christ I'm hit! You can't do this to Fifers.

"I sat up, and as I sat up another Indo sat up too and he was that close I could see he had a tiger's head shoulder flash and if I'd had a bayonet I could have stabbed him; and I thought well I've got to get this bastard quick because he was fumbling with his rifle. It was an old-fashioned bolt-action Enfield, or maybe a Mauser or a Springfield, but I didn't have time to see properly. Mine had been knocked out of my hand. His eyes were wide open and so was his mouth. I could see he was shit-scared . . . could be because I was covered in blood and yelling fit to bust, I don't know why. He was a very young guy. I found my Armalite, which still had the safety-catch to automatic, and gave him a long burst and he went down."

Thomson's decisive action probably saved his Sergeant's life as well as his own, and opinion in the Regiment conceded that he had been "very quick." He thought, where the hell's my leg? It seemed to have gone completely because it was nowhere near the other, and that conclusion was given weight by the altogether terrifying evidence of brilliant arterial blood pulsing from where his leg should have been, in great sprays not inches but feet long. Medically trained, he knew he was watching his life pumping itself away through the huge femoral artery, and that it would be gone in a minute, perhaps two, unless he decided and acted correctly within that time; yet his objectivity remained unimpaired, and just as well because he was stuck on a dilemma with two horns that propelled him in divergent and apparently irreconcilable directions.

Such bleeding could only be held by a tightly-bound tourniquet, so he quickly felt his thigh for a stump around which to apply one; no stump, no hope, no problem. There was. But bullets were still flying and he must not stay where he was; Sergeant Don Large had said, and he was a man one listened to, "When you're hit, move; you won't feel like it, but if you don't you're going to be hit again." So, which to do first for

Christ's sake? The bleeding gave him a minute, a bullet a split second. Move.

That the decision was made and acted upon in less time than the nearest Indo could resolve whatever problem he in his turn may have had, can be attributed to the sort of intense training that accelerates already quick wits to the speed of a computer, rigorously suppressing irrelevant thoughts like fear, or "What's my old Mum going to think of this?" He started crawling back and to his right behind the clump. As he moved he knew he still had a leg of sorts because its inert mass was wrenched to follow the rest of him and protested, audibly it seemed to him, by grinding pieces of the shattered femur against each other until it trailed behind him.

The clump was thick, its cover good, and he got to work. Take sweat-rag, put a lumpy knot in the middle, press firmly against the artery in the groin, tie round the limb, commando dagger through, twist to tighten and stick through trousers to hold steady. The bleeding stopped as he knew it would, yet is there not a touch of the miraculous in putting theory into practice and finding it works, especially if your life depends on it? Then a shot of morphine; that was the drill, because although pain had not yet obtruded it soon would, and the drug would also slow his heart and the bleeding.

Finally, he made a soldierly all-round inspection of the tactical scene. There was his Sergeant, lying quite still, with blood drained from his face and hands but all over the rest of him.

Eddie "Geordie" Lillico's eyes were brown with clear whites and a high polish. Because they were also round and usually wide open, not because they popped out on stalks, they were likened in the sergeants' mess to organ-stops, and through them shone a palpable and infectious enthusiasm. The enthusiasm was for his profession, and to a degree that excited comment even among his fellow enthusiasts. His shelves at home carried more books on military history and thinking than would have done justice to a retired general; it was even said that his lady friend could discourse on Ney's tactics at Waterloo with well-briefed authority, so that Thomson was evidently misled in thinking that his idea of a pinup was a Centurion tank coming through a smokescreen.

His eyes had been wide as he watched Thomson slip through the bamboo and the stillness was shattered by two bursts from what he thought was an Armalite. "But it wasn't," Thomson reported, "it was a Russian RPD because I seen it"; and Thomson certainly had an eye for weapons.

"The way it came to me," says Lillico, "was Head-on Contact. We had a drill for that so you didn't have to sit around thinking what to do." This was the SOP known as Shoot-and-Scoot, one of the most important though not necessarily the easiest to interpret. The aim was clear enough, to prevent casualties when there was no point in fighting to hold ground, and in a surprise encounter like this a patrol was directed to put its pride in its pocket and run away. That, however, was easier said than done because to turn your back would only present it to an unruffled enemy, neither would your friends be helped to disengage. Far better would be for every man who could see a target to react instantly and violently, and only then, while the enemy was adjusting his thoughts, to scoot independently for the emergency rendezvous; but if a man was incapacitated after all, with chilling logic the rule said leave him, at least temporarily, to prevent even more casualties.

Thomson being to the left of the bamboo clump, Lillico leapt to its right and ran forward to do his share of the shooting. He saw no one and could not understand how he was apparently kicked in the backside; it was not a powerful blow, he might even have knocked into one of the thick stems, but he went down nevertheless. Irked at the check, he made to spring up and forward, but the movement was only in his mind; his body stayed where it was, immovable.

Did Lillico pass out? Neither he nor Thomson can recall events precisely, gripped as they were in the full shock and trauma of hideous and potentially mortal wounds; Lillico cannot remember losing consciousness, but it may be observed that a feature of passing out is not remembering and Thomson's memory of his apparent death-mask is horribly vivid. But either way he was static and vulnerable, and almost certainly owed his life to Thomson, who had killed Lillico's assailant before the latter could fire again.

Thomson was keen enough to scoot, as was his duty, insofar as he could match his snail's gait to the ill-suited word, but he was even keener to help Lillico. He did the latter and perfectly illustrated the hazards of laying down rules for hypothetical contingencies because events proved him right, even though he thought at first that the only melancholy service he could render his commander would be to confirm his death and remove the operative parts of his rifle; but as he drew near to the supposed corpse, the eyes opened, wide of course, and Sergeant Lillico was back in charge.

The shooting phase, envisaged as lasting only seconds, was being prolonged by their enforced presence on the battlefield, leaves and even branches falling about them amid the juddering racket. Taking comfort from their mutual presence, Lillico and Thomson continued the fight. Never mind that their legs were useless, their prone positions were ideal. No longer surprised, they used their expert marksmanship and determined will to convince the enemy that it was he who had lost and had best retire. Fierce and hard with the joy of battle, they were a formidable pair of cripples.

The clearing lay open before them. Thomson reoriented himself from his new position by noting the tree whence the guy had shot him. He could then scarcely believe his eyes, for there was the guy coming out from behind it, clearly under the impression that he had eliminated his enemy. It was an error of judgment.

"Bugger-r-r-r-r-U!" The staccato roll of Scottish "R"'s matched the merciless clatter of the Armalite and the guy fell, dead.

Lillico fired two rounds in quick succession ("double-tap routine, gave you a slight spread of shot, needed a bit of practice") and a fleeting movement across the camp ceased.

"D'you think . . ." Lillico asked between bursts, " . . . you can get back to the RV?"

"Och aye, I'm fine."

He's a hard little guy, thought Lillico; quite good really. Quite good, that is, by SAS standards in which only the best is acceptable and praise rare. As for heroes, they don't believe in them.

All suddenly became quiet, so suddenly that awareness lagged behind the event. Lillico wondered whether the enemy had temporarily surrendered the initiative. Possibly, but even so they would certainly return sometime if only to recover their dead, quite soon if it was just a matter of regrouping, or later if reinforcements were sent for; and if he and Thomson were still there when that happened and had not already succumbed to their wounds, they would surely die.

Since Thomson could move and his presence would not affect the inevitable outcome, he must go. That did not mean he would be the only one to benefit; not at all. He might well die alone and miserably of his wound or by the enemy's hand. Even if he were to reach the rendezvous a near-mile back by driving himself with a supreme effort, he would take so long that the others would certainly have left to do whatever they had thought right. But every yard he covered away from the enemy and nearer to friends must increase the chance of his being found, and that would not only be fine for him but improve Lillico's own chances greatly; from negligible to slim. The decision, however, though reached with the impersonal deductive logic which was Lillico's stock-in-trade as a sergeant, meant sending away the last friendly face he thought he would ever see, and surprised him by being difficult to take.

"On your way," he ordered. It had to be an order.

Alone and more than ever alert as he covered Thomson's withdrawal, Lillico's suspicion that the enemy had retired was quickly proved premature. Again, he detected movement across the clearing. This time a man came into the open; two men, and a third. Lillico opened fire; the first dropped and lay still, the second fell into undergrowth, while the third had just enough time to make himself scarce for which purpose the jungle is accommodating. What had they been doing? Not attacking, surely, because their movements were too indecisive; but no immediate danger suggesting itself, the answer could wait because there was other work to do.

First, move from a position known to the enemy, as Thomson had done. Again Lillico was helped by his friend, who had joined in the battle from some yards behind. Never mind that he could see no one; he knew where Lillico was and saturated everywhere else with stinging bullets and blistering invective. It was reassuring, and Lillico tensed to drag the inert mass which was himself into and under the bamboo where he should be almost invisible. When there was something to grip the effort was tolerable, but without a handhold his clawing fingers scraped impotently, sweat extruded under pressure, his breath rasped, and he was weak, weak; but domination by mind over matter improves with practice and, fortunately, SAS training had anticipated the need.

With one trial surmounted, the next presented itself; more would follow. The end was unpredictable, except should he fail to meet any one of them. So be it, take them singly. He was aware of his left leg as a lump of rubber, but there was no sensation in it; his right he could feel, but no effort of will could make it move, and blood, warm and viscous, filled his pants. It did not spurt like Thomson's but there was a lot, too much, and it felt comforting, which was even more dangerous. Action was needed.

The wound was gruesome and ominous. The bullet had made a small entryhole just in front of the left hip, half-severed the great sciatic nerve so paralysing and desensitizing the left leg, and expanding as it left through the pelvic opening had destroyed a three-inch mass of the right buttock muscle and with it all power to that leg too. "Fortunately"—Lillico's constant good fortune may be hard to appreciate, but to him it was real—"it missed the artery because there was no question of a tourniquet there." Blood welled through the lacerated flesh all the same, "but fortunately I always carried two shell dressings so I got them both out. No trouble with the entry-hole because it was small but the other seemed to have torn out half my arse; however, I managed eventually to trap the dressing inside my slacks and shove it in the hole."

There was movement yet again, and with a burst of fire Lillico warned whoever it was to keep his distance. The noises came from a dip in the ground where he could not see—muffled grunts denoting exertion combined with frustration, and what could have been a soft but heartfelt groan of pain—and did not convey aggression, rather that the Indos were evacuating a wounded man while trying to keep quiet, and were not finding it at all easy. That would keep them acceptably occupied, and all Lillico needed now was somebody to do the same for him.

Meanwhile, he shared the battleground with three Indonesian bodies and thought there might well be more. A victory then, in effect by two men over at least six to judge by the volume of fire and its sources, and that after being ambushed unawares. Of course both Jock and he ought by rights to have died; and now that the immediate tension had partly eased, he remembered that they might still do so. He wondered whether "D" Squadron and the Regiment would ever hear about their performance and, if so, whether they would consider it to have been all right.

It remained only to resolve that if he was still there when the Indos returned he must die fighting, for to let himself be captured after Paddy Condon's murder (Chapter 5) was almost unthinkable. Lillico did not complain; the war's very purpose and justification was to preserve civilization from barbarism and his present plight merely highlighted the point. Fortunately, he could rely absolutely on the Regiment, as represented by Major Woodiwiss, not giving them up either, so he took a shot of morphine and settled down to wait. "I wasn't really in pain; the loss of blood left me lightheaded like being drunk, sort of mystical and at peace with the world, but the Army training in self-preservation kept me going and I didn't pass out or forget where I was." He stayed there for four or five hours, but nobody came; not even the enemy; fortunately.

Orders are for misinterpreting, even sometimes in the SAS. Thomson could not bring himself to believe that Lillico was totally immobile. He had expected to be told to carry out the standard drill of retiring a short distance and covering his withdrawal. He also wanted to, SAS sergeants not being of a different subspecies to troopers but companions in fortune or misfortune as well as lawgivers, not to be left alone to die without good reason. Whether the wish was father to the thought or the noise of gunfire had snatched away Lillico's words, which were perhaps less distinct than usual, Thomson deemed himself to have been so ordered and was thus able to take part in the last flare-up of the battle. That over, and man's strident intrusion slowly giving way to nature's harmony, Thomson awaited his boss's return, and waited in vain. The exchange of fire assumed a grim significance; "Geordie!" he called, and again, less muted, "Geordie!" The jungle's immensity enfolded the sound and vouchsafed no answer.

He himself was in redoubled danger if the worst had happened, so he did not speak again, which would have been foolish. It was also foolish perhaps to stay where he was, but that he did, alert and hoping against his conviction, which increased in certainty as time passed. How long he waited he cannot say; time in such circumstances is only to be measured in relation to the next event, and "after that" could mean a split second during the battle or an hour now. Judging himself at last to be irrevocably alone, Thomson turned to carry out his real orders.

He did not despair by any means. In the SAS you must not need to be part of a group to save you from cracking in times of stress. Motivation is all, and having been blessed with it you can further strengthen your resolve by schooling yourself in techniques like having the right boots, or psychological self-deception: "Don't keep looking at the mountain which never seems to get any nearer; switch off, think of sex, and you'll undoubtedly survive to be a credit to the Regiment."[1]

[1] Trad. Anon.

Hands forward with elbows akimbo, right knee up and out, heave! Hands forward . . . twelve inches in three seconds, a yard in nine, a hundred yards in fifteen minutes, a mile in . . . No, forget it. Right knee out, heave; and however far the rendezvous, he was a foot nearer to it.

He did not invoke the distraction or it might be the spur of sex because there was much to occupy his thoughts. His theoretical time to the rendezvous was not worth computing anyway, because there were too many unknowns. His strength was limited and must be husbanded by regular rests, blind unthinking perseverance, however gallant, only to collapse short of the goal not being the SAS way. Then he must release the tourniquet at intervals to prevent gangrene, risking further loss of blood and, consequently, energy; but although heatstroke, also a killer, could result from not drinking to replace the copious sweating occasioned by hard exercise in the tropics, the mere thought of even water passing his lips was revolting. Thankfully, food would not be important for several days.

As a trained medic, Thomson knew all this and more; for instance, that the broken bone crunching with every movement might kill him by severing more arteries. In civilized surroundings he would have prescribed absolute stillness, but here he might as well forget that. It was the pain that worried him most; the torture, if he could feel it, was only too easy to imagine and would impair his capability drastically, even if he could steel himself to bear it. But fortunately, when he had collected the patrol's medical pack at headquarters he had spotted twenty syrettes[2] of morphine on a table, and with the far-sighted providence of a good soldier—''might come in handy''—had scooped the lot, the normal allowance being two per man. Although not too sure about the long-term effects of exceeding the statutory dose, he reasoned that there was unlikely to be a long term at all unless he kept himself well fixed, and so he felt no pain and his blood-pressure stayed low.

Thomson's progress was also affected by concern for the enemy, who would certainly find the patrol's entry route which must therefore be avoided. The result was a curve of increased distance leading through unfamiliar jungle, but using the mountain and its contours as guides he was never lost.

He did not get far that day. ''I was knackered,'' and he meant it absolutely, like running out of petrol with the reserve can

[2]Small two-shot syringes operated by squeezing the flexible container.

already gone; and since there was no alternative to stopping or guarantee that he would ever go on again, he scribbled details of the enemy on the back of his map, in case his body should be found, with a detachment which surprised himself. "There was this pig-hole under a fallen tree; they dig these holes and lie in bowls of mud so I rolled up in it and covered myself, took a shot of morphine and waited for the night." And when that came he took another shot.

Lillico spent a happy day in the cool, dappled shade of the bamboo, mulling over his circumstances to be sure but in a disinterested sort of way and not worrying about a thing. He was thus clearly in a very bad way indeed from shock and blood-loss, but the enforced rest gave full play to the body's marvellous recuperative powers, and a part of him—the sergeant, one suspects—stood disembodied beside him to remind him of his duty, so that at some time during the afternoon he became aware that not only should he move but that now he could.

With his renewed strength, little though it was, he developed an elbows-only technique and covered 500 yards towards the border ridge, uphill all the way. The achievement was the greater because he chose a route through thick undergrowth for the cover it afforded. Known as "belukar," this was a previously cultivated area that had been abandoned when the soil had become exhausted some five years earlier. It impeded progress much as an overgrown English briar thicket would have done, the common factor being thorns in plenty though on very different bushes. But Lillico knew that such places were often the haunts of wild pigs who also like concealment, and rooting in the earth for food make tunnels through the scrub of just the right diameter for a soldier marching on his stomach. This one proved a maze of runs with the pigs themselves evidently prepared to allow him free passage; fortunately, because the best way of dealing with an angry 200-pound tusker surprised at close quarters was not clear. But the risks from animals was small compared with that from man, and his worst natural enemies were the humble leeches, which took full advantage of the easy access afforded by his earthbound body to clamp themselves on in swarms and suck away the blood he could by no means spare.

Towards evening Lillico's pig-run led him to a hole like Thomson's under a huge felled tree and there he stayed, again drained of vitality. A helicopter's rotor beat the air overhead but seemed to have no message for him, more interested as he was in a myriad huge shiny bluebottles clustering upon his wound and laying eggs that turned into grubs as he watched, absorbed and fascinated.

When firing first broke out the two rear members of the patrol sprang sideways for cover and then scooted for the rendezvous. In so doing they conformed precisely both to Shoot-and-Scoot and another key SOP that forbade shooting without a visible target, but they acted uneasily none the less, keenly feeling their recruit status which demanded such implicit obedience. The four already at the rendezvous had flashed a signal to base, ''contact—wait—out,'' but hard information was still lacking and the new arrivals could supply little; only as leaden minutes throbbed by with no sign of Lillico and Thomson did they understand that the news was hard indeed and so was their problem.

How best to act depended on the enemy's strength, since the rules allowed a forward probe at this stage if the risk seemed reasonable. But, again, inexperience told because they were all quite sure they had run into a major force. To them there had been just one hell of a noise, but Lillico even though wounded had instinctively broken this down into a number of sources, and with a finely tuned professional ear detected the types of weapon which told him much. There had, in fact, been only rifles and light automatics, indicating a small patrol; any larger force would certainly have included at least one machine-gun and a larger-still mortar. Lillico also knew, as the others did not, that the enemy had suffered a high proportion of casualties.

The decision was taken to ask for infantry support from the Company base at Sain, several hours march to the rear through which the patrol had entered, and to return there themselves in order to lead the infantry to the right place and avoid the considerable danger of mistaken identity.

At base in Kuching, Major Roger Woodiwiss tried to project his mind into Lillico's and Thomson's so as to do everything possible for them, never giving up; the morale and mystique of the Regiment were born of mutual confidence and the success of future operations would depend on his doing so. His worry was that he could not do more, as when he had guided a helicopter into enemy territory to lift out the survivors of Condon's patrol. The little possible was easy, backed as he was by seniors whose predilections were for doing more rather than less, his own Colonel, Mike Wingate-Gray who chanced to be in Borneo, and Brigadier Bill Cheyne commanding the district known as West Brigade. Woodiwiss had only to ask for the infantry to be alerted and the Royal Air Force to begin helicopter searches, both with permission to cross the border which was not lightly given at that time, and they were done upon the instant; after which he suffered for many hours the tortures peculiar to officers whose men are in trouble without them.

Night did not fall, it rose, to envelop first pig-holes, then undergrowth, and finally climbed the tree-trunks to the canopy. Above that the sky retained some light though it was of little use to creatures on the forest floor where darkness was nearly total, except those whose eyes nature has specially adapted, like mouse deer and scaly anteaters, but man is not among them. Movement was not impossible without a light in the days before image intensifiers; on well-worn tracks it was quite easy and, indeed, elsewhere there was nothing to stop one feeling one's way, but the going was both painfully slow and inevitably noisy so that when the enemy might be present it was just not done.

The game was therefore suspended for the long night. The pieces would remain in their respective squares and the only practical effect of the break was on Lillico's and Thomson's vital forces; they could either use the quiet hours to regain strength and live, or weaken and die as their wounds warranted. To state the alternatives was to recognize a challenge, and they lived. Lillico even tried to stand by pulling himself up with his arms. Although his legs would still not support him, the effort of self-mastery reinforced his determination.

Rested, and no longer preoccupied with bluebottle grubs because he could not see them, Lillico reasoned that since the SAS patrol had not come forward they must have gone back for the infantry, who would now not be far away. Similarly, almost exactly so, he had been well placed to know that the enemy patrol had not come forward either, indicating that they too had probably brought up reinforcements which might also be close at hand. Exercising the mind lubricated it and he remembered that the British infantry in question were the 1st Battalion of the 6th Gurkha Rifles, who, although shorter, lighter in complexion and of a different cast of feature to the Javanese, would not be readily distinguishable from them when behind a bush in the jungle shade. Clearly, he must lie very close, fully using the jungle's concealing properties whereby men have evaded detection at ranges down to two feet, and only reveal himself when absolutely sure.

Yet another sense of awareness drummed in his head and tried to form itself into a thought. The helicopter! Was he not carrying the search and rescue beacon (Sarbe) with which he could have homed the aircraft to him? Yes, it was still there on his belt. The realization was depressing, but it was not his way to dwell on it; fortunately, there would probably be another opportunity and then he would be ready.

Thomson, on the other hand, full of morphine and short of blood, was not doing a great deal of thinking. Remembering occasionally to release the tourniquet, he spent the night either unconscious or nearly so; but when the sun rose and drove the shadows down to him, and a great chorus of crickets and cicadas and tree-frogs and birds and monkeys and goodness knows what else greeted the event with exuberant vitality, he awoke fully and found to his surprise that he too felt fine, just fine. His contribution to jungle life was crawling and he set off without delay, knowing nothing for certain except that the Regiment would be trying to find him.

The thoughts of the Gurkhas and the enemy would have run on identical lines. Neither knew whether the other was present, but that was highly likely and every move must be planned and acted as though he were. Nor did they know if the two men were alive or dead or where they were; the task was to find them, and if alive the presumption must be that their trigger fingers would be very sensitive.

The Gurkha platoon commander accordingly ordered his men to turn their jungle hats inside out and expose the red bands sewn there for easy recognition; they would not blend so well with the background but better red, in this case, than dead. He also asked the six SAS to walk singly, a hundred yards ahead of his search line in the hope that Lillico or Thomson would see one of them first and identify a friend and fellow countryman. They were glad to do so, although it was a lonely job that risked blundering into an enemy force without immediate support.

Lillico awoke from a doze to the cheering and appetizing aroma of brewing Nescafé; "Well it might have been another sort of instant coffee, but I reckoned it was Nes; you develop your senses in the jungle." He did not, however, stretch out his arm and call for a mug; fortunately because the brewers were enemy soldiers of whom he now saw five or six some thirty yards away. They seemed to be looking for something. What, he wondered? Him! He shrank further under his tree and froze, presenting a profile that could scarcely be lower; only his wide eyes were mobile.

Prominent in his limited field of view, a durian tree overtopped the scrub. From its brown trunk hung bunches of big spiky ripening fruit whose succulent flesh is rarely enjoyed by Europeans because of the repellent odour which must first be braved, but it is prized by gibbons, flying foxes, and the jungle peoples who had driven climbing-nails into this particular tree for easier picking. A soldier climbed the tree, but not for the fruit. He wanted a better view. Sitting comfortably in a fork, he looked directly into Lillico's eyes.

Absolutely still now even to his eyelids, Lillico was afraid. Yet his fear was by no means numbing; he realized at once that although he could see the bloke, the bloke could not necessarily see him in his carefully chosen hole with plenty of foliage around it, dried blood caked with mud camouflaging his body to perfection. His chief concern now was for the unwelcome swarm of bluebottles, which might well intrigue an observant tracker; but for the soldier to see him and not give the least start of recognition would demand unusual self-control, and Lillico, reassured, allowed himself the further encouraging observation that the men on the ground were going about their search in a manner he would not have tolerated in his own Troop. Too much talking for one thing, and too far apart for another; at least twenty yards when five was the maximum in that thick terrain, if you really wanted to find somebody who did not want to be found.

The man's gaze and Lillico's attention were both diverted by a distant drumming which, approaching, resolved itself into a helicopter. In the citation for Lillico's Military Medal, Woodiwiss wrote: "He showed superb presence of mind and courage in not switching on his Sarbe and thereby probably preventing the loss of the helicopter and its crew"; but Lillico would have none of that. "It would have been stupid to switch on and bring it in. It was only a little Whirlwind and all those Indos could have shot it down easy and what good would that have done? The Sarbe was only a beacon. You couldn't talk through it and explain the position; but I knew they'd keep looking until they found me, they or Johnny Gurkha."

The enemy's coffee-break was not a long one; the bloke came down from his tree; orders were shouted—shouted! Lillico's professionalism was again offended; you never shout in the jungle—and the patrol moved off. The searching helicopter stayed within range of his Sarbe but he did not switch it on, calculating that a hovering aircraft would bring the enemy scurrying back. It may be thought that the longer the time since they had left him the greater was his courage.

Two bursts of fire came from not far away and Lillico's immediate thought was that the Indonesians had found Thomson.

Thomson crawled and crawled and his bone crunched and crunched so he jabbed yet another syrette of morphine into his other leg and kept on crawling and crawling, feeling no pain and with his mind as clear as a bell. Clear enough certainly to find his way up and over the border ridge, past Melancholy Mountain and into the rendezvous, a satisfying achievement of navigation in view of his worm's eye view of recognition features, circuitous evasion route, and other difficulties.

He made a very cautious approach because the enemy might have found the place and ambushed it, a common jungle tactic; advances of a yard or two in dead silence followed by longer spells with every sense alert disclosed nothing at first, yet that was no proof that the place was deserted as he knew from experience, none better. Pushing on ever more gently, he saw something unnatural and his heart wobbled, only to right itself at the next beat when he recognized his own bergen with Lillico's beside it.

Needing friends not things, the packs induced a sense of abandonment; dumped, shapeless, full of erstwhile useful articles now to be ransacked by pigs and honey-bears, rotted by damp and fungus, and at last obliterated by the remorseless growth of the jungle. That train of thought was inadmissible however, and a water-bottle lying apart promised better. His thirst was raging, and as the precious liquid softened his parched mouth and swilled around his acid teeth his assurance revived, only to crash even lower than before as his stomach utterly rejected the intrusion and returned it with the addition of evil-tasting digestive juices in that eruption of nature apparently designed to cause total desolation.

The choice open to Thomson was the same as the previous evening's but more pressing; he could either curl up and die, which a benign providence gently urges when his degree of weakness and hopelessness is reached, or not. He chose the latter because the former just was not done in the Regiment and he could not bear the thought of their even suggesting that he had "chucked in." Perhaps he had not fully appreciated before where all the training in endurance and perseverance, which he had enthusiastically accepted, was leading, but he did now; to the limit. Fair enough; if any bugger was going to let the Regiment down, it would not bc him.

He crawled on. Crawling was the opposite to curling up, but it may be that the clarity of his mind was becoming less bell-like than he thought because it might have been wiser to have hidden near the bergens, whose position would be known to any rescuers and must surely be the focal point for a search. As it was he plunged once more into the limitless jungle towards Sain, 5,000 yards away. He had covered 200 when he reached the limit of his self-propulsion.

Thomson pulled himself under some bushes beside a stream on the friendly side of the watershed and lay there comfortably, though not contentedly as Lillico had done. He wanted to be found, ever more intensely as the likelihood of his being so by friends seemed to diminish. The possibility of the enemy coming first possessed his mind so that it became the probability, and himself a hunted, wounded, snarling animal at bay. Images forced themselves into his consciousness; real ones without a doubt, but his evaluation may have been less than objective because of his troubled state of mind. There were the two parties of Indos who failed to see him because he took good care that they should not, but were they really Indonesians? There is no way of telling for sure, but the unhappy fact is that the Gurkhas certainly did pass that way to reach the rendezvous.

Then there was the helicopter. That it might be friendly and concerned for his welfare never crossed his mind, and certain that it brought enemy troops for his destruction he opened fire. Aiming at the noise through the tree canopy there was little danger of hitting, nor did David Collinson the pilot notice, but who would be an RSPCA inspector trying to rescue a wounded tiger? One's belief, whether true or false, dictates one's actions and misunderstanding is the more common especially when stress is present. The shots must have been those which Lillico heard and interpreted despondently.

The afternoon began to slip away, and so did Thomson. He was well accustomed to weakness and exhaustion, but, whereas those could be corrected by rest, this draining of the life force

itself was a new sensation; he recognized it for what it was
and this time he had no choice. Its nature was kindly and seduc-
tive, like the brook beside him curving smoothly over sandy
clay; downhill to be sure, but why should it want to go up?
Peacefully, he contemplated his glade and saw it to be beautiful.
Tall straight trunks of jungle giants culminated in heavy foliage
so that all beneath was softly shaded like a beechwood he knew
on Dinedor Hill outside Hereford, and shrubs grew only
sparsely, revealing their elegance. There were vine-stems
sweeping upwards, delicate two-ferns, a bush with spiky leaves
several yards long and only an inch or two wide, and another
with broad lush ones as in the foyers of grand hotels, palms used
by the natives for thatching their roofs and random coils of rotan
cane with which the British clear their drains; but although men
could venture there the great harmony was wholly independent
of him, owing him nothing, and Ian Thomson thought at last,
"What's my old Mum going to think because I'm going to die
here and be eaten by pigs and nobody'll ever find me?"

("Come off it!" taunted realist Bill Condie, pint to hand in
the Ulu Bar of the "David Garrick" at Hereford where the land-
lord, ex-SAS Sergeant Major Frank Williams, catered for the
Regimental thirst. "You were stoned to the eyeballs." And
Thomson excused his weakness; "Yes, it must have been the
morphine.")

He thought further and to better purpose. Even the Indos can't
do much to me now. What have I got to lose? And consciously
abandoning his ingrained policy of concealment, he fired three
deliberate signal shots into the air. The positive action annulled
the calm of resignation and he became a cornered animal again,
aware only of danger. He could receive clear impressions and
respond instantly and fiercely, but lacked the mental energy to
reason beyond the moment; and when the soldier came, feline
with sinuous movement and tense alertness, dark eyes in the
olive face scanning the ground minutely and rifle following the
eyes, Thomson had no thought but, Bloody Indo! Well, if I've
got to go, this bastard's going with me.

He could still raise and aim the Armalite under inch-by-inch
control without alerting his target. The range being short the
best point of aim was the head, a quick kill being imperative.
But having eased the safety-catch soundlessly and hooked his
finger to the trigger, he could not help but notice that the foresight was steady on a red hatband. He recalled only dimly that
this might have some meaning, but it was enough to make him

hesitate. The hesitation became a pause, and the pause prolonged itself until, with a sublime outpouring of bated breath
and griping tension, his weapon sank gently to the forest floor.
"Johnny . . . Johnny!"

When Lillico judged that the enemy had moved far enough for
him to bring in the helicopter safely it was no longer there, and
no amount of Regimental spirit could construe that as fortunate.
The stress engendered by his eyeball to eyeball near miss with
the tree-climber had left him weaker even than before. Few hours
of daylight remained, and although his resolution remained unimpaired, his chance of surviving another night without medical
attention had to be dispassionately assessed as small; and he
was still in enemy territory.

This last consideration offered him at least an excuse for action; and despite the Herculean effort needed to move at all
being compounded by the strain of unremitting wariness, that
was a great deal better than wallowing like a pig in far from
glorious mud with ever dimming hope. He moved a good 200
yards, right onto the border ridge itself where, although the
enemy might still be encountered, he was the more likely to be
found by friends. He had also made the helicopter's task easier,
a ridge being more negotiable than a slope. But although the
country was still "belukar" and the pilot could descend close
to the ground, tree-stumps, felled logs, saplings and undergrowth precluded landing.

Exhausted again, he could now do nothing but look, scent,
and above all listen. Wanting the precious daylight hours to pass
slowly, he made the mistake of checking their progress by the
shadows which the tropical sun, falling plumb from zenith to
jungle horizon, caused to lengthen very fast indeed. The forest
knew before he did that the light had begun to dim, and signalled
the event with a perceptible increase of insect noise that he could
have done without. Straining through the thrumming for not
greatly dissimilar rotor-beats, he could have imagined them at
any time had he let himself; but there was no question of that,
he was entirely in control of himself and intended to remain so.

Perhaps it was on this account that he delayed acknowledging
an alien sound until it had repeated itself, or that being tuned to
helicopters he was slow to adjust to something else. Thunder;
not isolated cracks but deep, rolling, prolonged and, when he
had assessed its implication, sinister. The light faded faster than
the sun decreed as a huge black cloud swept up from behind the

mountain and there were no more shadows to measure; a breeze stirred the treetops, bland at first but full of portent, and then lightning slashed the cloud and lit his hiding place. It would be no mean storm, though not unusual for Borneo; you could not expect tropical rain forest to grow without tropical rain, but neither could you expect a light chopper to fly through it, that was not reasonable.

Reasonable or not, suddenly there it was. Its noise, masked by the thunder until right overhead, roared generously and unmistakably. He had to fumble for the Sarbe, held for so long at instant readiness but recently laid aside. Even now he hesitated. How close were the enemy? Dare he use it?

Flying Officer David Collinson had spent two busy days flying over trees infinite in number and impossible to see through. Although well aware that an enemy on the ground could easily see him, he could not fly at above small-arms range for fear of missing any sign of the men. But his briefing had been that they were probably dead anyway, and as he quartered the ground for the eighteenth time the task seemed hopeless. Yet every task must be accomplished with maximum efficiency or no deduction drawn from a negative result would be valid and, if apparently hopeless, the spur was even sharper so as to counter any tendency to inattentiveness. And he was young, new to the game with only 200 flying hours, and those men below whether dead or alive were very real to him.

So when a call came from the Gurkhas to lift Thomson out and get him to hospital—quick—Collinson's frustration was hard to contain, because the trees were just too tall for his winch-cable. He tried place after place, brushing twigs with his blades and even depressing them a little with the down-draught, but the strop dangled bafflingly inaccessible from the ground and there was no nearby clearing to which the wounded man could possibly be moved before nightfall.

Accepting defeat with a bad grace, Collinson then saw the gathering storm, decided that his duty was to return to base before it broke—and did not. The light remained adequate as he grimly started his nineteenth pass, and barely had he left the high primary jungle for the "belukar" when Lillico's Sarbe bleeped, loud and close. Right! Collinson's mood angrily rejected even the possibility of a second failure and was admirably suited to the challenge presented by the tangled mass of scrub beneath him.

Lillico dragged himself clear of his log and waved. Collinson saw at once that he could expect no further movement which might simplify his own manoeuvring within the constraint of utmost speed dictated by nightfall, storm and enemy. The strop must be placed within arm's reach, and this he did by descending clear of the man where the growth permitted and then backing his hovering aircraft like a car until the tail rotor was neatly parked between two high and jagged tree-stumps.

But Lillico's severest trial was still to come. He fitted the strop snugly under his armpits, that was all right; grasped his rifle and signalled to hoist, and that was all right too; but as he rose he realized with alarm that one hand could no longer support the weapon, and with dread foreboding when both together did not prevent it slipping. Yet again he called forth all his determination to force his body to his will, and would have succeeded had it not been for the friendly roughness of the crewmen who were concerned only to get him safely inside. The rifle fell, and nothing in his future mattered but the sheer awfulness of reporting back to the Regiment without it. How could those airmen just sit there grinning? But, of course, they did not understand.

He said to them, "Don't hang around, there's Indos about."

They said to him, "The Gurkhas have got your mate. He's all right."

Relieved at last of responsibility for themselves, the end of the story for Lillico and Thomson was a series of vivid but often unconnected pictures of those who had taken over. Collinson flew Lillico first down the hill to the Gurkhas' jungle post at Sain, where the Medical Officer inspected his wound and prescribed immediate evacuation to Kuching Hospital 45 miles distant—if possible. It was, just. Lashing rain made the darkness total except when lightning flared and the gale buffeted the little aircraft so that Collinson had to fight it every inch of the way, with the jungle below awaiting mechanical failure or a false move. But that was not Lillico's job. Then he was watching Matron cutting away his trousers, professionally undeterred by filth, blood, flesh and grubs; that was not his job either, so he left her to it and the scene faded.

Thomson feared at first that he had been mistaken after all because the Gurkhas would not come down to the stream for him; but that was because they were professional soldiers and had first to check that the enemy was not using him as a decoy. Then Kevin Walsh was bending over him and he put his arms around his neck, which was significant because Kevin did not have the sort of face that naturally invited an embrace. The chopper came and went and the Gurkhas made him a stretcher with a poncho. It rained so they made him a tent with another poncho, and jabbed him with penicillin and streptomycin.

Then it was morning and four of those great little guys carried him on his stretcher. He remembered that all right because it hurt like hell; it was slow going too because the Gurkhas ambushed the track behind to ensure that the enemy was not following and then had to catch up. They cut down trees with their kukris and made a landing-point, but it was on a slope and when the chopper came again it could only get one wheel down while the other still hovered and the rotor whipped the shrubs on the high side. "But they shoved me in and Collinson was flying it and he got a Distinguished Flying Cross and deserved it.

"Then there was this wee Malay nursie coming at me with a pair of garden shears and I thought Jesus; but she just cut off my pants and there were maggots right through my leg. I was embarrassed in fact, I was embarrassed; but she didn't bother, she just sprayed these maggots.

"And the next thing was this guy saying, 'Jock, we're going to take your leg off,' and I said, 'No way are you going to take my leg off,' but it didn't come out that way; my mind was as clear as a bell but my mouth wouldn't do as it was told. I was gibbering like a maniac and they didn't pay any attention.

"But the Colonel came, Mike Wingate-Gray, and he's a Scot too, and he said, 'Take it easy Jock,' and I said, 'If you let them take my leg off I'll never talk to you again,' and he said, 'Jock, if you don't want your leg off, they won't take it off,' and it was as simple as that.

"I told him about the tiger's head flash on the first Indo I shot because that was important, but he couldn't understand; and then I remembered the guy looking at me, so young and scared, and I thought, poor wee lad."

Lillico was in an unhappy turmoil; of self-criticism for allowing his patrol to be ambushed and losing his rifle, and unease lest his wound should disqualify him from the SAS or even the Army. He might also be a cripple for the rest of his life, having always been superbly fit. The last straw was the money that a patrol commander carried for contingencies and had to be returned, but when he explained that it had been in his hip pocket and must have been burned with his trousers, he felt with bitter shame that he was not believed.

Woodiwiss and Wingate-Gray set out to reassure him. There had perhaps been some risk in revisiting the enemy camp, but the SAS was in the risk business and nothing would ever be achieved without it; he would be wanted in the Operational Research Wing as soon as he was well enough, so there was no question of his being thrown out; and as for the rifle and the money, hell take them. Listening to him and piecing the story together from all sources, the two officers became convinced that his leadership, bravery and self-sacrifice had been quite outstanding, indeed inspiring. They recommended him for a Military Medal and Thomson for a Mention in Despatches, which were awarded.

After a very long time, years, in the hands of the medical profession, for whose skill and devotion they are lavish in their praise, both men recovered. Lillico did so completely and resumed his front-line career with the SAS, but Thomson became "The Clog" with his left leg an inch and a half shorter than his right and not quite up to it, though he stayed in the Army for a period. After that he had to brave the world outside; and for one to whom the very breath of life was adventure, seeking challenge and surmounting it, risking his own life in a worthy cause, civilian existence was the greatest trial of all. As Sergeant Alf Tasker of "A" Squadron puts it:

"I can't talk to civilians. They don't know what I'm talking about and I'm wasting my time doing it. They can't understand why I like this job and I can't explain because I don't *know* why. It's crazy; know what I mean?"

CHAPTER 2

"IT'S A GREAT FINGER-POKING REGIMENT"

So says that repository of SAS wisdom Frank Williams over his bar at the "David Garrick," meaning that their fingers are poked mostly at themselves so as to learn from their mistakes in the unrelenting pursuit of excellence decreed by their founder David Stirling. Finger-poking from outside, however, is often less constructive. The accusation "murder squads" trips readily from the tongues of such as the IRA and those who wish to see Britain impotent against a threat to civilization of unprecedented magnitude; but it is not true.

What, therefore, is so special about them? "People don't appreciate the potential of what's in Hereford," says Eddie Lillico; and we are not going to learn much more either, but may at least be pleased both that the potential is there and that the evildoer will be the first to discover what it is. We are, however, increasingly aware of the SAS, no longer being surprised to hear, if only by rumour, that they are watching some disquieting event, ready to take action if ordered. The military meaning of the word "special" is hard to define since it can include almost any task that is not, well, ordinary, but is always sensitive and sometimes clandestine. Its essence is secrecy and its tools are small scale, bold initiative, surprise, and high skill.

Smallness, exploiting surprise to penetrate enemy lines and accomplish an otherwise impossible task, would be an unremarkable concept if just anybody could do it. Clearly, it demands special qualities, which Stirling enunciated with such perception in 1941 that his principles are still adhered to despite many changes in role and fortune since then. They are also important for those of us who are not quite content with stories of derring-do, but want to probe a little deeper into the make-up of these men.

26

First, the relentless pursuit of excellence. No qualification is needed because the words are explicit, uncompromising and daunting; and because excellence is unapproachable without deep personal motivation and few set themselves such a goal, those few must prove their commitment by surmounting a selection process so rigorous that Selection is spelt with a capital "S."

Next, strict discipline. That it may scarcely show on the surface is immaterial since it must spring from each man's *self*-discipline, which in turn derives from the motivation he has to show in order to join at all. It must impel him to lead as well as obey, and to act as the Regiment would wish in lonely, frightening and unforeseen circumstances. Should he fail, the only necessary sanction is RTU—returned to unit.

Then comes a precept as surprising as it was prescient in 1941: there must be no sense of class within the SAS. Only merit counts, because a unit, especially a small one, is strengthened operationally by each man's ability being put to best use, and in morale by excluding false values from man-to-man relationships. Even the wives conform; Stirling said they must.

It all means that the SAS has to be an élite. Although that is an admirable spur to excellence and comradeship, it contains also the seeds of smugness, which can blunt the cutting edge from within and provoke resentment from without. Stirling therefore prescribed the safeguard of humility, which is perfectly compatible with the self-assurance vital to high endeavour; the SAS is but a tiny part of the Army, which must on no account be let down, and excellence like an electric hare will never quite be caught, however hotly pursued.

Really testing, however, is Stirling's demand for smartness on parade, but even that is achieved with an effort—"we hardly ever have parades." Frank Williams again, complying with Stirling's final dictum that, lest all this relentless pursuing should lead the runners round the bend, humour—sharp and kindly, absurd and therapeutic—is indispensable.

But aren't they only a bunch of rather tougher than ordinary toughs? Why all this talk of high moral qualities? The answer is simple if paradoxical: the tough lacks the application to develop his skills to the utmost, the self-discipline to spare as well as to kill, the wit to decide which is right in the circumstances, and the dedication to endure to the end. The tough, therefore, is just not up to the tougher than ordinary job, and the moment he is recognized as such, he is out of the SAS.

* * *

Building on those principles, what had the Regiment become when it went to Borneo in 1963? In the first place, it was indeed The Regiment in its men's hearts, that almost holy entity to which each is glad to give his all, secure in the knowledge that others will do so as well. Tradition, however, was in the mind rather than the mess silver, finger-poking resulting in constant innovation in the pursuit of excellence and proving vital not just to success but for the Regiment's very survival.

For instance, the Army proper is wary of what it calls private ones, who have therefore to make a very good case for sending their wild young men out into the wild yonder to wreak who knows what havoc. Such misgivings are understandable since the only young men of use to the SAS are those who must seek adventure compulsively—even in the cannon's mouth—and, if no officially authorized cannon offers, they will be strongly tempted to have a go at another which is not.

Another recurrent frustration follows from the SAS being directly responsible to the highest commander. This is necessary because the Regiment can be employed anywhere on a variety of tasks, and its findings or depredations far beyond the battlefield may concern the whole campaign and influence major decisions. Thus, an intermediate senior officer under whom an SAS unit is placed for a particular task must endure its commander (however lowly in rank), disregarding his orders as unsuitable for the precious SAS and appealing directly to the top. Some find this trying, although restraint on both sides for the greater good of the whole usually achieves a working harmony; but, all in all, the SAS has learnt that, even with the strictest self-discipline, it must fight and fight again for the privilege of doing its duty and even of existing.

Sure enough, having fought in every conceivable terrain behind every line in the Second World War with many specialized skills painstakingly pioneered and believing its value to have been proved, the SAS Regiment was caught on the wrong foot by the peace and disbanded almost without a struggle. On being reformed rather tentatively for the Malayan Emergency as the 22nd Special Air Service Regiment, a characteristically confusing title which may serve to imbue its opponents with awe while being logical and precious to its initiates, its first resolution was that never, never must that be allowed to happen again, and for good practical reasons as well as sentiment. Indeed, the climb back to Stirling's standard of excellence was unnecessarily protracted, but so, fortunately, was the Emergency. During its course a new father-figure emerged, Major John Woodhouse, one of the Squadron commanders who, with other dedicated officers and NCOs, strove for an even higher peak. His methods were austere; such as leading the first Selection course over the Welsh mountains while suffering from a severe bout of malaria, which normally incapacitates completely and can kill, causing the thoughtful to murmur, enlightened, "so that's what it's all about."

Malaya is mostly a vast primary jungle and the best possible training ground for Borneo. Aboriginal tribes lived in the far depths and on these the communist terrorists battened to provide secure bases by means of food and early warning of attack. The SAS task naturally became to go in and break up the organization. That could be done by killing enough terrorists to persuade the rest to go away, except that it was impossible to find any to kill unless the aborigines revealed where they were; there was even a danger of the natives betraying or killing the SAS, who would always be at a disadvantage however clever they might school themselves to be in the jungle.

So began a fundamental element in the repertoire of the modern SAS—in General Templer's immortal phrase, the winning of "hearts and minds." To do so, special training and equipment proved necessary; for instance, an SAS medic had to be as well prepared for midwifery and dentistry as gunshot wounds. Material help obviously played its part, but lavish aid patronizingly administered would generate no loyalty under stress. Far more important, as the SAS soon discovered, was that truly to win hearts they had to give their own. There was no alternative to staying with the people and learning their language; not scorning their primitive way of life but living it—germs and all, but with many useful tips on the credit side—and, above all, respecting them as intelligent fellow humans, which proved quite easy once Western conceit was seen to be quite unwarranted. Then they would gradually accept the SAS and, using their incomparable jungle skills to share in their own defence, bind themselves ever more closely to the common cause.

The task was hardly one for licensed thugs, and to judge the SAS by their appearance would have been misleading. Living with the natives meant doing so for three months at a time without any breaks of which the enemy could take advantage. Four-man patrols searched the jungle incessantly, living like animals but looking a great deal worse because men must wear clothes which are not regenerating like the body and can actually rot away under such conditions. They also cause the body to smell even more horribly than it would otherwise, retaining the odour; and although by a strange and merciful dispensation of providence that cannot be smelt by those in a like state—whose delicate nostrils can nevertheless easily detect a far more subtle waft of hair cream—to a helicopter pilot, fresh from his bath and tasked to lift such men out of the jungle, it can verge on the hazardous.

The way of life was surprisingly bearable for, after all, man is a viable wild animal and especially in the forest whence he emerged not so many millenia ago; he has a good turn of speed, sufficient to evade a charging elephant, as Ian Thomson can vividly testify; his senses are keen and positioned advantageously five feet from the ground; his hands are unmatched in nature for usefulness, enabling him to rectify his lack of an organic weapon; and that is all before he starts thinking.

Like an animal, too, man could subsist on jungle fruit and meat, but since that took all day and the man was there to do a job, he had to carry his own food, only four day's supply with the standard ration of the day. That meant he had frequently to be resupplied by air, which restricted his movement and revealed his position. To "go always a little further" the SAS had to be innovators as well as sloggers, so Woodhouse experimented with concentrated and light-weight rations. For himself, the outcome was simple, since his own spare frame could be supported indefinitely by will power and little more than one tin of sardines a day; one hopes he actually liked sardines as that would be a glimmer of human frailty with which one could identify, but fears they just did not matter so long as the task was accomplished. His parting gift from the Regiment is a silver sardine tin, which symbolizes what in Borneo he would make a standard operational requirement: that an SAS patrol must be able to vanish for a fortnight, unhindered by apron-strings to friends or the need to reveal itself to foes.

Many jungle skills were mastered and new techniques developed, including parachuting into trees and then abseiling to earth, which was dreadfully dangerous and cost three lives. But one acquisition was of greater value than any, as Frank Williams says: "Living like animals for three months brings out the best and the worst in people"—though never mind the worst because RTU would soon take care of that. Sergeant, then Trooper, "Gipsy" Smith narrows the point: "When you're muddy, wet, hungry and tired all the time, that's how you come together."

And he should know; to a ruggedly individualistic horse-dealer who was dragged protesting into the Army when trying to evade national service, togetherness was a new and pleasant experience. In the SAS later he learned how to evade properly, but no longer wished to.

The aborigines talked and kills resulted; then they denied their support to the terrorists and even killed some themselves with their blowpipes. Silently and unspectacularly the enemy withdrew, though the SAS do not claim to have played any but a very small part in a very large campaign, and most other people had not, as yet, so much as heard of them.

Their true achievement had been to find themselves and set their standards, but only in a jungle environment. Now, in 1958, with Lieutenant-Colonel Deane-Drummond in command, the question began to be asked whether they had any part to play elsewhere. Disbandment threatened ominously and must at all costs be forestalled. Were their present skills too limited? Why then, develop more. Was there no scope for their present role? Find another, or several. Deane-Drummond looked around and discovered an interesting war in far-off Arabia, where rebel chieftains were threatening the Sultan of Oman from the top of a slab-sided plateau called Jebel Akhdar which had not been stormed for a thousand years, and then the Persians had lost nine out of ten thousand men. Now, the small British force, which was all it was deemed politically expedient to send, was baffled, and Deane-Drummond was asked whether the SAS could help.

They could; they must, though on the face of it the proposition was absurd. Trained only for the jungle where the visibility was at most twenty yards, they would now operate where it was usually twenty miles, and in an infantry assault, which was not their proper role. Yet Deane-Drummond knew they could pull it off; their physical toughness needed no acclimatization, and their mental toughness, well practised determination and adaptability would soon accustom them to very different terrain and tactics.

They did it by guile and toughness; the toughness being essential to the guile and the guile to the toughness, exploiting mind and body to achieve the utmost of which a man is capable. They marched by day and countermarched by night further than the enemy would think possible; scaled escarpments he would assume to be unscaleable; fed him false rumours; and finally

surprised him into surrender with hardly a shot. In the bright
desert light their quality was clearly seen as it could not be in
the jungle; they established their ability to go anywhere and do
anything, and although they lost "B" Squadron, leaving only
"A" and "D," there was no more talk of disbandment.

There followed a period of comparative peace that the SAS would
not normally have welcomed but now used to prepare for whatever might lie ahead in a worldwide role.

The nominal strength of each of the two Squadrons was about
70 officers and men, the precise number varying with the task
and, in practice, with the fully qualified people available. There
were never enough at this period of the Regiment's development
and in no circumstances would shortages be filled with light-
weights. A major in command was assisted by a warrant officer
second class as Squadron sergeant-major, a quartermaster sergeant for logistics, and signallers, drivers, storemen, etc. as
needed, sometimes attached from other units.

"A" Squadron comprised 1, 2, 3 and 4 Troops, and "D"
16, 17, 18 and 19, which, like the Regiment calling itself the
22nd when there was only one (regular), baffles the logical com-
prehension of the outsider who must nevertheless take them as
they were. The four-man patrol having become established as
the basic unit, always including a signaller and a medic and often
a linguist, demolitionist or other specialist, a troop of sixteen
men could field four. A captain in command (not always present
since junior officers of the right calibre proved hardest of all to
find) and a troop sergeant were included in that number as commanders of their respective patrols. The keynote of the organization was flexibility, though the intimate little family that
constituted a patrol was undisturbed as far as possible.

To work then; what was needed? Keeping fit, by which they
meant being in Olympic condition all the time; constant practising with a dozen different weapons to ensure hitting split-
second targets at five yards or five hundred from every possible
altitude; mastery of skills such as communications, demolition,
medical aid to a standard not hitherto attempted by soldiers;
parachuting in all its forms and applications; abseiling; learning
to live, move and fight in deserts, mountains, jungles, snow and
cities; fluency in the languages of countries where they might
operate; practice and development of tactics through exercises
and discussion both organized and endlessly around the bar,
"shop" being life to an SAS soldier; surmounting mental as

well as physical hardship as in escape and evasion exercises over rugged terrain with no resources and every man's hand against the lone soldier, followed by pitiless interrogation when drained of strength and vitality.

By 1962 the Regiment was ready for Borneo—"have bergen, will travel"; and when Lieutenant-Colonel John Woodhouse assumed command its readiness increased, as may be imagined. But, satiated with training, it would not remain at the peak without the element of real challenge, and there was as yet no war in Borneo, or anywhere else.

CHAPTER 3

"ARCADIA"

Java had once been the centre of a great empire, and such memories are cherished. That was before the Europeans staked out empires in their turn, of which the Dutch, British, French and American were in full vigour until the Japanese seized them all in 1942 to their great shame and ignominy. They fought their way back, but their reception by their old vassals depended on their popularity and likely value. The Americans were readily accepted in the Philippines, as were the British in Malaya who then demonstrated their goodwill and effectiveness by settling the Emergency before beginning the process of withdrawing from their empire. The French, however, were not welcomed in Indo-China and the long drawn out tragedy of Vietnam soon began, while in Indonesia the Dutch were met with armed resistance and had left by 1949.

The charismatic and visionary rabble-rouser Soekarno emerged as President of Indonesia, flushed with victory and grandiose dreams of fresh worlds to conquer. Not that he had the least hope of governing his own nation effectively; one hundred million people of many sub-ethnic groups often jealous of each other and living on a thousand islands spread over three thousand miles of ocean would have baffled a far greater man. Bored with humdrum practicalities of administration and economics, which alone could have brought some amelioration to his teeming poor, he loved to invent words like "Maphilindo" and distract the people from their troubles with a mystical vision of Malaya, the Philippines and Indonesia in one great Asian Utopia.

His neighbours would not have worried too much had he meant something like the European Economic Community in which the members subscribed to fine principles of unity and

34

then continued to act independently exactly as before, but much more was apparently intended, including the British relinquishing their military bases as well as their colonies. That would be unacceptable, and not only to the British, because Tunku Abdul Rahman of Malaya and Lee Kwan Yew of Singapore also wanted them to stay in view of the threat from communism to the north. And now it seemed that a threat was developing from the south too, for whatever "Maphilindo" meant Soekarno clearly intended to be the boss of it. This concern was intensified by communism having become a strong and growing force in Indonesia.

Time and again the Tunku asked Soekarno what he was getting at; but wily as he was, or woolly, he never explained. The implication could only be that he wanted the British out of the way for no good reason and must therefore be taken seriously, particularly since Indonesia had ten times the population of the British territories combined and was well armed by Russia. The Tunku's reaction was to invent his own world, Malaysia, preserving the Commonwealth grouping of Malaya, Singapore and the three Borneo territories Sarawak, Sabah and Brunei as a viable political, economic and defensible unit, and the idea gradually caught on. Only Soekarno demurred, angrily, though no one was threatening him. It may be that he saw himself presented with an unsatisfactory choice between waiting until the British had gone before taking what he wanted, when Malaysia would be a recognized nation and his action overt aggression that might provoke outside interference, or doing his utmost now to prevent its ever being formed so that its individual states would remain weak and amenable to pressure.

He took the latter course and, misleading himself that the colonial peoples yearned to throw off their yoke and join Indonesia, opened his campaign by setting up subversive cells in Malaya and Singapore and interfering with their fishermen. He does not seem to have appreciated in the early stages that British Borneo offered him a better chance; perhaps it was too small beer for one who aspired to change the world, and contemporary sources agree that the Brunei Revolt in December 1962 took him as much by surprise as it did everyone else.

Brunei was the original native name for the whole island, though the Europeans of course knew better and called it Borneo. Comprising mountains, rivers, swamps and universal forest, it is the third largest island in the world and proved too big for the corrupt and ineffective rule of successive Sultans, great pieces being sliced off until in 1890 the map appeared as it remains today. Two-thirds, first Dutch and now Indonesian, is called Kalimantan. The rest was British, acquired absentmindedly in the nineteenth century by different means; Sarawak (second syllable pronounced "r" and accented) to the southwest, where the first Rajah Brooke was entreated by the locals to free them from the Sultan; Sabah (pronounced *Sar*ber) to the northeast, where there had been virtually no government until it was settled by the British North Borneo Company. Both were now colonies, and between them two tiny enclaves were all that remained of Brunei; she was still a hereditary sultanate, now a protectorate, and her affairs had taken a turn for the better since fortune had presented her with the only oilfield on the British part of the coast.

The Revolt was quickly suppressed by British troops flown in from Malaya in a very efficient little operation with few casualties. Since the SAS were not involved and the issues were mainly domestic, there is no need to master its oriental complexities except in one regard. Its leader had strong leanings towards Indonesia, where many of the unfortunate rebel "soldiers" had been "trained" and, after the event, Soekarno's propaganda supported the uprising bombastically. It was, therefore, only prudent to assume that Indonesia was the instigator as part of her anti-Malaysia campaign. The British force was ordered to remain and be ready for whatever might happen next, not only in Brunei but in the whole of British Borneo.

Major-General Walter Walker was appointed Director of Operations and rarely can a general have been so absolutely right for a task and been given it. He was a fighting general who won his battles, fierce and aggressive like his Gurkha soldiers with most of his active experience having been in the jungles of Burma and Malaya. Walker was also a soldier's general, that high accolade which meant, in his case, that he drove his men hard but himself harder and that they mattered to him and knew it. With those at the head of affairs such as governors, administrators, police chiefs of the three territories he could be embarrassingly terse when they failed to see things his way. Yet he was also essentially an English gentleman: polite, interested in others' opinions and capable of inspiring that cooperation among his colleagues which was vital in the circumstances. Even with the armed forces his position could be difficult. Exercising the new doctrine of Unified Command over all three services, he was responsible only to the commander-in-chief in Singapore and not to their individual commanders on whom he relied to support him but who did not always like being left out.

As Walker took charge in Borneo, Lieutenant-Colonel John Woodhouse waited in Hereford for a call to join in what seemed a promising affray. The SAS do not wait long in such tantalizing circumstances, so Woodhouse called at the War Office to find, as he fully expected but which shocked him too, that the Regiment had not even been considered, despite its readiness for instant deployment and its outstanding jungle experience. He therefore importuned, as all SAS commanders must learn to do, and succeeding at least in having it included in a list of units available to General Walker should he want them, went home to the Dorset downs for Christmas. On Boxing Day the hardest winter for many years took a grip on the south of England, so that when the summons at last came, the first leg of his journey to the steaming jungle was made on foot through a blizzard and banked-up snowdrifts.

Walker was convinced that trouble must be expected from Soekarno, though most opinion held that Borneo would soon settle down once the revolt had been tidied up. Some even said, and there are always such, that Walker thoroughly enjoyed his grand command and wanted to develop it; but once peace has been disturbed, violence tends to persist, and although there was little positive Intelligence of Indonesian activity, Soekarno would surely deduce that if one group of people was prepared to rebel there might be others whom he could use. British Borneo could thus become a more attainable target than Malaya, and attractive in that success would emasculate the hateful concept of Malaysia.

There was indeed such a group, a very large one known as the Clandestine Communist Organization (CCO). Predominantly Chinese and mainly in the towns of Sarawak, quietly it built up its strength and influence with total dedication and harsh discipline in readiness for the day of action, whenever that should come. Soekarno was not a communist, but they wanted to frustrate Malaysia just as he did. The dilemma, which Walker clearly saw, was that his security forces would be hard pressed either to contain a large-scale internal uprising, in which case the Indonesian Army would be free to march in, or to hold the frontier and thus allow the CCO a free run behind it; but they must be ready to do both and never must the two enemies be allowed to meet.

Walker's initial directive laid emphasis on a first class Intelligence organization and included the remarkable imperative, "Dominate the jungle." What, the whole of the nine hundred mile frontier with the equivalent of six infantry battalions and local forces? Not everywhere at once, perhaps, but wherever it mattered, and success would depend on knowing where that was through Intelligence in all its forms. The SAS could help in that function, but Walker had sent for Woodhouse with something quite different in mind. Some of the larger jungle villages had airstrips that were vulnerable to Indonesian airborne assault, in which event he would want soldiers who could parachute into trees to restore the position. Could the SAS do it? He had not worked closely with them before, despite both having fought simultaneously in Malaya; few had, for when the SAS were on the job they tended to vanish and it was usual for their capabilities not to be fully understood. But Woodhouse did not argue; much more important was to impress the General with enthusiasm and get a Squadron to Borneo for whatever initial purpose. So yes, of course the SAS could do the airstrip job, especially as it seemed they were the only available unit trained to do so; though perhaps General Walker would also like to consider using them on the frontier itself, where they could stay for long periods, get to know the locals and find out what the Indonesians were doing.

A signal winged homewards as fast as light. Almost as fast, "A" Squadron skimmed down on their skis from the Welsh mountains where they had seized the opportunity to train in arctic warfare while rescuing snow-trapped sheep. Within hours, two in the case of those furthest away, bergens were packed with tropical shirts and slacks, jungle hats and boots, long jungle knives called "parangs," mess tins with hexamine for cooking, insect repellent, sardines and other necessaries, and the men were gone, ready to march into the jungle even as they stepped out of their aircraft. They had no time to kiss goodbye, and could not have told their loved ones that they were going, far less where, even if they had; but they did not mind, they liked it, and would have done so even had they known that nobody really wanted them in Borneo and that it was their own Colonel who had put them to the trouble. That attitude is perhaps not quite ordinary, even a little special.

Commanding "A" Squadron, Major John Edwardes was surely the archetypal SAS officer, and yet not quite because the rest describe him as wholly mad, which implies a difference of degree in an outfit where all are necessarily mad to some extent. His wife says he knows no fear, which may be madness because it ought to be dangerous, yet he has survived one adventure after another to which he is inexorably propelled by that irresistible urge that is indeed typical of the SAS. Take, for example, the one when he was a London policeman and hurled himself on top of a stolen Jaguar with nothing to hold onto but the radio aerial while the driver accelerated and swerved wildly. Surely that was mad, yet it was but the beginning, for he then smashed the windscreen with his truncheon which should logically have caused the instant deaths of the pair of them. But no; they hit a low wall, the malefactor popped out through the hole into a garden and Edwardes, always a jump ahead, intoned, "Anything you say will be taken down. . . ." He was awarded the George Medal "because it attracted a certain amount of attention in Kensington." Well yes, idle people will indeed stop to stare at almost anything rather than go about their business.

Similarly in Malaya when his Gurkha patrol was ambushed and his reaction was so fast, fierce and fearless that five terrorists were killed, they having started with all the advantages. Snakes were his fascination, picking them up and putting them in his bergen as he went along so that there was never any bunching in his patrols, a fault common with soldiers new to the jungle. He took them home, and once found himself blinded by a spitting cobra that he had taken from a roomful of those engaging creatures, holding it in one hand while his wife—"who did not really like snakes"—guided him with the other where to throw it back preparatory to shutting the door. Then there was the capture of "Georgie Girl," a 25-foot python, in unarmed combat at dead of night, again assisted by his wife who illuminated the hissing, cursing, writhing mass with candlelight. "Candles!" she says. "Can you imagine?" There was only one species of snake that Edwardes never caught, the King Cobra or Hamadryad, which can grow to twenty feet and kill in as many minutes. "You really need a stick for them."

The Squadron was held up at Singapore and told to acclimatize. It was a very necessary precaution for most troops, but the SAS took a pride in not needing to and were irked. Then more inactivity awaited them at General Walker's headquarters on Labuan Island where they were kept as an emergency parachute force; but the pause enabled Woodhouse to advise the General on how they might best be employed, very tactfully because a

Gurkha officer does not easily acknowledge that anyone can do anything better than Gurkhas.

The immensely long border needed watching, but how? The problem had never arisen before as it had always been friendly, and indeed of no great significance because nobody had any cause to go there except the local tribes to whom it meant little anyway. There were even parts that were thought never to have been visited at all. On a small-scale map it was easy enough to see where it ran, but the larger the scale the greater the areas with nothing marked but what was visible from the air: mountain peaks and ridges, rivers wide enough to divide the canopy, and trees, trees, trees. Where it was mountainous the frontier usually followed the watershed between the Kalimantan and British river systems, thus recognizing the jungle way of life in which rivers are the arteries of trade and communications and all communities live near them; but elsewhere the line tended to be drawn with a ruler on the map though not on the ground, neither did British and Dutch maps always agree.

In a few instances rivers crossed the border and could be negotiated by boat. Elsewhere, one had to walk, but there was no particular hardship in that apart from climbing to the dividing ridge if there was one. Tracks could be classified like roads: six-foot wide trade-routes with carefully maintained bridges and convenient handrails, single tracks with just logs, and ways barely discernible to the foreigner and only occasionally used by hunters and foragers. Animal tracks abounded and were useful, but movement was by no means limited to tracks, especially in primary jungle where shade inhibited undergrowth and walking could even be pleasant. Swamp and secondary jungle, however, were another matter and there were some such areas along the border itself.

Thus the Indonesians could come across almost anywhere, concealed from but a few yards on the ground and completely from above so that modern technology would be powerless to detect them before they reached their objectives. The needle/haystack ratio was so extreme that if all the British soldiers had been posted on the frontier they would have been 400 yards apart. There was thus no alternative to keeping them in the rear, poised to react once the enemy had shown his hand. That would be bad for the people's morale because some might get hurt before help arrived, leading to the inevitable conclusion that the British were powerless to protect them. Some form of early warning would therefore be priceless, and Woodhouse offered it; the border tribes themselves, guided by the SAS, must act as eyes and ears.

The plan followed directly from the Regiment's success with the aborigines in Malaya. A jungle dweller was a finely tuned sensor of all that happened in his minutely familiar area; even the behaviour of some individual animals and birds was observed, so that a strange human or group of them trying to pass was a conspicuous and noteworthy event. The information would be doubly valuable because the tribes were just as much at home in the Kalimantan border villages where they traded and intermarried, but it would only be passed on if they liked the soldiers and trusted them to prevent possible reprisals.

The SAS had trained themselves to go and stay in far off places for long periods, whether to fight or make friends or both, living off the country if possible, but otherwise needing little resupply. Their various skills matched this requirement; there being no point in going had they not been sure of being able to report what they found, their high frequency radios were specially chosen for long range, lightness and reliability; their medical attainments were high and many of them spoke Malay, the lingua franca of the tribes. Over and above soldiering in all its forms, these three skills were specialties and everybody had to master one, though many had more. It would now have become clear to the General that no infantry regiment possessed them to anything like SAS standard, far less would it have been able to split itself into three- or four-man patrols and include them all in each one. Whether he was convinced, or merely hoped that they might do some good, he kept to himself, but he let them go. "A" Squadron hoisted its bergens, stepped into the unknown and found Arcadia.

John Edwardes set about establishing his patrols, assisted by his Squadron Sergeant-Major, Lawrence Smith, who in the absence of an officer as second in command doubled in that role too. He was one of those who felt that the fewer officers there were the better, unless, like Edwardes, they measured up to his own standards of vitality and competence, being more than prepared to take on any of their tasks himself. He liked being a Sergeant-Major in the SAS because the conventional duties of square-bashing, gingering people up and putting them on charges just did not arise, and his high position would enable him to take the most interesting patrols.

Also helping were two civilians who knew the borders and

their tribes better than most: John Warne, a police officer in
Sabah, and Tom Harrisson, the world-famous anthropologist.
Both had parachuted into Japanese-occupied Borneo in the Second World War and persuaded the people to resume their ancient
though latterly discouraged practice of taking heads; ten bob a
nob, but only if Japanese. They did not need much persuasion
for it used to be an essential part of their religion in which there
was now a gap. If one asked how much headhunting went on,
the quick, official answer was "none." The slow answer was
"hardly any," at least that ever came to light, but how could
one tell? One way of telling was by tiny but revealing tattoo
marks on the forefinger, and there were such. Was there then
danger in going among them? If you were British, none whatever. A more charming and hospitable people could hardly be
imagined, and every longhouse, even some thought never to
have been visited by white men before, displayed a prize picture
of the Queen, garlanded though it might be by their other tro-
phies—skulls; Japanese, of course.

Edwardes spaced his patrols at intervals, which varied with
the potential threat in different areas but were never less than
twenty miles. Accompanied by Warne or Harrisson he would
usually take them in personally, introductions would be made
and then the patrol stayed for three months to become in many
cases more knowledgeable about the area than anyone else. District Officers with vast regions, outstandingly dedicated though
they were, could but come and go and not necessarily everywhere; but the SAS made it their home, earned the people's trust
and set them to gathering information about the Indonesians.

They added many essential details to their blank maps: wa-
tercourses showing limits of boat navigation, tracks classified
into main, secondary and hunting with distances in both yards
and hours marching, contours and accessibility of individual
areas, primary jungle, areas under cultivation ("ladang") and
secondary jungle previously cleared but now reverting with thick
undergrowth ("belukar"). They wrote a Domesday Book of the
population, describing their races, habits, customs, what they
ate, their state of health and whether they had enough salt (so
essential in hot climates), what shotguns, boats, buffalo, pigs
and chickens they possessed, and who among them were influ-
ential for good or ill. In particular, they noted ambush positions,
border crossing-points, and places for parachute dropping and
helicopter landing, some of which they cleared.

Edwardes worked methodically along the border, starting at

the eastern coast of Sabah. Here lay Tawau, an important town by Borneo standards of 15,000 people and the centre and port for a considerable area of enterprise such as rubber, timber and hemp, employing many Indonesians, which was worrying. It was also very close to the border, which first runs through islands, actually bisecting one, and then across the combined estuaries of several rivers on both sides where the land is flat and swampy for 25 miles until hills start to rise and soon become mountains; patrols were clearly needed here, in part waterborne.

The next stretch of 40 miles posed a problem because it was not just uninhabited but virtually unexplored. Known as The Gap, its rugged mountains and lack of navigable rivers made it uninviting even to the local tribe, the Muruts. As the border could not be watched without their help, it had to be given a miss for the time being. Eventually something would have to be done about it, primarily because access was easier from the Indonesian side but also its magnificent wildness challenged the SAS pilgrims irresistibly.

Westwards again, to a region that was centred on the village of Pensiangan and was still satisfyingly wild with peaks up to 3,000 feet and great areas of primary forest. Much of the border was watershed ridge, but there were two gaps where a large Indonesian river and its tributary flowed across, and further dividing provided the Muruts with the main condition for community life. The villages were isolated and vulnerable, and Sergeant "Tanky" Smith commanding 3 Troop, in the quite usual absence of an officer, went in to redress the balance. The Troop split into patrols which did not see each other again until the end of the tour, Smith taking one. In his maturity his impressive perception, experience and lucid ability to express them call to mind a tranquil elder statesman, and it is only an involuntary twinkle that makes it just possible to envisage his earlier boisterous irrepressibility, of which those whose duty it was to try and repress speak with much feeling.

Smith's experiences were typical. "When we arrived at this village near the border a baby looked as if it was dying and I said to my medic, 'You'd better get this right or we'll be kicked out.' He gave it a quarter of an aspirin dissolved in milk and it got better, so we were made welcome and that was a good start. It was a happy time, better than Malaya because although I loved the abos they weren't so civilized as the Muruts, who took us into their hearts and homes."

The Muruts had a reputation for hard drinking, but they worked hard too. In their "ladangs" they cleared the jungle and cropped the land until it was exhausted, rice (dry "padi") and tapioca being their basic diet; they foraged for jungle fruits such as figs, durians, mangosteens; they hunted wild pig, deer, birds, monkeys and other animals with blowpipes, traps and the odd shotgun, and they fished the rivers. They built and repaired their own houses with materials from the forest, and could be completely self-supporting as they had had to be during the Japanese occupation. But trade improves any economy, and jungle products like timber, rotan, swiftlets' nests for Chinese soup and jelutong for American chewing gum could be exchanged for the products of so-called civilization such as clothes, paraffin, baked beans, shotguns, or corrugated iron for roofing, which offended the occidental aesthete but kept out the rain much better than palm leaves. There was also trade between the villages to balance surpluses and shortages, so the boat people and porters were hard at it too, the border being no obstacle.

What more natural and sensible, therefore, than that the Muruts should take three days' off a month for what the Army calls rest and recreation, and the SAS would have won no hearts by refusing their hospitality, though "Tanky" Smith had to steel himself to endure it; "What they do is split a length of thick bamboo and fill it with uncooked pork, salt and rice; then they bury it for a month, and when they dig it up it's called 'jarit' and, oh God, the pong. But we had to eat it. You just could if you'd drunk enough 'tapai';" though Lillico adds, "even so I had to go outside and spew it up. The things we did for Queen and country." "Tapai" was wine, for want of a better word, made from rice or tapioca, and looked like rough cider because the Muruts could not wait for it to ferment out or clear, but drank it through straws out of huge Chinese dragon jars as soon as the alcohol content was sufficiently fiery. "Great climate for wine-making"; comments Frank Williams the publican. "Anything would ferment, even your socks."

"Tanky" Smith relates another sore trial. "After a month the headman said we'd been away from home for a long time and would we like to refresh ourselves with four of their girls who rather fancied us? I said we'd be delighted"—and there is no reason to disbelieve him for these people were primitive only in consequence of their environment, and he would have been less than a man who was not awakened by the girls' intelligent sweetness and bare-breasted charm—"but there's a snag. Even if they themselves fancy us, they've probably each got a boy friend so we've made four enemies, and those four will have families so we may have twenty enemies when we're supposed to be here making friends. Besides I didn't want a blowpipe dart in my back and my head added to their collection. My youngest unmarried trooper said, 'Speak for yourself, I think it would be impolite to refuse'; but I told him, 'No,' and that was an order. It was a talking point for an evening and then we got on with something else; though I did just wonder which one had fancied me.''

There being as yet no enemy and, consequently, no warlike tension, the tour took on the nature of an idyll among people living in a state of nature, with nature untamed and dominant. The SAS felt themselves enfolded by the vast harmony of the jungle and its peoples, the more palpably because in sad contrast to modern, western values. There, a ''jungle'' means a concrete waste and an ''animal'' a hooligan, whereas the real jungle is alive to the smallest twig and no animal would be so stupid as to seek pleasure in violence. A myriad miraculous life-cycles intertwine to render each dependant on all and all on each; and man can only make his life there if he forgets or has never learnt that he is the zenith of creation, wisely submitting himself to the salutory and life-perpetuating law of the jungle. The SAS found it exceedingly satisfying.

All patrols were ordered to cache some rations for use in emergency, and secrecy was essential. Not that the Muruts would have betrayed their friends from malice, but every happening however small was news which they loved to disseminate, and the information would soon have crossed the border; so the patrol took four days searching for the wildest spot and covering its tracks with all the jungle skills acquired in Malaya. On return to his village base Smith was cheerfully handed his ''porter money,'' an immense fortune to the Muruts, which he had left lying about and not even missed; trust grew, and the soldiers, having set out to win the Muruts' hearts and minds, involuntarily surrendered their own. Their main offering was medicine; ''It was a great thing to see a man's disfigurement which he'd had for years clear up in a few days when you gave him penicillin; or the father of that baby, his first child. No way could they be anything but your friends for life. We only had to say what we wanted and they'd rush over the border to find out.''

Medical aid was not one-sided. In a neighbouring patrol Trooper Roger Blackman contracted lepto-spirosis, a tropical disease foul in all its aspects from its origin in the urine of rats borne by water, which is why it was not only permissible not to bathe but desirable. Raging fever, violent headache, severe abdominal pain with vomiting and coughing blood combine to cause death more often than not.

Blackman was very ill indeed, losing two stones in ten days. His life may have been saved by the aureomycin that the medic dispensed; but the whole village was deeply concerned for him, too, and their witch-doctor was in constant attendance, professionaly attired, with spells and incantations administered with that intensity of faith which we are told can cure and may, who knows, have helped. As convalescence supervened, he continued unflagging in his ministrations, bringing comforts of all sorts and delicacies to eat which happily did not include "jarit," but even eggs with half-formed chicks inside proved too much for poor Blackman. He declined weakly as graciously as he could, but his complaint was judged to be frivolous.

"You eat chickens don't you?"

"Yes."

"And new laid eggs?"

"Yes, but . . ."

"Well then."

Another bank holiday weekend came round and the headman said to "Tanky" Smith: "That 'jarit' you put out so carefully last month must be just about ready and we thought you might like us to bring it in. We know where it is." Ethereal among the shadows, hunters had watched the patrol's every movement, intrigued that putting tins up trees was the British way of making "jarit." A pause ensued while Smith, who was rarely at a loss for words, recovered himself sufficiently to reply, "Oh that's the long term stuff, takes three months"; but without conviction as he pondered the implication thus vividly presented. To win hearts and establish an efficient Intelligence-gathering organization could indeed prove the key to defence, but what if they were lost to the enemy? Not only would information be denied, but how could even the SAS survive on the frontier? It was a solemn thought.

Moving on westwards the hinterlands of Long Pa Sia and Long Semado were so rugged and mountainous as to be uninhabited; they were, however, accessible from either side and long-established trade routes crossed the border. The area was thus vulnerable to incursion and proved later to be a thorn in the flesh, but at this early time border surveillance depended and could only depend on the skilful and willing cooperation of the locals, so that, where there were none, patrols had to be stationed well back where people did live and hope to profit from reports of hunters and traders.

Southwards into Sarawak the mountains soared even higher, river navigation to the coastal plain was blocked by falls and rapids, yet where one would expect to find another Gap there existed as near an approach to Arcadia as may be found in the twentieth century world. The massifs encircle a fertile plateau to which in distant times the peaceful Kelabits had been driven by warlike enemies, and here they had developed an advanced form of agriculture centred on rice from wet "padi" in fields irrigated by an ingenious and complex system and ploughed using water buffalo. They were highly sophisticated in their ideas too, not being content just to follow tradition but constantly experimenting and innovating, as Tom Harrisson found to his admiration when he lived with them during the war.

The plateau embraced the border, Ba Kelalan and Bareo among many smaller villages on the British side with Long Bawan and Long Medan on the other, and of course it meant nothing to the Kelabits. But the area was crucial to defence, commanding the narrow waist of British Borneo with oil-rich Brunei at risk. As elsewhere the patrol wrote their Domesday Book, made friends and had fun. A particular hearts and minds winner in the Kelabit Highlands was cosmetic surgery. Beauty had traditionally demanded the piercing of a baby's ear lobes from which were hung increasingly heavy rings until the extended loops of gristle dangled to the shoulders or below, the longer the lovelier; but now that outsiders had at last arrived, many youngsters yearned to have neat ears like theirs and the SAS medics were happy to oblige with a quick snip and a few stitches.

That particular importation was undoubtedly an improvement, but the same could not be said for all. As in ancient Arcadia where the rustic paradise was often disrupted by gods descending uninvited and pursuing their incomprehensible activities among the shepherd boys and girls, so did Christian missionaries descend at Be Kelalan by light aircraft and with selfless devotion to duty succeed in introducing conflict where there had been none before. One half of the village was teetotal and took its recreation at prayer meetings with hymn singing, while in the other the usual large quantities of "tapai" was consumed to a less restrained type of entertainment. Smith could not detect any difference in quality between the two, their general standard of morality being in any case higher than many allegedly civilized communities, but there was no doubt which was the more cheerful and content.

Progress, so-called, is inexorable however, and, enjoy themselves as they might, men as perceptive as the SAS could not but be saddened at the prospects for the border tribes to whom they were becoming increasingly devoted. Lieutenant-Colonel John Woodhouse saw the danger early and briefed his men to do all in their power to allay it. The coming frontier war would greatly accelerate the opening up process, the effects of which could be disastrous to the tribes' own self-contained and almost perfect economy, especially after the departure of the British. Medicine was the one major service the outside world could provide to improve their lives significantly. Once accustomed to it, how terrible if it were to be cut off. Perhaps saddest of all was the thought that they, so happy and free of stress—which were blessings the soldiers learned to admire and indeed envy— should be introduced to western pressures and anxieties.

Such sensitivity for the welfare of simple dependant peoples was peculiarly British. Those representatives who had reached the Kelabits and their like—Rajah Brooke's District Officers were not even allowed to marry the better to serve them, devotees like Tom Harrisson, many excellent missionaries among the cranks and now the SAS—were dedicated to the good of the tribes. The people were certainly not overburdened by government, but there was enough of it to impose that absolute fundamental, the rule of law, between the tribes. Nothing approaching Arcadia had been known on the island in the savage, headhunting, pre-colonial days when fear and stress had been the norm.

The tribes envisaged no change for none was wanted, and when it was mentioned, as honesty demanded, that the British were planning to leave, they were first incredulous and then dismayed. Such loyalty boded well for the coming war, yet it also became clear that the tribes did not regard the other alternatives to the British as much better than the Indonesians; the Malays were the traditional aristocrats, but they tended to look down on the jungle people and were in turn disliked, and the Chinese were either ruthless traders or communists.

* * *

Southwest-wards from the Kelabit Highlands Sarawak widened into its Third Division, watered by the great River Rejang and its tributaries. Here the Kalimantan border was 100–150 miles from the sea and ran through wild and mountainous country where there were no settled villages and only the really primitive semi-nomadic Punans were occasionally found. It was difficult to gain access from the other side too, and an intruder would then have to cover a great distance in Sarawak to reach any significant objective, so SAS patrols were again deployed well back where villages began. Captain Bill Dodd of 2 Troop was given this considerable responsibility; he placed one of his patrols at Long Jawai under Corporal George Stainforth, who because he was lent from "D" Squadron stayed there until the summer.

The SAS were thin enough on whatever ground they occupied so it was important to place them where they could do most good, and a glance at the map will show that it was in the First and Second Divisions of Sarawak that both the Indonesian threat and British vulnerability were greatest. Kuching, the capital, was but 25 miles from the border, which was crossed by innumerable trade routes with easy access from both sides. Much of the land was cleared for cultivation, making possible the deployment of major military formations. Half the country's entire population was concentrated there, including many Chinese of whom a substantial proportion were undoubtedly clandestine communists. Maximum SAS effort was thus called for.

Patrols went into the Second Division where the Ibans lived, after the Chinese the most numerous race in Sarawak. They were a warrior race, having entered the country as invaders, and were also called Sea Dyaks because they had not been averse to piracy either. Tattooing and headhunting were their specialties, the latter indulged without restraint until the Rajahs Brooke clamped down on it; but when restrained by the rule of law, military aptitude can be a virtue, and many Ibans had been recruited as trackers for the Malayan Emergency and would now contribute more than any other local community to their own country's defence.

The First Division, strategically the most important of all, was screened by what might be thought a very thin red line indeed, though by 1963 standards in Borneo it was lavish, the whole of 1 Troop commanded by Captain Ray England. No fewer than sixteen men watched the equivalent of the English border with Wales. Put another way, this amounted to six miles a man, though in practise the 16 were divided into four patrols about 25 miles apart with about 25 villages to each.

Like Wales too, the First Division was where early refugees, Land Dyaks in this case, had been driven by waves of aggressive Ibans. Their historical aim was to keep out of trouble, often building their longhouses on defensible hilltops while being more reliant than other tribes on good spirits to protect them and help them prosper. Such spirits, being good, usually cooperated without being asked. It was the malign ones who had to be pacified, driven away or avoided by complicated and time-consuming rituals. Some of these the SAS learned and observed, thus gaining in respect, but it could nevertheless be frustrating to go exploring with Land Dyak hunters and be told that because a hornbill had flown from left to right across the track the expedition must be cancelled; though as understanding grew it was sometimes possible to invoke some good spirit to neutralize the evil one.

England established his base at Padawan, an outpost of civilization where there was an Anglican Community Centre comprising a school, a medical dispensary, an agricultural adviser, a chapel, and a football pitch, which would later be handy for helicopters, though in these early days those invaluable workhorses were rarely seen. England did not spend long there, however. Leaving his signaller as a receiver of local information and a link with headquarters, he journeyed constantly with the other two men to map the country and meet the people. Peace was as yet unbroken so he used the tracks, but as the first incident could occur anywhere at any time, he required the patrol to be always alert, well spaced, and ready to melt into the bush either to offer ambush or avoid it.

On first visiting a longhouse, England would engage the headman in conversation:

"I'd explain who we were and they'd nod, though I don't think they really understood until I said we came from Padawan and mentioned someone they knew there because that was the centre of their world. Then we'd talk about the weather, what stage the 'padi' had reached, how many coconut palms they had, what were their specialities such as pineapples or cucumbers which were rare luxuries. After that we'd get onto sickness and they'd be quick to tell us of their complaints; toothache was common, and so were septic cuts as they had no conception of hygiene but rubbed tobacco into wounds. We did all we could for them.

"At last I'd tell them we'd come because the Indonesians might caught trouble and we wanted to help them. They were already apprehensive enough of the Indonesians to have curtailed their cross-border traffic, and that was a pity so I encouraged them to start again and tell us what we so badly needed to know: all about the local people, topography, and of course the least sign of Indonesian soldiers. I'd ask them what they'd do if the Indonesians attacked, and perhaps because there was little they *could* do but run into the jungle they promised to tell us all they discovered. This they did and a steady stream of reports flowed in, sometimes by runner and often by people coming to Padawan on their ordinary business."

In only one village were the people inscrutable, a Chinese one where the Dyaks' rubber was traded for other goods. It is not that the Chinese are naturally inscrutable, far from it; their sense of fun and zest for life are normally as well developed as anyone's, but here there were distinctly cagey overtones. The Land Dyaks murmured incomprehensibly, "puttisup," as though the place harboured an infectious disease and should be avoided. They were not far wrong, for their meaning when finally divined was Party SUPP, Sarawak United People's Party which was the legal front organization for the clandestine communists; and here, as everywhere, even among people who could have no understanding of what communism meant, they had managed to make themselves unpopular.

Sarawak geography ends with Cape Datu jutting north into the China Sea with the border running along its spine. It being obviously important, Edwardes extracted his Sergeant-Major, Lawrence Smith, from Bareo and sent him there to reconnoitre. Smith went there expecting to live rough, but found instead a Chinese millionaire and dined sumptuously on delicate bird's nest soup, fragrantly scented tea and all that went between them, accompanied by five-star Cognac. Intimacy was slow to blossom, however, because his host thought Smith must be a government inspector sent to investigate his fleet of motor-junks in which he imported rubber from round the point in Indonesia and then distributed it to the world without wasting time and money on customs formalities. The barrier between the two men was swept aside, however, when Smith perceived that here was the chance to go a little further; indeed, the Hereford Clock advocated crossing "that glimmering sea" as a proper way for a pilgrim. He accompanied his host on a voyage which, with its bracing air, good living and stimulating company, Smith found a memorable experience. He also discovered that no Indonesian military activity was in train on that part of the coast.

Having sent in his patrols, Edwardes went in himself, by himself, and walked the better part of that 900-mile frontier; coming out only when he reached the uninhabited areas and then going straight in again. Only brisk walking would cover the distances, so he took no pack; just his Armalite, water bottle, emergency kit, and sardines—because he liked them unashamedly though the tins added weight—but otherwise relying for sustenance, succour and survival on the tribes along his way. He proved that he was justified in doing so by surviving alone the perils of the jungle, such as elephants, swarming bees, falling branches or sprained ankles; snakes too, even for him, because they must not be allowed to take the initiative. "The trouble with being alone is you can't guard yourself against man or animal; two are all right. You have to become like an animal yourself, very, very alert; I slept in a little hidey-hole because that was less obvious than a basha."

There was no strain in this, just piquancy; he slept well and enjoyed himself thoroughly whether sitting snugly between the buttresses of a big tree watching the animal life or being entertained in the longhouses. Though unannounced, his coming was never a surprise, indicating that his approach had been stealthily observed, which might have been disquieting had he given any concern to the watchers being headhunters by immemorial custom.

Out of consideration for his hosts and his own comfort, though heedless of lepto-spirosis, he plunged fully clothed into the last river before arrival to wash off the worst of the stench and filth; and on stepping, dripping, out of the jungle he would find that all was prepared for his reception. The ladies took his clothes to dry them, leaving him in a state of near nature, but that only conformed to the fashion; "tapai" appeared, or it might be "tuak," "borak"—different longhouses, different brews, but there was never a shortage—girls were presented, drums throbbed, the aroma of roasting mouse-deer excited the palate, and the party began. Great were the rewards of enterprise, a little hardship, and of being British. Only once in the entire Odyssey was there an undercurrent of reserve to the hospitality and, sure enough, communists had been at work.

When Edwardes met his SAS patrols, he was fully briefed on their areas, and adding his own observations returned knowing the whole frontier better than any other individual. Viewing it with the eye of a soldier, he could both inform and advise General Walker, and the General was impressed.

As in ancient times this modern Arcadia was not to be left in pastoral isolation, and in January 1963 the Indonesian Foreign Minister said: "We cannot but adopt a policy of confrontation because Malaysia is the accomplice of neo-colonial forces pursuing a policy hostile to Indonesia." He used the jargon of the aggressor in which anyone who defends himself is hostile. Similarly, at international conferences convened to resolve the issue sensibly and peacefully, he was pleased to cooperate just as long as Indonesia was given everything she wanted. She was encouraged by news that the Malaysian idea was slow in taking shape, the intended members being wary of Malay aggrandisement at their expense, and was hopeful that judicious pressure might abort the half-formed foetus.

General Walker became aware that Indonesian troops in Borneo were moving towards the frontier and that the CCO were active and well prepared for operations. His commander-in-chief in Singapore, however, worried that the Vietnam war might get out of control and spill over into the rest of Southeast Asia, ordered Walker and his headquarters back to be ready for the next crisis wherever it might break. But even as the latter was making his reluctant farewells, on 12 April 1963 a platoon of Indonesians attacked the police station at Tebedu in 1 Troop's area in the First Division of Sarawak and clarified minds wonderfully.

One unfortunate policeman was killed, two were wounded and the armoury was ransacked, the raid being clearly intended to test British reaction. If we were to vacillate, morale throughout the territories would surely plummet, the CCO would be encouraged to rise and Malaysia would be still-born; but we stood firm, to the relish of General Walker and his troops, now hastily reinforced, who feared only that the war would fizzle out before it had properly started. So began a colonial campaign in which the element of possession was totally absent. True, we stood to gain from the area's continuing stability, but we should also be doing a service to international peace and, above all, discharging our trust to our dependant peoples. Wars, even small ones, are costly in lives and treasure, and in the devious field of international politics this one was an uncommonly honourable exercise.

* * *

Satisfying as it would be to relate that the SAS knew all about the Tebedu raid before it happened and then frustrated it, that was not the case, but for good reasons. First, Tebedu was only two miles from the border so the scope for early warning was negligible. Secondly, it had a road whereby the Queen's Royal Irish Hussars could quickly arrive in their armoured cars, which they did, so it had to take a low priority in the attenuated SAS coverage.

What then had "A" Squadron achieved as they prepared to hand over to "D," apart from enjoying themselves? Where they had been able to go they had built up encyclopedic knowledge of the border country and secured the people's active cooperation. Great tracts remained to be explored and many villages to be won over, but there was an immediate and impressive pay-off of which the contribution of Ray England's patrol was typical. He was able to make the following reports from information passed to him by his Land Dyaks.

"*13th April 1963*

Inhabitants of Sidut and Gun have been ordered to clear and improve tracks between them and clear camp sites for 100 soldiers each who are expected shortly.

"*15th April*

Headman was stopped by Indonesian soldiers on his way to Entakong and his shotgun confiscated. 70 soldiers are based there, dressed in jungle-green uniforms with automatic weapons, and spend much time patrolling. A Land Dyak border-crosser met an Indonesian Land Dyak near Kapala Pasang who said there were 20 soldiers there. 100 Indonesian soldiers have now moved into both Sidut and Gun where their camps are precisely located. 100 soldiers are also stationed at Sekajang and Suroh.[1]

"*17th April*

3 men from Gun killed some Indonesian soldiers who had been pillaging and have been arrested by the Indonesian District Officer."

If soldiers can win the hearts and minds of the people among whom they campaign the benefits can hardly be exaggerated, in logistics, communications and security as well as Intelligence. They are freed to concentrate on their own tasks and their morale, that battle-winning factor, is significantly raised; whereas

---

[1]These Kalimantan villages were on the Upper Sekayan River opposite Padawan, but are not all shown on the maps.

the fate of the Indonesians at Gun neatly illustrates the consequences of failure.

If General Walker had been a little sceptical when the Squadron went into the jungle, he was quite the reverse when they came out: "I should like to congratulate you on your excellent performance. You have been deployed in your classic role over a 900-mile front to provide me with my eyes and ears. Above all the work of your signallers and medical orderlies has been quite outstanding and they have made a significant contribution both to our Intelligence sources and to our efforts to win the support and loyalty of the tribes. We have enjoyed having you with us and hope should the need arise that you will come back."

They too wished nothing better. Indeed, Ray England was extracted from Padawan only with the greatest difficulty. Enchanted with the life, the country and the people, like Odysseus on Circe's Isle he found he had acquired a corresponding aversion for western civilization, despite the strong calling of home.

CHAPTER 4

"CONFRONTATION"

"D" Squadron's First Tour, April to August 1963
"A" Squadron's Second Tour, August to December 1963

"D" SQUADRON

Tebedu was the first of many hit-and-run incursions, and from then on confrontation was spelt with a capital "C." General Walker's reaction was prompt and uncompromising. Implemented by keen and efficient troops, it ensured that few incursions gained any success and most suffered casualties.

In the areas of greatest threat the British infantry began to be based in jungle forts close up to the border whence they patrolled constantly, "dominating the jungle" as Walker had instructed them and assuming responsibility for the locals and border surveillance. Some of the SAS were thus released and set to train an irregular force, to be called the Border Scouts, from the best of the jungle people's young men, using their uncanny skills to good effect and giving them an important role in their country's defence. Volunteers flocked, and Major Tom Leask, commanding "D" Squadron, found himself with a formidable task that almost exclusively occupied him and his men in the First and Second Divisions.

Frank Williams, now a mature veteran, was the Squadron Quartermaster-Sergeant, an unsought-after post—because it debarred him from operations—but a vital one. Patrols must be supplied instantly with what they needed, whether it was available or not. It was a job that demanded a keen sense of anticipation founded on long experience, constantly projecting the mind into those of the troops, and aggressive rapacity. But now, with the patrols established, he found himself motoring pleasantly up the river from Simanggang in the Second Division with the aim of recruiting a local unit of Border Scouts, but not quite knowing how to begin:

56

"Ten years earlier in Malaya, we had Iban trackers. My three were Roh, Ejok and Jalan. We got on very well but they left in 1954 and I'd thought that was that; but would you believe it, there was Ejok coming the other way in a dugout, so I reversed engines, he back-paddled, and we had big talk on a sandbank. Then he plunged into the jungle, returned with Roh and Jalan, and the unit was founded."

The initial training was thought afterwards to have been too formally military, yet basic discipline was essential if all were to work to a plan. The warriors had also to learn refinements such as not pointing their weapons at anyone except the enemy. One instructor remembers: "It was hairy, had to clout 'em a bit, needed a lot of patience. One guy thought he was invulnerable because he'd paid his witch-doctor 40 dollars for a good-luck charm; we put it on the target and blasted hell out of it and he was upset, wanted to claim his money back. But they were keen and fit and did very good info-gathering work on the border."

And that was their proper job. They were not soldiers but scouts. Within a few months their uniforms were discarded and with bare feet and shotguns they became ostensibly hunters again. They were also a great deal safer should they meet the enemy. Gradually the scheme spread through Sarawak and then Sabah. Before the end of "D" Squadron's tour, a few Border Scouts were added to each SAS patrol, thus enlarging the area it could cover and greatly improving communications. Finally, Border Scout training was turned over to the Gurkha Independent Parachute Company. Their commander, Major John Cross, had a wonderful touch with native peoples and spoke, it seemed, every language under the eastern sun.

Conferences and incursions took place concurrently, the Indonesians clearly trying to make the point that they could operate inside British territory at will and must eventually have their way. Nevertheless, an agreement was signed in July 1963 for Malaysia to be set up in September. Only Brunei chose not to join, preferring to remain a British Protectorate. She was economically viable with her oil revenues, but cooperated wholeheartedly in resisting Confrontation. Soekarno raged at the fait accompli, proclaiming that "Maphilindo" was now formed and vowing that the New Emergent Forces would triumph over colonialism in some peculiarly Asian way; though Tunku Abdul Rahman of Malaya observed that if Soekarno did nothing at all the colonialists would leave quietly on Malaysia Day instead of waiting to frustrate whatever knavish tricks he might try.

Then the Tunku was specific. Communism, he said, was a religion more destructive than imperialism (as he had good reason to know from Malaya's own experience); its increasing power in Indonesia was the most alarming factor of all and he would resist it. Surprisingly, an agreement was reached whereby the United Nations would ascertain whether the Sabah and Sarawak peoples wished to join Malaysia, and such was Soekarno's genius for confusing and misleading that it was generally believed he would be content with the findings even if contrary to his own wishes.

The Sultan of Brunei's keen cooperation extended to lending a house of his own to the General and a haunted one to the SAS; the latter being where the Japanese equivalent of the Gestapo had conducted its unsavoury business, and its ghost a young girl foully done to death in bygone times. The Haunted House was admirable, for as well as providing space for operations room, communications centre and accommodation (with showers) for patrols returning from the jungle, it was shunned by the populace. That was good for security and helped to enhance the aura of mystery and invincibility with which the SAS found it tactically expedient to surround themselves. Even the ghost moved out when they moved in, an understandably prudent soul.

Whenever Border Scouts were not being trained, patrols continued with the same aim as before, border surveillance, though with a much more wary eye on the Indonesians. They rarely spent a night in a village, but camped in the jungle to avoid compromise, never in the same place twice. Their rations were cached in places calculated to give them tactical flexibility in their main task of tracking incursions. But their daytime visits were very important; first for hearts and minds, in which the main element was medical aid with medical stores forming the bulk of their resupply demands; then there was information to be collected and reported, landing-points to be cleared, assistance to be given to the civil administration and police, especially Special Branch, an aircraft crash rescue service to be organized, and Domesday Book ever to be expanded. It was hard, physical and mental work.

Bob Turnbull, the strong and notably silent Sergeant-Major of ''D'' Squadron, took a patrol to eastern Sabah where estuary country gives way to hills. Ian Thomson was included, and he had occasion to wish that his leader was a little more communicative with his accumulated jungle lore, which was legendary in the Regiment. On being instructed, by a gesture, to collect water from a stream below their stopping place, he found himself rubbing shoulders with a wild elephant engaged on the same errand. He was surprised on two counts; first, because someone had told him there were no elephants in Borneo, which was true only in their not being indigenous, but many imported working animals had been turned loose when the Japanese came; secondly, it usually is surprising to see one in the jungle, for despite its bulk it blends well with the background and what you think is a small tree that looks oddly like an elephant's leg, turns out to be just that. Prompt action is then advisable; most creatures can detect and evade a blundering man long before he becomes dangerous, but an elephant's sight and hearing are so poor that it may only sense him when he is within that critical distance where the instinctive response changes from flight to counter-attack.

The little eye blazed with fury, the great ears flicked wide like the wings of a dark angel, and a scream whose blood-chilling horror might have paralysed a lesser man set Thomson off along the bank with all the impetus of SAS training and two good legs. But the gap did not widen and the thought of tripping prompted an immediate change of plan. The charging beast would be upon him before he could turn to use his rifle, so with a well practised football swerve he turned through a right angle and raced up the hill; the lumbering giant crashing on and soon losing interest. Thomson regained the camp to pant with pained irony, "There are no bloody elephants in Borneo"; but was much more disgruntled to learn that Turnbull had known there were some in the neighbourhood all along, having noticed patches of mud eight feet up tree-trunks and "how else could it have got there?"

Thomson was with Sergeant "Mo" Copeman when they found a train. Yes, a railway train with steam locomotive and six wagons, pierced and smothered by the jungle, so they laughed; expecting the unexpected was all very well, but really! Then they discovered graves with still decipherable Australian names and understood that this was a solemn and sinister testimonial to Japanese occupation. Sadder still, not a soul in Tawau had heard of it.

THE GAP

Eddie Lillico's patrol began the tour in the eastern part of the Pensiangan district. He became ill with another potentially lethal tropical disease, tick typhus, and with the impersonal logic and obedience to orders of a good soldier had himself lifted out by helicopter, was cured, and returned. That was becoming easier to arrange; more aircraft had been made available at the insistence of General Walker who realized that they must form the core of jungle operations in the 1960s, since a helicopter could move troops as far in five minutes as would take them five hours or more on foot.

Lillico's area merged into the lost world of the Gap, and when the call came in June to explore it, he was the natural selection. "I took a young officer with me," he says, in the manner of what the officers called "The old Malayan Sergeant" who needed no direction from a younger man with negligible experience; yet the view was also held that young officers were not entirely useless, the more broadly educated mind being better fitted to look at new problems from new angles and accept more readily that established practise was not always the best solution. Personalities alter cases; the officer in question, Andy Dennison, probably thought that he was taking Eddie Lillico with him, but since both were solely concerned to do the job with credit to the Regiment, harmony prevailed. Also in the augmented patrol were "Mau Mau" Williams, whose nickname dates him but certainly does not describe his methods, "Yanto" Evans, three hand-picked Muruts and two Ibans from among the SAS circle of friends, and five constables from the Sabah Police Field Force. They were gone for six weeks and did all that was asked of them.

Intrepid Anglo-Dutch surveyors had delineated the border many years before, but there was no record of anyone else having been there; the map was almost blank and Major Tom Leask's directive might have been intended for Captain Cook. The patrol was to report on the topography and its penetrability by friend or foe, the flora and fauna for its general interest and its capacity to support a military force, and the races, characteristics and customs of the people encountered "of whom little is known." The phrase is revealing, clearly indicating that nothing at all was known for nobody lived there. Finally, recommendations were required on how best to patrol the area and deny it to the enemy.

The country was certainly rugged, like an immense cauliflower Lillico thought, with hundreds of unmapped streams and rivers in gullies and ridges up to 4,000 feet, where it was so cold at night that they wished they had brought blankets. It was up and down, up and down all the way; much more so than usual, for with a reasonable map it is often quicker to detour round difficult places, but with few features marked and those inaccurately, as they soon proved, they could not have been sure that they had regained their track. They marched therefore on a fixed compass course until they came to a truly impassable obstacle, when they made a definite alteration.

Navigation was one of Lieutenant-Colonel John Woodhouse's innovations and he used the term advisedly because there was much more to his system than just map-reading. It needed endless practise, but the SAS were accustomed to that. Speed must be estimated accurately, a rough guide was 2,000 yards an hour on a track and 1,000 through bush that did not have to be cut, but you could school yourself to become ever more precise. Your course could never be absolutely straight in the jungle; you were always having to dodge round something, and so you looked at your compass at least once a minute and tried to ensure that your mean course was the right one. In the Gap they marched for fifty minutes in the hour. When they rested, Dennison would assess the direction and distance travelled since the last stop, making use of the others' opinions, for all had to participate. They hoped that at last they would find a feature by which they would check their position for sure, but despite that rarely happening in the Gap they were never lost. "You may not know where you are," Sergeant-Major Lawrence Smith taught, "but you're not lost; keep your head and use it and you'll always get back on your track eventually."

Accuracy was important, however: to pinpoint the features they found, to keep their side of the border (which was sometimes as little as a mile away on their right hand), and to home-in their resupply aircraft. The latter was due every seventh day, its arrival being an important event though they could no doubt have survived without it; at the appointed hour they sent aloft an orange marker balloon which floated miniscule above the tree-tops and awaited the murmur of engines with studied carelessness. As though by a miracle the Twin Pioneer always found them and dropped its manna: food, medicine, new boots or anything they had asked for, collected by Frank Williams at whatever inconvenience to himself and others, and most precious of all, mail. Therefore, they blessed the seventh day, and hallowed it by doing no work thereon like other travellers in the wilderness before them, but here their environment was surely more wonderful than anything Sinai could offer. "Oh beautiful!" says Lillico, "Primeval forest that nobody's ever been in before"; and the latter attribute certainly enhanced the appreciation of those who, having eyes, saw. Loveliest of all were the riverbanks; peaceful too, but only if the camp was sited to conform with two immutable principles of jungle lore. Falling trees can kill, and do so far more often than charging elephants or anything else; "deadfall" is the menacing word, so look upwards before you spread your poncho. And then look downwards at the river, guess how high it could rise in a flash flood caused by torrential rain high up in its "ulu," double it, and if you have to cross, do so while you may. Even Lillico underestimated once and they had to scramble when their river rose 30 feet in a night.

Otherwise the peace was only disturbed on one occasion, by a 20-foot python; and yet it was not the snake that caused the trouble for it was merely proceeding on its innocent way which happened to cross the hump of a sleeping policeman. The man it was who objected and turmoil ensued, the snake expiring under slashing "parangs" in a welter of gore; but Lillico barely remembers the incident, a lot of fuss about a creepy-crawly if you ask him. Tiger leeches, as Dennison called them, were far more annoying; spectacular two-and-a-half inch beasts with orange bellies and irridescent green stripes down their backs which came looping towards you like little drooling Draculas, and "if you didn't feel the nip as they latched on, they gulped blood a tot at a time."

All these were but the normal inconveniences to set against the delights of jungle life. They were certainly no worse than rail strikes, traffic accidents and blocked drains. But this nature trail was unique even to Lillico, because man was such a rare species here that the animals came out of the bush to look at him. There were great sambar deer with antlers like Scottish stags, smaller barking deer and charming mouse deer only twelve inches tall, wild pig, innumerable sorts of monkey, an orangutan as big as the Murut who met him, five-foot monitor lizards and many others; even fish in the rivers swam towards them. It seemed a shame to kill, but they did so for the pot; an evening meal of, say, venison was more nutritious and better for morale than anything provided by Frank Williams. Monkey meat was preferred to pork, which places it on a high level of excellence. Snakes were best curried.

They came at last to the headwaters of the River Serudong and found a 500-foot high waterfall, a more than sufficient obstacle to permanent habitation. After that, signs of humanity began, then Muruts; the first they saw ran away thinking they were Indonesians, which was significant, but when they shouted that they were British they were welcomed as usual and given boats and paddlers with which to end their journey in the style of Sanders of the River, luxuriously.

Dennison's comprehensive report was praised by General Walker. It was not true to say that there was never anyone in the Gap because they had seen clear signs of occasional hunters. These were probably not only from Sabah because the border was crossed by two sizeable rivers which, although unnavigable, offered easy access. Where hunters could go so could Indonesian soldiers. Should these come, they could live off the country and need never be discovered until they fell on some unsuspecting objective far to the rear. Dennison proposed four forts with landing-points as patrol bases, manned largely by Border Scouts, and the steps that were taken as a result of his report contributed to two enemy raids being frustrated later in the campaign.

From Labang, across the border from Pensiangan, a team of runaway rebels from Brunei set out to return home with arms and ammunition. The first part of their journey was entirely in Kalimantan, yet their progress was noted and reported at every stage by Muruts from SAS villages going over and listening to their friends' gossip. Willie Mundell commanded the SAS patrol at Ba Kelalan. He had already earned a reputation for knowing more about events across his border than anyone else, and when the rebels reached his area he fixed their position and likely movement so nearly that on finally infiltrating into Sarawak they were intercepted by the infantry. The achievement was praiseworthy, said the General.

But also in this area there occurred a calamity for the SAS. On 4 May a helicopter took off from Ba Kelalan on a round of visits to patrols with Major Ronald Norman the second in command of the Regiment, Major Harry Thompson the Operations Officer, Corporal "Spud" Murphy and others, and crashed killing everybody. Frank Williams had been turned off the aircraft at the last moment in one of those whims of fate which seem afterwards to be inexplicably significant. He took a patrol in at once, establishing that death had been instant.

Thompson had been earmarked to relieve Woodhouse in command at the end of 1964, so his loss was particularly serious, but over and above that the Regiment was collectively and individually upset. It would be reasonable to suppose that always living close to death they would somehow become impervious to it, but that was markedly not so. There was a strong family element in their relationships, the whole Regiment at this time comprising fewer than 200 men who knew each other well both in pleasure and adversity. Within the two Squadrons the affinity became even more intimate, and closer still in the Troops, while the four men in a patrol after a tour like this one, knew each other, as Williams observed, better than they knew their wives or than their wives knew them. Now, as then, deaths are felt as they would be in a family, and the utmost pains are taken to avoid them. That may be a weakness; John Woodhouse thinks it is sometimes, yet since the SAS do not recoil from danger, it encourages thoroughness in preparing for operations. What it also does is strip away the unfeeling image and reveal them as warmly human.

George Stainforth was still at Long Jawai in the Third Division of Sarawak; that is to say, he was in and around it because he and his men patrolled huge areas, made friends, and established beyond doubt that an enemy build-up was taking place on the border. He too earned the General's appreciation by arresting two high-up Brunei rebels, which of course came about through his being so intimate with the locals that no stranger could pass without his being told. When at last he and his patrol left in August after six months continuously in the jungle, the General guessed that the Long Jawaians must be feeling lost without him, but could not know how right he was to prove.

Lawrence Smith's luxury holiday on Cape Datu had been well publicized and "D" Squadron raffled the job as being the best on offer. But the winning patrol must remain anonymous because the brandy proved too much for one member, who first entertained their Chinese friends with stirring British ballads of the bold and free and then crashed out cold beneath the table. The others stayed conscious but euphoric until somebody thought, "Crikey! What about the weapons and radio?" Their host, doubtlessly out of solicitude and possibly enlightened self-interest (but it was still a remarkable gesture), posted six of his own men with shotguns to ensure that their rest and equipment were undisturbed. And this was against a new background of a strong Indonesian patrol on the other side of the point with whom the SAS had arranged a non-aggression pact through the locals, which they themselves were bound to keep because they were not allowed to cross the border anyway, though the Indonesians had no need for such restraint. All in all, it was a lapse.

Nothing happened, and in due time the patrol was moved, through Long Jawai in the Third Division to the "ulu" Rejang to investigate some of the primitive nomadic Punans, whose company they also enjoyed. The liquor was less tempting, being flavoured with ripe fish, but the meat was excellent, fresh-killed by blowpipe, which the SAS learned to use and added yet another weapon to their armoury. The eight-inch and almost weightless bamboo sliver would have been deflected by the slightest draught, but of course there was none in the forest and accuracy was astonishing; a monkey 150 feet up, barely grazed but stunned by the virulent nerve poison, would cling for a moment and then fall to its death, its meat uncontaminated. "Double-tap" too, whereby one dart was pushed well up the bore and a second held in the teeth, the thrusts coming from the powerful bellows of the whole lungs. They traded beads with the Punans, the Punans offering the beads, and of course enlisted them as allies. Although more backward than the other tribes, they were by no means unintelligent and would play a valuable part.

It was all fun, but it was also hard, serious work to create a viable defence. The rest of the Army, the Police, the Royal Air Force, the Royal Navy, Intelligence services and all the many agencies concerned with military operations were hard at work too on an immeasurably larger scale. As they expanded and extended their activities, there was less need for the SAS on the British side of the frontier. Woodhouse was quick to advise General Walker that their proper place was beyond it, to harass the enemy and disrupt incursions before they started. No action was taken and the seed thus sown lay dormant, but it was his job to sow it.

August came, and it began to seem as though Soekarno was confronting the hated neo-imperialists with little more lethal than hot air. To be sure, minor incursions continued, but most had been hit hard by the infantry and consideration was given to withdrawing the SAS, who were not properly employed in a static role. They had always to be ready, and trained, for those emergencies for which their special skills were designed.

Then, Major Peter Walter, an SAS veteran now serving with his own battalion was uninhabited by that, arrived in Borneo for the shooting. Tom Leask suggested he might like to see the Border Scout training camp at Song, a small town of some importance on the middle Rejang, a long way from the Haunted House. Simultaneously, the Indonesians chose Song as the objective for their first large-scale deep-penetration incursion. Walter therefore grabbed all available men, dashed unbidden into the "ulu" and took part in the battle with distinction; the SAS shrugged their shoulders and said it was typical of Peter Walter to be on the spot, some people were like that; the 2/6th Gurkha Rifles, whose area it was, said he was poaching; but General Walker said he liked that sort of sportsmanship.

The enemy were badly equipped and led, and the Gurkhas harried them for a month, killing or capturing many. They never looked like reaching Song, but the attempt had been significant and now it seemed there might be a real war after all. The SAS was not withdrawn, and an idea even began to be canvassed in General Walker's headquarters that more of them might be extremely useful. One cannot be sure who did the canvassing, but Lieutenant-Colonel John Woodhouse certainly raised no objections.

Leask's time in command of "D" Squadron was up before the tour ended and Major Roger Woodiwiss came out to relieve him, full of enthusiasm for what was regarded as the best job in the SAS. He would be close to the men with every chance of leading them on operations, and senior enough, being SAS, to command the attentive ears of important people and influence the Squadron's destiny. In appearance and brisk manner he resembled Field Marshal Montgomery strikingly, but not in public relations for he hid his light under a bushel so that it shone only downwards at the men who, always the best judges of an officer, rated him as highly as any. To Lillico, he was a soldier's soldier, which included among many qualities complete identification with them, the Regiment and the trade of war, while excluding with a shudder of distaste any concern for the politics of self-advancement.

"A" SQUADRON

"A" Squadron took over in August 1963, this time temporarily commanded by Captain Bill Dodd. He was not happy with the static task he was given; to concentrate entirely in the approaches to Brunei, which was thought to be still under threat from her rebels. 1 Troop (Ray England) was based at Long Semado, 2 Troop (Captain Iain Jack) at Bareo, and 4 Troop (Sergeant Maurice Tudor) at Ba Kelalan, where Squadron Sergeant-Major Lawrence Smith went too, thinking the place "interesting." 3 Troop was elsewhere in the world doing something or other; who knows what? In dealing with the SAS, one gets out of the habit of asking unnecessary questions.

The Troops in Borneo were reinforced with infantry detachments and Lawrence Smith was tickled by havng an officer under his command, "a good lad." They patrolled their areas as usual, supervised the building of landing-points and defended bases, and evolved a drill called "Step-Up" for quickly deploying infantry by helicopter should an incursion be detected by the SAS or their retainers. But Troop Headquarters were always in their bases near the airstrips and felt that they were being misemployed; the Indonesians were known to be building up their strength, but the SAS were not allowed to get involved.

The first thing that happened was Malaysia Day on 16 September, a United Nations team having visited Sabah and Sarawak and reported that most of the people wanted the Federation. Ray England watched the celebrations at Long Semado which were jolly but less than fervent; a good excuse for a day off, certainly, with some polite flag-waving encouraged by the local government officer and the schoolmaster, but the people made it clear that they wished the British were staying.

The Indonesian capital Djakarta was a more exciting place to observe the impact of Malaysia's inauguration. It happened that the SAS was represented here in the person of Major Muir Walker as British Military Attaché. Soekarno's propaganda about British neo-colonial perfidy in sponsoring Malaysia had fomented tension in the city, and the communists incited a crowd of students to hurl abuse at the inmates of the British Embassy and stones at its windows (of which it was officially noted for guidance in future embassy design that there were far too many).

That was nothing out of the ordinary; but the mood changed ominously when Walker seized an offensive weapon, bagpipes, and marched, skirling, through the hail of missiles in SAS uniform with inflammatory composure and, doubtless, phlegm. The crowd could not endure it and became a mob, rushing into the city with frenzied cries of "Death to the imperialist old-established forces" and "Crush Malaysia," there to whip itself into a state of "amok" and return two days later with enhanced fervour and fury. The embassy was stormed, sacked and burnt while the staff looked on, murmuring with well-bred disdain that somebody really ought to stand up to these people.

A strong anti-colonial feeling existed among ordinary Indonesians and it was exploited by Soekarno. He refused to recognize Malaysia, and this time the hot air was accompanied by a determined military raid against, of all places, Long Jawai, where Stainforth's SAS patrol had not been replaced.

The SAS were most unhappy at not still being there; perhaps they would have fared no better than the six men of the 1/2nd Goorkha Rifles, three policemen and 21 Border Scouts who were attacked without warning by a 150-strong enemy force, but it had been their place and they felt they should have stood by it. The defenders fought extremely bravely, five being killed including the two signallers so that the survivors had to trek through the jungle for four days to pass the word. The battalion's counterattack by helicopter to well-chosen cut-off points ahead of the retiring enemy was a model of jungle skill applied with ruthless determination, and the Indonesians suffered heavily; but something seemed to have gone disturbingly wrong with hearts and minds, for the enemy had infiltrated the village two days before attacking, and not a soul, villager or Border Scout, had dared breathe a word to the Gurkhas. The lesson was thus rammed home; win hearts as you may by being thoroughly nice guys, minds will be overridingly influced by force majeure when the choice is between life and death. The locals must be shown beyond all doubt that it was the British who had it. In practical terms the rapid reinforcement of isolated patrols by infantry was vital psychologically as well as tactically, and training for it was intensified.

Lieutenant-Colonel John Woodhouse was in the habit of writing to all SAS wives from time to time, trusting them with more information about their husbands than was vouchsafed to other civilians. The trust was never misplaced; SAS men tended to marry girls with comparable intelligence and courage who knew what they were taking on and were prepared to endure it. Many found that when their men were on operations it was more loving to keep them in the back of their minds, instead of in the front and suffering constant and useless anxiety; and that also helped them to avoid the terrifying risk of letting slip sensitive information and endangering their precious lives. "Where's your husband?" a neighbour might ask. "I don't know" had to be the reply, normal and understood in wartime, but this was so-called peace and the reaction was often clear though unspoken, "Ah, another marriage breaking up." Life could be hard, but everything possible was done to make the wives feel part of the Regiment.

What the wives most wanted to know was when the men were coming home. It was Woodhouse's atrocious luck to send his letter after Long Jawai had been attacked but before the news had reached headquarters; he told them that "A" Squadron would be home for Christmas and that "D" was unlikely to be going out again. Prudence and precedent suggest that foretelling the future of military operations should be left to astrologers, but that, if it must be done, any reference to Christmas is best omitted.

Also in September there was a small incursion south of Bareo in 2 Troop's area. Although they did not themselves make contact, their previous groundwork and tracking enabled the infantry to catch the raiders. Otherwise all was quiet on the SAS front, irritatingly because reports were continuous of Indonesian activities elsewhere, and Dodd constantly urged more profitable employment for his Squadron. By the beginning of November, General Walker was quite certain that things were going to happen, telling the SAS he would not release them before the end of the year and probably not then; he went further, to their delight, and recommended officially that their overall strength must be increased if they were to fulfill their role in Borneo.

3 Troop rejoined and the Squadron was largely redeployed, partly to the Third Division, where they discovered a large enemy camp on the border from which the Long Jawai attack had been mounted. In Sabah, Lawrence Smith and 4 Troop were put in to walk the Gap again, this time from east to west and much more as a fighting patrol in case the enemy had infiltrated; they were also to cut landing-points. It was a less pleasant trip than Lillico's; navigation worries, the resupply aircraft not always

finding them, perpetual alertness with heavy packs in what should be re-emphasized was dauntingly rugged country, felling jungle giants with hand-axes, and a sense that the Haunted House was preoccupied with other things, made it much more of a strain. Any trace of the enemy would have been stimulating, but there was none, and moments of light relief were rare.

The animals still came out to watch, however; including another big python which hung motionless from a branch, as pythons do when waiting for something to turn up, and looked as like a small tree as an elephant's leg though of the sort blotched with many-coloured lichens so common in the jungle. Half the patrol walked by at arm's length without noticing, but an Iban was not deceived and lunged with his "parang"; the snake resented that and letting go the end, coiled, reared, and launched itself at great speed in the direction of Sergeant Maurice Tudor, the Troop commander. From the latter's viewpoint, the mouth, so small when closed but now unhinged, agape, huge and full of backward slanting teeth was raised four feet and, advancing rapidly like an advertisement for a horror movie towards which one is remorselessly carried by an escalator, expanded to fill his universe. He so far forgot himself as to scream before diving sideways, and his loyal band laughed immoderately as the SAS do when one of their number encounters misfortune, even their superior officer.

Preoccupation at headquarters concerned the enemy. During 4 Troop's six-week journey through the Gap, the Indonesians concentrated substantial numbers of troops along the border to the west of them as far as the Kelabit Highlands. In the Tawau district to the east, there were strong indications of an imminent assault, but no SAS were deployed there.

There was also the matter of "Home by Christmas." "A" Squadron were decidedly tired and a shade edgy, occasioned by unremitting exertion at frustrating jobs that achieved little. This showed itself in a way that might seem surprising, but was really to be expected of any good unit. Woodhouse sought to fulfil his promise to the wives by proposing to bring home at least the married men, and that was received with an angry, "No way!"—from the married men. In the event, the turnover from "A" Squadron to "D" was achieved in relays, with a fair proportion of both home for Christmas or Hogmanay, according to race. Woodhouse himself came to Borneo and spent the holiday in the jungle, attached to a patrol, because he could not have borne to be anywhere else.

During the changeover, a large body of Indonesians attacked Kalabakan, upcountry from Tawau, defeated an outpost of the Royal Malay Regiment and were themselves almost wiped out by the 1/10th Gurkhas; but the SAS had no part.

So ended an irksome tour, not least for Bill Dodd who, nevertheless, did a significant service to the Regiment by ensuring that "D" Squadron would immediately be deployed where they could use their skills to best effect, in the most rugged and isolated parts of the threatened border.

CHAPTER 5

"CONTACT"

"D" Squadron's Second Tour, December 1963 to April 1964

Border areas sufficiently threatened, isolated and rugged to be suitable for the SAS were the Third Division of Sarawak, Sabah south of Pensiangan, the Kelabit Highlands and, between the last two, the uninhabited Long Pa Sia Bulge where Sabah, Sarawak and Kalimantan met, and Brunei was but 25 miles behind. Lieutenant-Colonel John Woodhouse told Roger Woodiwiss to detect, report and track incursions as his first priority; his second being to help the infantry intercept, both on the enemy's way in (to thwart his purpose) and on his way out (to inflict condign punishment). Landing-points and cut-off tracks were to be cleared, and the infantry met and guided into ambush positions; but extreme care must be taken never to risk chance encounters with friendly forces.

High jungle skill and nerve are needed to track an enemy force, because one must constantly move towards it, and to move in the jungle where hiding is so easy is to ask for trouble. True, the enemy must also move to fulfil his mission, but he would have rest periods when his men would melt into ambush, as they would do at any sign of abnormality. It was to mitigate the potentially dire effect on a four-man patrol of meeting such a force unexpectedly that Woodhouse devised the "Shoot-and-Scoot" standard operating procedure. Finally, one had to be able to extract every scrap of information from tracks once found.

The "old Malayan Sergeants" were well up to the task, and three of them commanded patrols in the Bulge: "Smokey" Richardson, Eddie Lillico and Bob Creighton. Opposing them were no fewer than three Indonesian battalions based in and around Long Bawan, and behind them the 1st Battalion, Royal Leicestershire Regiment stood ready to pounce. Woodhouse spent some days with Creighton in the River Moming area and told him that this was where the enemy would come; Woodhouse had a nose for such things.

THE ADMIRABLE CREIGHTON

The enemy came, and on 22 January Creighton spotted their tracks leading north. The discovery resulted from the SAS practise of patrolling parallel to the border and keeping constantly on the move, which was all they could do without locals to help. It might seem as though their chances of finding anything over a six-mile front were slim, yet although a single individual walking delicately could indeed be almost undetectable, greater numbers offered compensations. The jungle floor is rarely thick with leaves which, there being no seasons, are shed throughout the year, but comparatively few at a time, and those are then tidied away by armies of ants or rotted by fungi. It is thus unusual for the cover to be more than one leaf thick and footprints tend to show clearly, the earth being nearly always moist. A body of men following each other soften the ground further, and prints show better. Someone is bound to kick and mark a rotten log, snap a twig or bruise a leaf, even if he avoids committing a disciplinary offence like dropping a toffee paper, and a track is formed.

Creighton's first reaction was to freeze, with every sense alert. As far as he knew, the tracks might have been freshly made with whoever had made them still close by. Having been quiet for several minutes, he listened carefully to the insect noises, which always diminished when men were moving; no sign there, nor did any man-made smell hang in the still air. He checked also that the cobwebs suspended horizontally across the track were still intact. Now he could relax a little, though not much because a track once used could be used again in either direction. He placed his three men in ambush, told his signaller to make an initial report, and he himself observed and interpreted every clue, but without leaving any sign that he had done so.

Some prints were of bare feet, but many were booted and of a pattern; soldiers, without a doubt—no one else wore boots in the jungle—and heavily laden ones, for they trod deeply. How many? Creighton looked for a place where the tracks were particularly well marked, took an extra long stride himself—to one side, of course—and knelt to remove the leaves and count the footfalls within it. He checked heels and toes separately so as not to miss any and took the highest number, 35; then he halved it, because each man would have stepped twice within the measured distance, and added an estimated allowance for prints obliterated by those behind; say, 20 men.

When had they passed? That it had not been this morning was confirmed by the edges of the prints being blurred by rain, and it had not rained since yesterday. Creighton's experience gave it longer than that, two if not three days. When he looked for snapped shoots and bruised leaves, they still exuded sap, though slowly, and gave him the same time-scale. He replaced the ground leaves in a natural way, signalled his findings, and followed the line of the track northwards. Towards evening the track crossed his patrol boundary at a point very near a preplanned infantry ambush position. The rule against crossing such a line without double-checked clearance being of the sort that is best obeyed, he stopped, made a last amplifying report, and awaited further orders.

With Creighton's first report the whole area sprang to arms. Colonel Badger of the Royal Leicesters ordered intensive patrolling, and to good purpose. The following day, the 23rd, a team of Border Scouts found tracks to the east of Long Miau, again for twenty men, and following them north discovered a camp where no fewer than 200 men had stayed for two nights before continuing their journey on the morning of the 22nd. The infantry were redeployed to cover possible enemy routes; helicopters were positioned to lift them rapidly in response to new reports; and Woodiwiss moved patrols ahead of the enemy to provide such reports.

Creighton was sent to stand by at Long Pa Sia. When he reached it he found that Lieutenant Peele and eighteen men of the Leicesters had set off after the enemy and were now out of touch, their VHF radios having insufficient range in mountainous jungle country. This was not the calamity it seemed, however. A truce that the United Nations had appealed for was now in effect, Soekarno having agreed to it, though for his own reasons. Several incursions by Indonesian forces were at large in Malaysia at the time, but were being given a rough ride by British security forces. A cease-fire would prevent further casualties, while great propaganda value could be had from infiltrators remaining in Malaysia and being represented as liberators. General Walker trusted Soekarno not an inch, but had to give orders for incoming incursions not to be engaged except in self-defence, while those going home should be left entirely alone.

Happily, Peele knew nothing of all that. Following the trail into what might prove to be an overwhelming ambush, he came upon forty Indonesians having dinner, and with ten men charged in among them with consummate courage and verve, firing from the hip. Five of the enemy were killed, the rest fled leaving half-a-ton of arms and ammunition. Best of all, the main enemy force abandoned its mission and quietly retired. Creighton met Peele returning from the fight and searched the area. He picked up two woebegone survivors, who were delighted to carry his bergen for him and told him that the objective had indeed been Brunei as General Walker had long anticipated.

Good coordination of Creighton's skill and Peele's resolution, assisted by the latter's inadequate radio, resulted in a minor classic of its kind. Peele earned a Military Cross and Creighton was commended by Woodhouse for a first-class tracking job; admirable, he might have said.

The Long Miau incursion coincided with a visit to Borneo by the Defence Minister, Peter Thorneycroft, who saw for himself the value of the SAS in at least one of their roles. His attention had been carefully drawn to the matter lest it should escape him; and General Walker voiced a much quoted tribute which, because it is often misquoted, is given here in full:

"I regard 70 troopers of the SAS (one squadron) as being as valuable to me as 700 infantry in the role of hearts and minds, border surveillance, early warning, stay behind, and eyes and ears with a sting."

If an SAS trooper takes that to mean that he is as good as ten private soldiers, even he would be well advised to say so with caution, but it was certainly true that infantry skills did not match those concentrated in just one four-man SAS patrol. In the First and Second Divisions, where the infantry were watching the border, many more men were needed. But there they were also guarding it, which the SAS could not do. The equation fitted better in the wilder parts, where if the infantry had been strung out along the border, they would not have been strong enough to defeat a determined probe at any one point; it was the SAS who enabled them to remain in reserve, fully mobile and ready to move in sufficient force against a known threat. The SAS knew perfectly well that they were only part of a team and, while being trained to a pitch that gave them calm self-confidence in performing their own tasks, were not given to idle boasting that they could outdo, or even equal, those of others;

besides, they never knew when they might need the others' help. Still, it was pleasant to have such a compliment on the record, and from a man whom they had learnt to respect very highly indeed.

General Walker's good opinion also had practical effects. He continued to press strongly for a third squadron to be formed, but that would take time. The limitless Borneo frontier could absorb more SAS or SAS-type men than would ever be available, so it was also decided to train the Guards Independent Parachute Company in the SAS jungle role, with the wild Third Division particularly in mind. Later, the Gurkha Independent Parachute Company too was retrained and added to the strength.

Individual recruiting to 22 SAS improved as well when the need became manifest. The problem was not so much to whip up volunteers but to open the door to men who needed no urging. There are always a few such, able, adventurous and mad; but most young officers and soldiers knew little about the SAS in 1963, and most commanding officers were quite content with that, not wishing to lose their best people. Now the curtain was lifted, and Woodhouse was soon able to report that the Regiment was up to strength except for the second in command's post, which had been left unfilled since the tragic helicopter crash. Woodhouse intended that whoever filled that would take over the Command from him when he left at the end of the year, so the right man was worth waiting for.

Now he appeared, Mike Wingate-Gray, with the coldest pair of baleful, ice-blue eyes you ever saw in your life. Here, you thought, was unfeeling ruthlessness if ever it existed and you could not have been more completely wrong. In fact, he was scared stiff. Never having served in the SAS before, though his war and subsequent record showed the right combination of daring and success, Woodhouse insisted that Wingate-Gray's appointment would depend on his passing Selection. The thought of that is enough to turn the bowels of the bravest to water, yet Wingate-Gray, even at 42, would not have had it otherwise: "Commanding that outfit was going to be difficult enough anyway, but if I hadn't proved I could do what they'd all done, it would have been bloody impossible." At the very moment of his arrival, they gave him the "bergen packed, truck waiting" treatment and soon he was out on the hills in January with no advantage from seniority but the ability to read a map better than younger soldiers so that he never went a step too far, and an inflexible determination to think of, well, anything except defeat. The effort paid off and he was both accepted and respected.

Woodhouse had come home to see about all these matters, but before he left Borneo he told "D" Squadron that their tour would be a bare four months—thought to be the period beyond which efficiency would deteriorate in jungle warfare—and that they would be home in April. But, again, it was not to be.

At a Foreign Minister's conference in February 1964, Malaysia hoped to take the truce a stage further. She asked when Indonesia was going to withdraw a force that had penetrated the First Division, apparently with orders to lie up and await developments, and which although it was being harried was still there. For once Indonesia gave a straight answer: it and others would stay; and two weeks later she escalated this arrogant initiative by demanding the right to resupply her troops by air, finally announcing her intention of going ahead with a parachute drop whatever Malaysia might say. Malaysia said "No," set up an Air Defence Identification Zone supported by fighters and no more was heard of that project; but at yet another meeting on 4 March when Malaysia firmly demanded withdrawal, Indonesia equally firmly refused and at last the position became clear. Whether war was declared or not, which it never was, there was undoubtedly a war on, and Indonesia set about proving it with a series of raids into the First and Second Divisions by strong forces of well trained regular troops. She tried it on again in the Long Pa Sia Bulge too, but there Sergeant "Smokey" Richardson and his SAS patrol took a hand.

THE THREE CAMPS, MARCH 1964

The Bulge was so completely wild, mountainous and unpopulated yet of such strategic importance that Roger Woodiwiss was convinced the enemy would come again. So wild was it that near the border that the map showed nothing but the line itself and even that was suspect; this was intolerable in the circumstances, its true position must be established beyond doubt and searched for signs of the enemy.

The task, virtually without a map, would be testing, but Richardson was an old friend as well as an "old Malayan Sergeant" and Woodiwiss knew he could do it. Short in stature, "Smokey" because he smoked constantly, he had the reputation of an excellent all-rounder rather than a specialist. He was to walk the supposed border from Ba Kelalan in the south and eventually meet Bob Creighton's patrol on the River Plandok.

Tony "Lofty" Allen was an old Malayan Corporal; serious, sensitive, and Richardson's contemporary and particular friend with whom he could debate freely and so use their combined experience and intelligence while being assured of complete loyalty when the time came for decision. With them were two youngsters: John Allison, an ebullient Scot, and James "Paddy" Condon from Tipperary. The latter was short, slight, and very quiet, which made it easy to miss the enthusiasm and drive that had led him to join the British Army, against his republican family's wishes, and become champion recruit of his batch in the Parachute Regiment. Now, a member of "A" Squadron, Condon had volunteered for an extra spell in Borneo in response to an urgent request from Woodiwiss for a signaller. His job meant not just operating the radio but carrying it, maintaining it, and guarding it with his life; so integral was it to SAS operations that it had acquired a half mystical value like a regimental Colour of old.

The walk would be a long one, so they took three weeks' rations, and a high one, so they needed blankets. What with spare radio batteries, ample medical pack and all the rest, each man carried over 70 pounds and felt it as he climbed to the 5,000-foot ridge. But the extent of the challenge was not fully revealed until they reached the top; not only did the map show nothing, but having looked forward to panoramic views, which would indicate the border and their route, they found they could see nothing either. Ridges usually carry trees to their summits, but where the sides are steep, glimpses are afforded past soaring, elegant, branchless trunks rigged with searching lianas through a leafy frame that is often delicate like English ash and very beautiful; but here such gaps were few, and those immaterial because the ridge formed its own clinging cloud which rarely lifted. The near environment was eerie as well as thus confined; heavy rain alternated with thick, moist fog, so that all was permanently wet, with tousled sponge-like club moss hanging on trees and covering the ground to give slippery footholds and a sense of desolation; they called it "moon country" in consequence, but, unlike on the moon, growth was dense and cutting ceaseless and gruelling.

Days passed, exhausting and depressing, though at least the nights were cool, and they slept well in their blankets. But where were they now? On a ridge certainly, but what ridge and where did it lead? Ridges branch, and one such major divide should be evident where Sarawak, Sabah and Kalimantan met. Although no others appeared on the map it would be most unusual if none existed, and their planned track was not on just any ridge but the threatened frontier with an aggressive enemy. Richardson could only hope he was on it, though all he had to reassure him was the patrol's combined but unsupported estimate of direction and distance marched along the zig-zag crest. They called that "dead reckoning."

Another week went by at two miles a day, the ridge curving to the northeastwards as the map showed. Then the first strange thing happened. Its oddity was compounded by nobody thinking it the least odd, except that it began with a climbable tree coinciding with a clear sky which was certainly unusual. At last, Borneo was revealed in its immense magnificence—and they might have been just about anywhere in it; but they might also have been where they thought, between the rivers Paling and Plandok. Indeed, there was a glint of water in more or less the right position.

Badly needing a resupply and the opportunity now offering, they descended the north side of the ridge. There they found a suitable place to make a landing-point where several deadfall trees had begun the work; but it still took them two days of hacking with "parangs" to complete the task, which added to their fatigue. All being ready, they signalled their position with a list of requirements, and delivery was promised for the next day, 10 March.

They all listened keenly at the appointed hour, for while being not too unsure of their position, they were not too sure either; but the Whirlwind flew straight to them without even the benefit of a balloon, far less a radio beacon, which had not yet been issued. It brought good things from Frank Williams; and five letters from Allen's wife Sue, who wrote one every day as a good Army wife should, numbered because they might arrive in any order, anywhere, at any time. Allen posted his own, which was quickly borne aloft through the crowding trees and home, where, as he now read, his daughter Tracy was doing all the things to be expected of a one-year-old in the orderly routine of a country at peace. Then he burnt the letters.

Better even than the welcome stores and mail was the pilot's implied corroboration of the patrol's position, justifying, it seemed, modest pride in their navigation, which even the commanding officer might perhaps concede was up to standard, and he was hard to please. The 11th was a rest and sorting out day, and on the 12th they started north along the River Plandok, as it must surely be, to find Creighton. They had walked only 300 yards and reached the left bank when they saw a line of bare man Friday footprints on a sandbank. Was that odd? Not really; the Bulge may have been uninhabited, but hunters liked it on that account.

They pressed on for another hour under dark primary forest and then halted beside a small tributary, easing out of their bergens. Allen crossed the stream alone to probe ahead for a hundred yards. Then the third odd thing happened; Richardson saw a man, quietly fishing on Allen's side of the water, some twenty yards upstream from where he had crossed. The three of them rolled silently into firing positions, which was how Allen found them when he returned, having seen nothing abnormal; they gestured to him, and following their muzzles he saw the man too, no longer fishing but looking at him perplexed, as well he might. His olive-green shirt could have been a soldier's, but that evidence was far too flimsy to warrant shooting him, so Allen called cheerfully, "Selamat petang, ada baik lah?" ("Good afternoon, how's things?") He was a qualified interpreter, but something about him—perhaps his white bearded face surmounted by a piratical yellow sweatband, the civilian shirt he wore for comfort, or his speaking Malay instead of Javanese—terrified the man, who fled, shouted to somebody, and disappeared.

Oddness became suspicion; they had been sent to find the enemy and it began to look as though they had done so. Richardson conferred with Allen and decided to investigate at once, so they crossed the knee-deep stream to find what was clearly a concealed sentry-post, indicating that fishing had been only a secondary and time-passing occupation. They followed the sentry's track, at instant readiness for action and using every skill at their command. They moved slowly, but soon became aware of man-made signs. Then they made out an obviously artificial entanglement of split rotan cane, which was often used as a delaying obstacle around jungle camps.

Such outworks were usually accompanied by viciously sharpened bamboo stakes called "punjis," which could pierce a clumsy foot and cripple it. There might also be mines, tripwires, hidden pits and devilish contrivances of all sorts, but, if your training had been thorough, you knew what to expect and progress was possible even if barely perceptible. The camp itself began to show: bare poles of poncho-type bashas, then more, some with palm-leafed roofs, slit trenches protected by logs and earth, still more bashas, and the ashes of several fires from one of which the faintest wisp of smoke snaked upwards lazily, implying much.

It was a big camp, but the more they saw of it and the longer they watched the less it seemed to be occupied. Richardson and Allen crawled forward, covered by Condon and Allison. On seeing the whole extent for the first time, they estimated that 100 Indonesian soldiers had stayed there; regular troops probably and, it had to be admitted, quite efficient to judge by the professional siting, tactical layout, and tidiness emphasized by a single exception, a belt of ammunition left lying carelessly. That and the smouldering fire were puzzling. All other signs pointed to the enemy having left at least two days before; but the way he had gone was clear enough, a heavily pounded track leading southwestwards.

First, Richardson sent an emergency signal reporting the startling find of a large enemy camp on Malaysian territory; and the authorities, duly startled, alerted all forces in the Bulge. Then he led back over the stream, and north to relocate the enemy track; but what he found—and it was as well that his nerves were unconductive of emotion, particularly fear—was another big camp. The same professionally cautious approach revealed that this too had been empty for several days, but had housed a very different type of unit; the irregular guerilla force called the TNKU, which had launched the Brunei Revolt. This was proclaimed both by the initials carved boldly on a tree, and an irregular mess of unburied litter and general sloppiness. The patrol wondered whether the fastidious Indonesian imperialists had positioned these unsavoury natives 300 yards from their own immaculate residence as much for social as military reasons.

The next discovery pointed to the military reason, but much more besides. The big track from the main camp did not end here but swung north, and at least 150 men must even now be deep into Sabah. It was an exciting moment, justifying their perseverance and, indeed, the Regiment's existence; but their enjoyment was marred by the sharp recollection that they themselves had been compromised. And there was something more; superimposed upon the beaten track were the marks of three individuals fresh that very day, one in army boots, one in studded hockey-boots and one barefoot. That, then, explained the wood-smoke and abandoned ammunition; the sentry must have been one of a stay-behind party that had hastily made itself scarce, and messengers were even now hurrying after the main body to warn it of an enemy in its rear.

It was evening and not a moment too soon, quite enough having happened in one day. Taking more than usual care to leave no signs, the patrol basha'd down in thick undergrowth; but the night was far from restful because Richardson decreed that all four should lie on the ground under just one poncho with bergens packed ready for instant flight. Sleep became ever more elusive as they mulled over their prospects. Condon cleared his momentous report without trouble, and the reply came back that they were to follow the incursion track, as Richardson expected and as he would have done anyway. The worry was how best to do it. The aim must be to shadow the enemy as closely as was consistent with reasonable safety so as to give the infantry the best possible data on which to intercept him; but when the messengers reached him, he might well come bounding back, 150 men against four and between the four and their base. The patrol must therefore be ready to fade away before meeting the Indonesians head-on and move like ghosts, accepting the slowness and nervous strain.

Looping was inexpedient because the growth was inpenetrable without noisy cutting, so they walked very quietly on the track itself, widely spaced in the depressing hope that not all of them would be annihilated in an ambush. All ears were strained to hear an approaching enemy before he heard them. They stopped often, melting into the bush, and were fortunate in their timing because they were hidden when sounds approached, sure enough from the north. Whoever it was came crashing through the undergrowth in a thoroughly undisciplined manner, grasping young trees whose tops shook visibly, and clearly lacking jungle experience. Tensely on aim, Allen saw what first looked like a brown uniform shirt and then resolved itself into an enormous, ugly, patriarchal orangutan, waddling by as though he owned the place. In normal times he would have done so because *pongo pygmaeus* has no natural superior, but now *pongo britannicus* had the edge on him without his knowing, and he was a lucky ape not to have blundered any closer.

Such was their stress that the men were not at all amused, and they continued northward with even faster pulse-rates. In the afternoon they stopped at the top of a ridge, though the track pressed menacingly onwards, so as not to become embroiled with the infantry. Woodiwiss at base was also concerned to prevent that happening since he knew that the 2/7th Gurkhas were even then placing their ambushes. He told Richardson to stay where he was for the night and then go back south out of the way.

In the early darkness of the jungle night, they again had time to discuss their circumstances, this time with a twinge of unease that things might not be entirely as they seemed. What was it that insistently checked the smooth flow of deductive reasoning; the sentry? However incompetent, he would hardly have been fishing if he had any concern for his own safety, so perhaps he had none? The camp fires? Wood-smoke in jungle is trapped beneath the canopy, spreading far and hanging low, and to make it when trying to remain undiscovered in enemy territory would be a stupid and quite unnecessary risk. And now this ridge they were on, entirely unexpectedly? Could it—just conceivably—be the border itself? The thought was extruded painfully, because it inexorably implied that they, not the Indonesians, had been in enemy territory.

The unthinkable having been thought, they felt in their bones that it was true. To return south would, far from keeping them out of trouble, plunge them right back into it and they did not like the idea at all. Yet there was no proof that justified a signal to Woodiwiss. Wherever the border was, the enemy incursion had certainly crossed into Malaysia; and Richardson had his orders, which, contrary to a widespread misapprehension, are obeyed in the SAS as they are throughout the forces, all else confusion. So, on the morning of the 14th, they retraced their steps. They moved slowly as before to avoid discovery and slower still because heavy rain had partly obliterated the track.

Now, Woodiwiss too began to feel disquiet, for his jigsaw of evidence was not fitting together either, and important pieces were missing; Creighton had moved southwest from the Plandok to find the enemy track but had not done so, neither had it reached the River Berbulu where it reportedly led. One thing only became clear, that Richardson was not where he thought. Where was he then, and where in consequence was the enemy? Most likely further to the east between the rivers Plandok and Moming, yet how was the successful resupply to be explained? The helicopter had flown direct from Long Semado for only twelve miles, which gave little scope for gross navigational errors. Here was a puzzle whose solution just had to be found.

By afternoon the patrol was back in the camp area, their last stopping place before entering automatically becoming the emergency rendezvous in case they should become separated. Tired and strained, though with due professionalism, they looked first at the TNKU camp. It was presumably sited so that a British force following the incursion track would attack it first, the TNKU being expendable, and allow the Indonesian élite to exploit the diversion. Nothing had changed either there or in the main camp, showing that the enemy force was still at large. Having done their bit and the day ending, the patrol continued eastwards to find a suitable place for a really good night's sleep.

The area was new to them, but it was good and thick; gratefully they discarded their bergens and stretched luxuriously in the evening twilight. Allen even permitted himself the voluptuous pleasure of taking off his shirt; in a jungle environment shirts are always wet and clinging whether from sweat, rain or both, and fresh cool air on sticky skin is a rare delight. But he went further, back into the bush whence they had come, with no shirt, no weapon, just his "parang" to cut poles for what would be such a bed as would carry him softly to oblivion. None suited in the immediate vicinity so he went a little further, and then further still; it was madness, an aberration caused by utter weariness, and incomprehensible to himself afterwards.

Four men—soldiers—armed—were looking at him; and what they saw was a white man, chalky white because there is no tan to be had in the jungle. Allen switched on and ran, looking over his shoulder once and seeing that they were running too, away, obviously to report. "Move!" he barked to the others as he burst into their circle. They bundled their clobber together and did so without wasting time in futile questioning, stopping after a short distance to dress and resume battle order. Then they heard voices ahead, just where they would have run to had they continued for another few yards; normal, unexcited conversations and domestic sounds of men preparing for the imminent night. Not *another* camp? Jesus!

More voices, behind them now and of altogether different timbre; sharp, tense, executive, and close. Richardson, Allen and Condon had their bergens on but not Allison and there was no time to pick it up. They whipped round, Richardson leaping to the front, and lay down with rifles at the ready; Allen's face nearly touched Richardson's bootsoles, then came Allison, and finally Condon with the precious radio. They lay very still, hoping to be missed in the half darkness though they were clearly being searched for. At first they could hear not voices but rustling, then a single bush waved sharply and unnaturally amid the stillness; that was followed by others, and murky figures appeared fleetingly, recognizable as human only because they moved; four of them—no six—ten—more, advancing directly towards them in extended line. Finally, in screaming silence, two broke cover completely at twenty yards.

Allen saw only one, through the circle of his backsight, an Indonesian with a light automatic who may have been an officer by the red patches on his lapels. He saw Allen and they both froze. Richardson was apparently aiming at the same target so Allen waited, not only to allow his commander the initiative but, more significantly, because his trigger finger was limply impotent. He had trained and trained again for this moment but, now that reality had come, it was just not real.

The man stood staring, helpless because he had not raised his weapon at the first suspicion as a good jungle soldier should. As he stared, Allen could read his thoughts with absolute precision because they were on the same ultra-strung frequency as his own. At first there was a startled wide-eyed awareness of danger, followed by frantic calculation of what to do about it. Then came the realization that there was nothing to be done, nothing at all, and the eyes grew wider like a dog's when about to be punished. Death, immediate and personal, now forced itself to the front of consciousness. Wider yet, the eyes half hoped, half pleaded that Allen would not shoot. But he would, he must, the impasse admitted of no other outcome. Death was now certain, but it was not accepted. The eyes were huge, and awful.

Richardson fired, but the man remained erect and Allen thought, "He's missed!" Though he had not because he was engaging the other target, who did fall. The spell was broken; double-tap. Both bullets struck slightly off-centre, and what must already have been a corpse before it was enfolded by the jungle was spun and hurled backwards as though by the punch of a giant; but the eyes did not die for Allen, and never would.

This was a Shoot-and-Scoot engagement and the drill was well understood and practised. The shooting had been satisfactory if a little slow, though probably not so slow as it had seemed to Allen. Allison, as third man, was making a formidable contribution by standing up and firing his SLR in rapid from the hip over the two leaders. They were not aware of that, and when they sprang up to scoot were in mortal danger from which only luck and quick reaction by all three saved them. They raced away, sideways and to the rear. Each took a different direction at first, according to the plan, to mislead the enemy as to their escape route and to disperse his fire, which now began in earnest; but they were soon out of sight and unscathed.

They re-converged on Richardson, or rather Allen and Allison did, heartened to be of one company again. It seemed as though Condon was conforming too for they all glimpsed him, but then he swerved to the right and was gone. Why, no one could tell, then or afterwards when the others spent many hours in wretched speculation. They all knew, as he at the rear probably did not, that the enemy's line reached to just where he now headed. The firing redoubled in violence, shredding branches and saplings which fell about them, then slowly died away.

Richardson headed for the sentry-post; with enemy camps on either hand and the main river in front, there was no alternative to blasting a way through with speed and firepower if necessary. But nobody was there. The enemy did not pursue so they crossed the stream and set course for the rendezvous, where Condon would go if he was all right. Darkness overtook them, however, and they huddled into a thick bamboo clump for their most miserable night yet.

Paddy Condon was lost, possibly wounded, but they could do nothing for him until dawn. Furthermore, he had the radio, and the serious implications of its loss became apparent. Between them and their base were hundreds of men and a large enemy complex through which they must look for Paddy; the enemy would surely use the night to organize a massive search for them in the morning but the patrol could not report their plight or ask for help. All they had for comfort was the certainty that Roger Woodiwiss would spare no effort on their behalf as soon as he realized they were in trouble, but as yet, he would only know that they had missed their evening call which was nothing out of the ordinary. No radio was infallible, a patrol commander might well think it imprudent to transmit when close to the enemy, and only when three consecutive calls were missed did emergency action become mandatory. Woodiwiss was worried nevertheless and spent as sleepless a night as the patrol; even if he wanted to send reinforcements, SAS or Gurkhas, where should they go?

Dawn broke on the 15th and the second call was missed, but the Haunted House operators strained to hear something and thought they had. "The sets only had an output of 0.8 of whatever it is sets have outputs of," recalls Woodiwiss, a Devon and

Dorsets officer, "and you had to be clever to hear them, though my operators were." Nevertheless, he was scarcely reassured, and as the day progressed with no further crackle, he asked for a helicopter search to be flown. It found nothing. Even if it had gone to the patrol's landing-point it would have found nothing, because Richardson and his men were not at all concerned with being lifted out, only with finding Paddy. The lengths they went to and the risks they ran placed them in the noble company of those who risk their lives for their friends. "He was an 'A' Squadron lad," Allen explains, "and we felt a special responsibility for him."

The patrol spent its fourth day in close proximity to the enemy, now alerted. Allison was left to guard the bergens while the other two prowled around the rendezvous, Camps 1 and 2, even the area of the contact itself. There they found the new footprints of the soldiers who were looking for them but whose skill at tracking and concealment did not match their own. Rain fell depressingly without stopping and the stream rose to breast height, which made it difficult to ford. But, on balance, the downpour was advantageous, because the leaves were softened and their own sounds were drowned by its noise. Nevertheless it was a dreadful day of tension, and hard physical effort demanded by slow, gliding movement with every muscle under precise control. Added to all that had gone before and their present failure to find Paddy, they had been reduced to near exhaustion when they reached the token refuge of the bamboo clump. It had been no fun for Allison either; alone, listening, and afraid.

Without Allison's bergen, shortage of food became a worry. The only safe and certain way home was back on their tracks, which would take many days; so, since their search for Condon could hardly have been more thorough, the time to start had presumably come? Had it hell! They could not comprehend that Paddy might be irretrievably lost. He must be hiding somewhere. The luck of the Irish would pull him through. They couldn't just push off and leave him.

The inactivity of the night, cold, restless, uncomfortable and wet, did little to revive their bodies and nothing at all for their spirits; mind over matter having been their spur for several days, they had now to exercise mind over mind as well, and their reserves of mental energy were very low. Allison again guarded the two bergens, a lonely and fearful responsibility; and Richardson and Allen found Condon's, slashed and rifled. It might have been booby-trapped, so they lay hidden and watched it, considering. In theory, it did not necessarily mean the end; to slip the clumsy pack when being chased was standard practise, but in the circumstances of the enemy having been so very near at the last fusillade, and they themselves having searched everywhere that Paddy might have hidden had he survived, they knew in their hearts that hope was negligible. Their gloom was leaden and proved too heavy for nerves already strained beyond reasonable limits; they snapped, allowing hate and fury to flood in where self-control had held sway for so long.

Richardson jumped upright, shouted "I'm going to get the bastards who killed him," and strode noisily and purposefully out onto the big track between Camps 1 and 2. Allen's gorge rose too, but he soon became alarmed; to think such things was one matter, but actually to do them quite another. Perhaps it was easier for him to reimpose restraint upon himself, because the strain borne by a leader is double that on the led; common sense surged back and it was terrifying.

" 'Smokey,' stop!" he called, but Richardson pressed on, adamant. Allen ran and used all his greater height and weight to throw him to the ground and into the bush.

"Don't be bloody wet, there's hundreds of 'em."

"I'll get as many as I can before they get me, let me go."

"What good'll that do Paddy?" Allen asked, still struggling, "or me and Jock either?"

There was no response and he had to keep talking; "Look, we haven't been back to the landing-point, he might have gone there." The tension eased slightly, and the fight between friends began to seem ridiculous; there was a pause.

The trauma ended, and Richardson went straight back to duty as befitted an SAS soldier; except that he was now more like a Guards Sergeant on parade, marching at the quick with head up, chest out, shoulders square to the front, heedless of lesser beings who might be in his path for they would surely scurry out of it—and if there were any, they did. Allen hastened to follow, at first timorously and trying to pretend he was somewhere else, but then, in a strange metamorphosis, his stress and fear fell away. "Smokey's" outburst had revealed not weakness but absolute fearlessness, and he a man to be followed with supreme confidence; so Allen, too, straightened up and fell into step.

They heard a helicopter, but could not tell from the sound whether it was friend or foe. In fact, Woodiwiss was in it; an emergency was now in force and the Gurkhas were keen to mount a search in strength, but he wanted first to use his own judgment, instinct, and considerable knowledge of the Bulge, which he had built up by constantly flying over it visiting patrols. Furthermore, like Richardson, he had pierced the mental barrier of the physical border, becoming ever more inclined to think that the patrol was on the wrong side. His pilot was "Chunky" Lord, an old friend who conformed to his every wish and whim. He flew the helicopter up and down what they believed to be the border, dropping into every landing-point and edging well over into Kalimantan, but without ever a sign of the patrol's new clearing.

Richardson and Allen collected Allison and the bergens and marched to the landing-point. The rain and the wind stopped, making their every movement audible. The sun came out, tripling the visibility on the ground, and all the old tension returned as they approached their goal, where they fully expected the enemy to be waiting for them. But there was no one; now, surely, self-preservation would become their duty?

"We're going back for Paddy," said Richardson; "Come on."

They left Allison again, and were gone four hours, finding nothing. SAS training has been criticized for unnecessary hardship, which has sometimes even resulted in death on the Welsh hills. But these men had far outdone the worst that Selection or the harshest escape and evasion exercise had ever imposed, and they would have been ill-prepared and so endangered without them. "The best form of welfare for soldiers," says Woodhouse, quoting Rommel, "is training."

When bad light stopped flying, Woodiwiss suffered the anguish that is the heavy price to be paid for the delights of commanding a Squadron; having complete responsibility for his men's safety, it seemed there was nothing he could do for them. At the landing-point too, all was again gloom; but anguish and gloom were moods, to be surmounted and dispelled; objective thinking leading to sensible action were what mattered. Woodiwiss and Richardson both spent the night thinking very hard indeed. Guided perhaps by common training and experience, mutual trust and the ability of each to put his mind into that of his friend, their thoughts converged.

Richardson and Allen might have concluded that they should start walking before the enemy found the landing-point or their food ran out; but they decided to wait because they believed that

Woodiwiss would somehow arrange for a helicopter to come where one had been before. Woodiwiss might have reasoned that air search had failed and the Gurkhas should go in. Though where would they go? And what about that 150-strong enemy force swanning about somewhere? There *must* be a way of finding the landing-point; and as so often when a problem seems intractible the answer comes by wrenching the mind to a completely new approach. Of course! Don't waste any more time probing from the north, but fly the route the patrol had walked from the *south*. Perhaps the terrain there would reveal the vital clue.

Accordingly, on the morning of the 17th, Lord flew Woodiwiss to Ba Kelalan, turned east, climbed to the border ridge at Ba Kelalan and followed it northwards, guided by Woodiwiss who tried to imagine how the country would have seemed to Richardson on the ground. Gradually the ridge curved northeast as it should have done, a bit sooner than expected perhaps but navigation could not be precise with no aids other than a compass and frequent short diversions to verify features and avoid cloud. And there, entirely logically, distinct in the turbulent ocean of otherwise virgin forest was a small circular hole. Felled trees showed the clearing to be man-made, but by whom? Lord circled tentatively before committing himself to what might prove to be a whirlpool, but Allen, at the vortex, realized his doubt and for the second time revealed himself without a shirt. Even from the air, Woodiwiss sensed the tension in the white, waving figure and was infected by it.

Down, with weapons protruding from the doorless cabin, a light landing, rotor blades held high at flying speed, and Allen was the first to hurl himself prone onto the floor as being the quickest way inside.

"Paddy's had it," he shouted; "get out quick, there's hundreds of 'em."

From elation to finding them to depression at losing one, Woodiwiss was nevertheless prepared for such news; and trusting Richardson to have done all that could be done, nodded his agreement without further questioning while the other two clambered aboard. They rose, excruciatingly slowly with the extra weight but bristling with augmented weapons. At just above tree height Lord urged every knot out of the little aircraft to present an impossibly fleeting target to anyone on the ground, swooping, soaring or skidding sideways into valleys to obtain the most cover and attenuate engine-noise. Soon they were clear away, but when, or if, they crossed the border they still could not tell.

Paddy Condon was dead; Indonesian soldiers in Long Bawan had boasted of having killed him and word came back. They had failed to do so in the fire-fight when he had run towards them, but wounded him grievously in the groin and captured him. They tried to interrogate him, but he pretended not to understand Malay, which he did well; except to indicate that the British patrol was fifteen-strong which may have deterred the Indonesians from following up, and have been intended to do so. Admittedly this was only hearsay relayed through the jungle telegraph, but it rang true to those who knew Condon. Allen and Richardson were in no doubt at all. Why otherwise should the enemy allow them to wander through and around their camps for two days? Or not seek to annihilate them at the landing-point, which he would have detected from the initial resupply? He must have fenced himself into Camp 3 and awaited attack. There was no other explanation.

Then, because Paddy Condon could not walk and the Indonesians could not be bothered to carry him, they killed him.

The Regiment mourned his loss and shook themselves out of any residual feeling that they were still picnicking in Arcadia. Woodhouse sent emissaries to the Condon family in Ireland to try and ease the blow, telling them the story that is always told, as it must be, that James's death was not in vain because the cause had benefited and others would live because he died; but in the chill of death's pallor, all passion spent, and such a long, long way from Tipperary, was it true?

Yes it was. A major enemy camp complex had been discovered, sited so as to launch incursions into a most sensitive area. One such sortie had probably been thwarted for it caused no trouble, nor did any others for more than two months. Thus, the cause was unquestionably helped and lives almost certainly saved. All the same, there are causes and causes, to each of which the proportion of acceptable casualties must be graded. In the battle of the Long Pa Sia Bulge it was very low indeed, and Woodhouse re-emphasized the "Scoot" in Shoot-and-Scoot. But he also told the SAS to plan for offensive operations across the border; and continued to advise General Walker that attack is the best form of defence, as the Condon patrol had unintentionally demonstrated.

* * *

By the beginning of April 1964 the incursions into Western Sarawak had been decisively defeated by the infantry and a lull followed. Soekarno had founded his whole Confrontation strategy, diplomatic and propaganda as well as military, upon the premise that the Malaysian peoples would welcome his troops as liberators. He was therefore aggrieved and genuinely surprised to find that the locals were actively helping the British, so that his only effective allies were the communists. They were a law unto themselves and not to be trusted; but the risk would have to be taken and the CCO thus became increasingly active inside Sarawak. Some crossed into Kalimantan to return as trained agitators and saboteurs, though Special Branch was active too and achieved some notable successes.

"D" Squadron had had a gruelling four months, despite Richardson's having been the only serious engagement. All along the Pensiangan and Kelabit Highlands fronts the enemy had built up strong forces that might attack at any time in an attempt to establish enclaves in Malaysia. Patrols were always on the move, sleeping rough and secretly. Tension ruled, since waiting to be attacked demands unremitting alertness, especially in the jungle where every tree may conceal an aggressive enemy, whereas offensive operations require courage to be screwed up only for the event. Indeed, Woodhouse had told Woodiwiss that the enemy might well attack SAS patrols which, small, isolated and near the border as they were, would pay them well *if* they could pull it off. Paradoxically, however, the tiredest of all were the six patrols in the far-out "ulu" of the Third Division with only the occasional Punan for company and no stimulating enemy activity at all.

The Squadron was more than ready to go home. Woodiwiss, though, was bothered by two niggles that he would have liked to resolve before handing over. Were those camps of Richardson's over the border or weren't they? And the incursion he had followed heading into the Bulge had not returned to its base during the five days he had spent there, so where had it been? Where, for that matter, was it now?

Woodiwiss need not have worried about leaving an unfinished job. Word now came that "D" Squadron would stay in Borneo until June, despite Woodhouse's earlier forecast, for reasons that seemed at the time to offer the best compromise between conflicting needs. The lull in Borneo coincided with the start of the Aden insurrection, which would culminate in the British leaving three years later. "A" Squadron was to go there; not, however, for immediate operations, but to train and reconnoitre in the mountainous desert of the hinterland, to be ready when the call came. In Borneo it was still hoped that as soon as the threat to Brunei was satisfactorily countered the SAS could be released, which just shows how hard it is to predict events with the limited information available at any one time.

They could not go yet, though. The four months' limit for jungle operations was only an arbitrary one, a longer period never having been tried, so it seemed reasonable to keep "D" Squadron out there for another two. That solution was also urged by the air transport people to save expense, an economy no doubt commendable to the taxpayer, but to soldiers on active service it was inflammatory. "D" Squadron officers looked sideways at their men to assess whether their morale could take the strain. The men were angry to be thus looked at. Of course they could take it, tired though they were. The decision was justified by "A" Squadron almost at once becoming engaged in bloody combat.

CHAPTER 6

"CRUSH MALAYSIA"

"D" Squadron's Second Tour, Continued, April to June 1964

Dogged but very tired "D" Squadron was consciously having to whip up that enthusiasm for operations which Woodhouse considered to be the hallmark of the SAS. When the enemy relaxed his pressure in late April and May 1964, Woodiwiss managed to allow each man ten days' local leave in Malaya. This was on the whole beneficial, though returning to travail and tension in the knowledge that hard-earned savings were no longer available for proper leave at home was sorely testing.

With the Indonesian communists in the political ascendant and encouraging Soekarno along the paths of unrighteousness, strident and belligerent propaganda accompanied a continuing military build-up opposite Western Sarawak, the Kelabit Highlands, and Sabah south of Pensiangan where the greater part of "D" Squadron was deployed. The country here was wild and rugged, peaking to 3,000 feet, with the villages widely spaced and isolated. Communications to the coast were poor because the river system on which they depended flowed over the border into Indonesia, where it became the big Sembakung and an excellent supply line for enemy forces. More convenient still for the Indonesians was its tributary the Salilir, which ran close and parallel to the border for twenty miles, supporting the military outposts of Lipaha, Nantakor, Lumbis and Labang. The Salilir also rose in Sabah, flowing through a gap in the border ridge near the villages of Kabu and Sakikilo, where Sergeant Alf Gerry and his patrol had drawn a winner if challenge and danger were the criteria of good fortune. Lillico too had an interesting beat centred on Saliliran and Talinbakus with an enemy camp just over the border.

The effort devoted to hearts and minds during the past year now paid well, the enemy's strength and movements being constantly updated by border crossers who were encouraged to continue their normal traffic. But the area was too large for the SAS to visit every community often, and the Muruts' chief concern being to survive in a dangerous milieu of warring foreigners, no one doubted that they told the Indonesians as much about the British as vice versa. Disturbed, though not unduly, the British did not punish such duplicity, but rather worked positively to strengthen existing bonds.

Gerry's patrol at Kabu was always within a few miles of 100 Indonesian soldiers at Lipaha. He had to assume that if the Muruts knew where he was, the enemy would very soon know too. Yet he or his Border Scouts had constantly to appear in the villages to collect information and develop close relationships; he would lose face either by not turning up or by letting himself be found, but to hide from Murut hunters meant never relaxing from the highest standard of jungle skill.

Woodiwiss made these points among others: "Keep on the move or you won't stay hidden for long, but don't let yourselves become physically exhausted so that senses are dulled and reactions slow. Six hours marching a day excluding halts are enough except in emergency; halt every half-hour and remove bergens, though halts are for watching and listening as well as resting. Each man's load must be strictly limited and supervised by the patrol commander; carry no more than seven days' rations and hide the rest extremely carefully, returning to the cache with the utmost caution. Wait until last light in stand-to positions before putting up bashas. Ideally the camp should be on a hillside (hammocks are useful for this) so as to be clear of ridges, away from water and at least 200 yards from any track; bury rubbish more than 20 yards away and so deep that pigs cannot dig it up."

The successful defence of Malaysian Borneo depended on the Step-Up drill for flying infantry in quickly when an incursion was detected, and it was constantly practised and improved. But a still more effective way of achieving security was indicated by a glance at the map of the Rivers Sembakung and Salilir. General Walker saw clearly that if the enemy were to be hit in his own bases and have his supply route constantly interrupted, he would be kept busy defending himself and have little inclination for raiding across the border. That, however, would be a bold political as well as military move which excited shock and dismay at all levels up to the highest. But nobody could deter Walker when he knew he was right, and he pressed the case with importunate vigour. Woodhouse, quietly gratified, ordered the SAS to make all preparations now.

BACK TO THE THREE CAMPS

The Long Pa Sia Bulge remained vulnerable to a considerable enemy threat. It was a very difficult area to patrol without locals to help and with only the barest outline map on which even the frontier was in doubt. Woodiwiss therefore made it his first priority to disperse this fog of war by sending another patrol to the three enemy camps; and because that would be even more hazardous than the first, and since he was sure it would mean crossing the border for which special permission was needed, he was able to obtain from his superiors the indulgence of leading it himself.

Woodiwiss then went down with amoebic dysentery, a foul and totally incapacitating disease, and the operation was delayed until his return to duty. On 27 May 1964 the team roped down from helicopters at a point on Richardson's old entry route, which they followed, led by Richardson himself and Allen. They were nine men in all, so that Woodiwiss could form two fully competent patrols should he wish to, carefully chosen as befitted the operation's importance. Bob Creighton went along, and another "old Malayan Sergeant," "Buddha" Bexton, whose nickname was an imaginative change from the many "Geordies," "Jocks" and "Paddys." The likeness was striking when he sat in front of his bergen without his shirt, smiling and benevolent.

Not having to cut their way, they progressed three times faster than before and reached the landing-point in only four days. There they found a pair of socks and some rations which it was not good SAS practise to have left these behind, but the previous exit had been hurried. The next morning, 1 June, they hid their bergens and approached the TNKU camp in fighting order. They found it to be again unoccupied though it had been quite recently. Richardson and Allen noticed that its layout and defences had been altered.

Pressing on past the sentry post, also unoccupied, Richardson whispered that the main camp was just in front. Woodiwiss took his word for it: "I couldn't see anything, but I'm like that in the jungle." For those who could, some of the bashas seemed to have been destroyed, but they were allowed no more than a glance. "Some chap loosed off at us, very close, missed and seemed more surprised than we were; we really took off." They scooted without shooting because there was no one to shoot at. Only the third man caught a glimpse of an enemy soldier in uniform and he vanished as soon as seen; they thought afterwards that he might have been on his way to the sentry post. The drill worked well and they all met again intact at the emergency rendezvous. Then they "leapfrogged" back to cover each other, and after retrieving their bergens, they headed north, fast.

There was no call for heroics this time, the main point having been established that the camps were still actively occupied; further details such as the number of enemy and nature of the alterations, presumably made to confuse an expected attack, would have been useful but did not warrant risking lives. What Woodiwiss really needed to know was the position of the camps and in that he was lucky; a rare combination of clear visibility and an uninterrupted view from a hilltop revealed a spur running north from the camp area to a high east/west ridge that was quite obviously the border, while a parallel ridge to the south was equally obviously the one that had misled Richardson. Between them flowed the River Pa Raya, though it would be some months before the British put a name to it.

Richardson and Allen recognized the spur as the route of the enemy track that they had followed, so Woodiwiss chose another spur further to the west and headed for the border. Night intervened, an uneasy one now that they were compromised in hostile territory and knew that nine men could not avoid leaving tracks, but they were unmolested. In the morning of the 2nd, they topped the main ridge into what Creighton realized was his old patrol area in the "ulu" Paling, and headed northeast to relocate the enemy track. They found it long before they expected, but there was no mistaking it for its great width. Closer examination electrified them by revealing that many soldiers had used it very recently, heading into Sabah. Woodiwiss's determination to resolve the area's mysteries was thus fully justified.

Darkness again dictated a halt. On the 3rd, Woodiwiss split his team, sending Richardson east to find the old trade route that led north along the Plandock to the nearest landing-point and Long Pa Sia, while he himself followed the enemy with Bexton, Creighton and "Dicky" Bird, the signaller. Creighton led, finding the way without difficulty by the sweet-papers and fag-ends that littered the track, one interesting packet being of a brand not sold in Sabah. "These Indos were supposed to be from a crack para outfit called RPKAD," he observes, "but they

seemed a load of rubbish to me''; which was a reasonable
enough judgement then, but premature.

Further acquaintance with the track gave the impression that
it had been regularly used for two or three months by small
groups as well as large, and Woodiwiss could only wonder, not
for the first time, whether the Condon incursion had stayed in
Sabah and had been regularly resupplied. A night stopping place
for ten men had been occupied a week earlier, and then Creighton came upon a muddy part of the track with bootprints that
were both military and fresh. Woodiwiss decided to call in the
infantry, who might well reap a rich reward if infiltrated between
the enemy and his base. To go any further now could forfeit
surprise so he returned south, rejoining Richardson who had
found the trade route.

To arrange a rendezvous with infantry in unmapped jungle
would invite failure. If by chance it succeeded, a real danger
existed of positive mutual identification being achieved only
when somebody was dead, particularly since the infantry in
question would be Asians, the 2/7th Gurkha Rifles commanded
by Lieutenant-Colonel Rooney. Woodiwiss therefore decided to
follow the normal Step-Up drill—reluctantly because it would
take much longer—which directed him to meet them at a landing-
point, guide them to the enemy track, and there leave them alone
with the certainty that no friendly troops were nearby.

Accordingly, on the 4th the patrol cut a lateral track eastward
to the trade route and then marched north to the landing-point,
having made a signal advocating reinforcement. In fact, several
signals were needed to reassure headquarters that the enemy
signs really were in friendly territory. Also, it seemed to Woodiwiss, to overcome a certain reluctance by the Gurkhas to believe
it possible that there might be a large enemy force in their area.
Time was thus wasted, but on the 6th a strong platoon at last
flew in. It was commanded by Major Brian Watkinson, whom
Woodiwiss was delighted to see for the two had not met since
they joined the Army together at Sandhurst. So did the ''old
boy'' net cast its meshes to the wildest ''ulu,'' which was no
bad thing for understanding and cooperation.

Creighton was now lifted out (for an Arabia course), which
displeased him much at the time and more later. Woodiwiss,
Bexton and Bird went south again with the Gurkhas, feeling
unusually secure among 40 heavily-armed soldiers. For their
part, the smart, quick, disciplined little men eyed these bearded
and threadbare guerillas with an interest that was at first critical;

how could they shoot straight unshaven? But their rifles were as clean as the Gurkhas' own and their desire to close with the enemy was as keen too, which is to say very keen indeed.

At the night-stop the differences between the two life-styles widened again. The SAS had basha'd down—their bashas being up—with their supper cooking a bare fifteen minutes from halting. Relaxed but wide-eyed, they watched the Gurkhas laying waste the jungle with their kukris and drawing great quantities of water as though settling in for a long stay. Woodiwiss could not but envy their commander: "He just sat down and waited for it all to happen; one chap built him a chair, another brought him a brew, while a third rigged his basha complete with mosquito net. He didn't even know what was in his pack. His orderly saw to that."

In fact, it all made good sense. Forty men could not pretend like the SAS that they were not there; their camp had to be tactically sited and organized for defence, and their commander honoured as a man apart on whom the fate of all depended. There is no reason to suppose he did not like it, but the privilege had to be hardly earned in times of lonely responsibility.

In the morning of 7 June the combined force traversed the newly-cut lateral track, the Gurkhas proving that they could be quieter than mice when approaching the enemy and a fight promised. They halted before reaching the incursion track, and the three SAS with Watkinson, his Platoon Sergeant and Section commanders went forward to reconnoitre and make a plan.

When the SAS showed the track to their friends, the veteran Gurkha Sergeant's slit eyes widened enough to gleam with expectancy as he saw the signs and pronounced them to be the real thing. Woodiwiss was modestly pleased with his achievement, a minor classic of tracking, interpretation, communications and organization leading to bringing in the infantry between the enemy and his base, apparently undetected. Now his job was done, but the thought of just walking away as the climax approached was quite unreal, even shocking; to do his job properly, he must surely show Watkinson the footprints in the mud as the most recent evidence of a certain enemy.

They tracked north with Bexton in the lead, "his eyes were sharper than mine," says Woodiwiss, who followed; then came Bird, and after a gap Watkinson and his team. They moved slowly and silently, fully ready for action but not expecting it or they would never have risked spoiling this rare and exciting chance of catching the enemy completely unaware in a full-scale ambush of all the Gurkhas. Afterwards, Woodiwiss wrote in his Squadron Orders: "To use a border track is dangerous, to return on it is twice as dangerous, but to follow up along a track recently used by the enemy is suicide."

Approaching the mud, Bexton eased himself over a bank and Woodiwiss lost sight of him for a moment, which became eternity. The forest's gentle hum was ruptured by a coarse shout expressing urgency and conveying dread. A burst of automatic fire clattered rudely, persisted brutally, and Bexton did not come back.

Woodiwiss and Bird scooted, though not far or for long; together again they turned and retraced their steps, but now pressing close to mother earth for dear life and worming their way forward like hunting lizards. Shoot-and-Scoot procedure made no provision for going back, but to do so was logical as well as brave; the enemy would be rash to follow up his own sprung ambush and was most likely to retire immediately because he could not know the size of the British force. If, therefore, a cautious approach revealed that the Indonesians had gone, Bexton might still be hiding nearby, probably wounded. It was not to be; the enemy were talking and moving about just where he had disappeared, so that unless he had escaped altogether, which was scarcely credible, he must almost certainly be dead or a prisoner.

As soon as Watkinson had collected his men, he took them through the contact area in line abreast, but met no opposition. The enemy, twenty in number, had left for the border by looping off the track and then returning to it; the opportunity of placing a decisive ambush further south had thus been missed but the SAS were grateful for the priority accorded to Bexton. He lay where he had fallen, instantly killed by many bullets.

To endure the sickening descent from high purpose to deep depression and continue with an operation that seemed to have already ended in dismal failure was hard but necessary; and, in the event, astonishingly rewarding. Later in the day and but 200 yards from Bexton, the Gurkhas found a camp where 90 men had spent the previous night. On succeeding days, when the search was reinforced, six more camps were discovered on Malaysian territory; all were unoccupied, but could have been used at any time for launching an attack in strength.

Woodiwiss, typically, did not think the point worth making that he had more than succeeded in his initial aim of clarifying the frontier situation. The price paid was Condon's and Bexton's lives; a fair one in strictly impersonal and military terms, but as usual the SAS mourned the latest names on their Hereford clock with tough outward realism and deep inner concern. "Nearly everyone on that clock is there because of some mistake," said one. "It's always tragic when we lose a man; even if you hadn't particularly liked him, you'd respected him for what he was and for what he'd achieved. We're such a close team and know each other so well, you feel numb—until the next 'op' and then you go at it just as hard as you can." But there was no question of anyone disliking "Buddha" Bexton, whose inherent geniality and helpfulness increased as hardship worsened; a manifestation of high courage.

Woodhouse felt the loss keenly too, the fourth death in as many months including two in South Arabia. He began seriously to wonder whether this rate of loss would unsettle his very small unit, which by no means regarded men as being routinely expendable; whether, indeed, this unexpectedly acute sensitivity might prove the Achilles' heel of the SAS. But the Regiment's effectiveness depended absolutely on intimate companionship, so all he could do was, on the one hand, crack down on sentimentality, and, on the other, try to avoid casualties by any means short of curtailing operations. Meticulous training, planning and preparation were indubitably life savers, and insofar as they could be raised above an already ambitious standard, they were to be, remorselessly; and since the aim of an SAS mission was rarely to stand and fight, Woodhouse stressed again the "Scoot" in Shoot-and-Scoot. Even so, the Long Pa Sia Bulge had not yet claimed its last victim.

When Woodiwiss returned to the Haunted House on 9 June, his Squadron's long tour still had a fortnight to run. The men braced themselves to endure it, ruthlessly suppressing any yearning to relax because all the signs pointed to the enemy's long build-up having reached the stage of action. The trail was much harder than starting up the Brecon Beacons for the third time. The mountains were twice as high anyway, and the physical effort alone of keeping constantly on the move with wasted bodies and months of accumulated weariness, trying to forestall the enemy by being everywhere at once, was not comparable. In addition, there was the mental stress of always expecting to be ambushed, a particularly disturbing element of which was nagging anxiety lest one should react incorrectly. Even success would not bring the clear-cut satisfaction of an offensive mission achieved; only a painfully gradual awareness that the enemy had not won.

All along the Pensiangan front SAS patrols were well briefed on the enemy threat, largely from their own painstaking work over the previous months. Other Intelligence agencies were also involved, which was normal, but co-ordination was initially poor; unhappily, this is often the case owing to the secret nature of the business and the need to safeguard sources. Lillico, at Saliliran, became suspicious of the comings and goings of one individual, wasting much time and effort until he discovered that this intelligent and resourceful man was already working for the British.

There was little that Lillico did not know about the enemy garrison at Nantakor, just a mile down the track; for instance, that two machine-guns were posted every day pointing north into Sabah. He had established their exact positions by going to look, crossing the border, which he should not have done, but: "only a little way. However, I was refused permission to take them out, which I could easily have done before NAAFI break. What annoyed me even more was that a young Royal Green Jackets officer had been over and nobbled one of these guns on another part of the front without asking anyone."

The obvious gateway between Kalimantan and Sabah was along the line of the main river between Labang and Bantul. To the east, a secluded side entrance was offered by the Gap, which Dennison and Lillico had virtually discovered a year earlier and where signs of an Indonesian reconnaissance patrol were indeed found. But when the enemy decided to test the British defences in greater strength, he went for Sergeant Alf Gerry's village of Kabu on the 11 June, and the first thing he did after crossing the border was to ask a Murut where the SAS were with a view to assaulting them, as Woodhouse had predicted. This incursion may have been just a reconnaissance in force, because later in the day the enemy withdrew, releasing the man whose message came straight to Gerry. The latter gulped, flashed a Step-Up signal to base, and moved on. The infantry, again the 2/7th Gurkhas—which illustrates the considerable length of frontier being covered by one battalion and the key role of the SAS in rendering it effective—came in quickly, to discover ample evidence that 40 of the enemy had been and gone.

Gerry and his two young troopers then began the most difficult and exhausting fortnight in his experience. "Have you ever tried to scream quietly?" he asks. Everything had to be done quietly up near the border with, for all he knew, the enemy between him and his base. While quietly chopping hammock-poles, he was startled by his mate quietly whispering that he thought he heard something, and slashed his finger to the bone—quietly. "No stitching needle and had to use a sewing one; left a lump.

"We lived like terrorists in hostile country. The Indos could look down onto the area from the hills either side of the river valley and came and went as they liked. They never found us although we knew they were chasing us, but it was dodgy. Only once had a good night's rest when we were surrounded by Gurkhas. Never went to the villages now, but kept in touch through my two Border Scouts."

The long-fostered liaison with the Muruts continued to work quite well. On 14 June another 40-strong incursion was reported southwest of Kabu; this time the enemy clearly intended to stay, but after a determined stalk lasting three days the Gurkhas made fleeting contact and the Indonesians retired. Lillico, too, had a moment of excitement when his Muruts detected a force approaching Saliliran, though it left hurriedly before it could be ambushed. Similar indications were found near Bantul, but only when the enemy had been and gone. Such irresolution was a poor start to crushing Malaysia, and is probably explained by the raiding force commanders finding themselves detected so soon after crossing the border that to continue meant heading into death traps. If so, they were likely to be right. In the Second Division of Sarawak, two 60-man raids were intercepted by the 2/2nd Goorkhas under their formidable colonel Nick Neill and lost nineteen killed. In Sabah the infantry awaited their opportunity with simple enthusiasm, frustrated only by the obfuscating jungle and the enemy's apparent timidity.

The Indonesian commander at Lipaha, however, was both determined and persistent. On the 22 June fresh tracks were again reported near Kabu, and again the Gurkhas flew in; but this time they were fired on at the landing-point itself. Unshaken, they reacted characteristically fast to seize the initiative. The enemy withdrew, but he did not leave Sabah and a confused and dangerous hunt ensued. That night, mortar bombs fell close enough to Gerry to make him believe he was the target, so he moved in the darkness, a difficult and anxious undertaking with the enemy nearby. The next morning when he was talking to the Gurkhas' Company commander, a burst of fire passed between them. The latter resumed the pursuit with vengeful vigour; but he had to endure three more days of nerve-racking intensity, such are the constraints of jungle fighting: critical decisions must be made from the slightest clues, the enemy is never seen until final contact, and the side which is moving at that moment is at a grave disadvantage.

The two forces at last met on the 26 June, which was Gerry's very last day on patrol. That he was really leaving after all those months would have seemed scarcely credible but for the fact that standing next to him, listening to the distant firing, were ''A'' Squadron's commander, de la Billière, and the second in command of the Regiment, Wingate-Gray, who had flown in to be briefed on what was then the most sensitive spot in Borneo.

The battle itself was not a murderous affair but another brush in a continuing war of attrition. Yet it is typical of such wars that hindsight would show it to have been decisive. Never again did the enemy make a thrust at Kabu, which was saved by the grinding, unsatisfying exertions of its own people, the Gurkhas, the SAS, and the teamwork between them. Then, however, the threat still seemed real and immediate to the inhabitants of the border villages. They began to wonder whether the British could really protect them; and whether it was wise to continue giving their whole-hearted support for fear of reprisals from the enemy. The change was almost inevitable, the enemy having come very close to home and the SAS being, apparently, scared to visit the villages; it was sad too, in breaking down the previously warm relationship, and serious in undermining the fundamental concept of General Walker's policy.

To put matters right would be ''A'' Squadron's first task, ''D'' having done its bit. General Walker said so, warmly, acknowledging that no enemy incursions had entered an SAS area without being detected; Woodhouse noted that it was becoming quite fashionable to take a favourable interest in the SAS. Back in the Haunted House, Gerry removed his jungle boots for the first time since the raids started. This was a significant act not only of high environmental impact and voluptuous relief, but symbolic of laying down a barely tolerable burden. Restoration to full health, vitality and motivation, however, would take much more than just peeling off the rotting canvas; Woodhouse had warned that when SAS soldiers showed signs of exhaustion, it would be most unwise to assume, after all their endurance training and having gone a little further and then a little further still, that they were not approaching total collapse.

With the cause of stress removed, the stress remained. Silence was tangible; conditioned to straining for the least sound that might spell danger, the men could not change their instinctive reaction and every noise now grated harshly. Friends who had scarcely seen each other for half a year with many adventures to exchange had insufficient energy to do so; even drinking was an effort. They hardly noticed Brigadier Harry Tuzo, under whom they had operated, when he kindly came to see them off from Brunei Town, nor even their journey by slow boat downriver to Labuan and air over one third of the earth's circumference.

Then they went home, to the concern of their officers that their wives would think the long separation unreasonable, and finding them skinny and listless would work on them to leave the Regiment. There proved to be no need for worry on that score, but the Squadron was unquestionably non-operational for the time being and pointed the lesson sharply that a unit must never again be run down to such a degree, except in the gravest emergency. Six months in enemy-infested jungle was too long, and four became the statutory limit.

Lillico, however, would not be so definite. "It depends how you look at it; some blokes lived on their nerves and couldn't sleep, but I always got a good night's kip in a thick bit of vegetation and woke up fresh next morning. I lost a couple of stone in weight like everybody else, but I don't think that does your health any harm if you're getting your vitamins and a balanced diet. Some of the married men got a bit agitated but I never got married, no time for two jobs; nothing against women, but it slows you up—perhaps when I retire. This is the job I enjoy and that means staying on it as long as I'm needed; proud of the Regiment and reckon it's up to us to set a style, a standard. Mind you, some people think I'm a bit of a nut; it's a matter of opinion."

CHAPTER 7

"PURSUIT OF EXCELLENCE"

"B" Squadron Raised and Trained, January to October 1964

Lieutenant-Colonel John Woodhouse wrote in early January 1964 that the project for expansion, zealously pressed and lobbied ever upwards in the Army establishment, had been tossed so high as to be out of sight; but before the end of the month it fell to earth right side up. The new squadron had to be "B," the one disbanded after Jebel Akhdar amid bitter talk of treachery in not having been allowed to go there and distinguish itself like "A" and "D." It is a moot point whether squadron loyalty is stronger even than regimental, but five years later survivors of "B" dispersed within the Regiment were still unswervingly faithful to their old mystic letter. Now, "A" and "D" would have to provide the NCOs for "B," whose morale would be all the better for having some members with an already established loyalty. Woodhouse had long preached that a man could not be a fully qualified SAS soldier in less than three years, but to pull its weight in Borneo, "B" Squadron would have to be deployed there in November. That meant putting between 60 and 70 barely trained recruits into the field throughout the Regiment. But no one knew better than Woodhouse how best to select the right men and train them; and if they were indeed the right ones, with the restless, irresistible urge and balanced confidence to achieve all things, they would, well led, surmount even a lack of training. Selection therefore, always crucial, became paramount.

First to be chosen were the leaders. The first of these was the Squadron commander, with whom there had to be no mistake. Major Johnny Watts was the man, and Woodhouse set about ensuring his availability when the Squadron was formed and ready to command. Of immediate priority were the NCOs, Woodhouse having conceived the idea that if they were to select

106

and train the actual men whom they would command operationally in troops and patrols, enlightened self-interest would ensure the best possible job. Their absorption in the challenging task would soon dispel any chagrin at being moved; and since the old squadrons' attitude to the greenhorns would be at best patronizing, a powerful incentive to catch up and overtake would be generated. "Tanky" Smith was one such Troop Sergeant.

At first it seemed as though the men themselves would be easy to recruit. Volunteers flocked, over a hundred in each of January, February and March, but, as usual, only one in ten survived the first three weeks. What then of the nine who wanted to pass and thought they could, yet of whom "Tanky" and his fellows could predict on the very first day that their hopes were vain? They knew well, for they were told the harsh truth plainly, that they would be invited to drive themselves to the point whence they could go no further in order to prove that they had the motivation to go further; but perhaps it is not possible entirely to comprehend such an idea, and certainly no one who has not been tested to the limit can be sure how far his motivation will take him.

Among those about to learn in the January batch was Jim Penny of the Black Watch, and his motivation was apparently somewhat less than sublime: "I was a fugitive from bullshit. Didn't know much about the SAS but had a friend in it so I volunteered; my CO wouldn't let me go and after six months I wrote to my friend who told Colonel Woodhouse who fixed it. Then I found out; bitter winter, snow and frost, but I couldn't go back to my Regiment after all that and face the finger of scorn, so I passed. Maybe that's a silly attitude but I reckon it gets a lot of people through; it doesn't matter what form your motivation takes so long as you've got it."

Yet Penny would agree with most thoughtful opinion that unconquerable motivation must derive from some profound, positive force, whatever the lesser impulse that tops the immediate hurdle; though even those who have it in full are hard put to say what it is. Love of country or freedom, hatred of tyranny and cruelty, religion or ideology, may be powerful influences but are rarely the whole story. Fame is certainly not the spur, and how the SAS hate it! Adventure? Only in part since too much ceases to be motivating. Courage, yearning to be tested? Of course, but what if the test is too severe? Duty? This surely is the key; for duty is greater than the individual and, at its highest, unstoppable.

More than 80 on Penny's course, some no doubt with loftier ideals than his and physically fitter, gave up of their own accord; not a few after the first short five-mile walk. After long experience the SAS were hardened to expecting such astonishing figures. They explain that Selection is 70 percent psychological, and the devil works insidiously on minds concentrated by hard, uncompromising reality. "Inner doubts creep in," says Penny. "Is this way of life really for me? Bloody though this Selection is, it's nothing to what they'll make me do if I pass. Am I prepared to give the total dedication they demand? Would my marriage stand the strain? God knows I need to prove myself to myself, but what if I go through all this and then fail? Much better get it over quickly."

The wily seducer's arguments were probably more forceful then than on an operation with important objectives and comrades depending on one for their lives. The deed was so easily done, merely by not forcing oneself to finish a march in the allotted time or, as Penny felt like doing, "throwing your bergen onto the truck and saying, 'Damn it, that's enough!' which is what the staff were watching for. Five minutes later with a cigarette and a brew of tea you wouldn't have done it but that's too late." Then the devil exults in his devilry; "You're no good, you'll always give in won't you?" The shock could be devastating, and when John Edwardes ran the course he made it his business to reassure the failures that they had not necessarily failed at all as individuals. They would more than likely fulfil themselves in some less crazy way of life where SAS qualities would be a positive disadvantage.

Shock or not, Selection had to be. There was no instilling motivation where it did not exist and the only way to detect it was by putting it to the test. That established, brain as well as brawn were needed to reach the objective, do the job and get home under SAS operating conditions. Practical intelligence tests were therefore woven into the exercises. These were particularly hard for the officers, who were set complex military planning problems when it was as much as the dead-beat wretches could do to stay awake. All had to have the right qualities, or the advanced training and much else—lives perhaps—would be wasted.

Those determined to succeed had much good advice to encourage them. The sage who advocated forgetting the mountain and thinking of sex for the honour of the Regiment offered other helpful precepts: "Don't envy the physique and vast experience

of the man who's obviously going to pass, it's such a disappointment when you have to carry his bergen back to the RV." "Don't
sit down half way up a hill but promise yourself a rest at the top,
where the wind's so damned unpleasant that you're forced down
to the next valley before pausing to get your bearings, which
you'll only find by climbing the next hill . . ." "If you give up
when you're completely shattered, you'll find out too late that
the Regiment is mainly composed of men who were completely
shattered." "Smile now and again; you won't tire out the face
muscles and might even fool the instructors into thinking you're
enjoying the course, which ought to make you laugh anyway."
Just plodding along is not enough by itself; keen observation
and hard thinking are needed to conserve energy by such means
as eking out rations, choosing the best route, navigating accurately, and then being flexible enough to see and exploit new
opportunities. Also, a constructively active mind has no room
for thoughts of defeat, which quickly lead to being defeated.

Only twenty men survived the first three weeks unbroken.
Before they took their longed-for weekend leave, eight more
were discarded for traits of character that the keen-eyed staff had
already spotted. The thug or killer types are anathema both to
the Regiment's image and to its operations. Soldiers must fight
and kill only when the task demands it or they will be more of
a threat to their friends than the enemy; and it may be that the
task is to make friends. An aggressively selfish man is obviously
impossible in a four-man patrol; an introverted "loner" too can
be very difficult since his aim may be more to justify himself
than to join with the others in serving the cause; the "big-
timer's" boasting probably conceals inadequacy; while the
"prima donna" type, however brilliant, flies into tantrums and
cannot be relied upon.

Thus was sought a disciplined will to do the right job in the
right way. "Tanky" Smith and his colleagues knew well what
they were looking for. So did John Woodhouse who, although
perturbed at the miserably low number of twelve passes when
he had to find 66, was not even tempted to lower the standard.
A man who had not proved himself so far as is possible without
an enemy might return from patrol saying he had been to the
objective but found nothing, when he had in fact ventured but a
little way from the dropping-off point and passed his time in rest
and quietness. The effect of such dereliction on a task linked to
a major operation could be truly awful, but mere words were

wholly inadequate to describe its impact on the Regiment's honour should it become known.

The twelve survivors were not yet admitted into the Regiment, and many more trials would have to be undergone before they were. They had, however, surmounted the toughest obstacle, for although what would follow might be even more gruelling they had proved their motivation and strength of will. But long before vanity could taint them they were swept into the never-ending pursuit of excellence, which would always make even self-satisfaction inadmissible. They could still be RTUd at any time, but then so could everyone, including the oldest and boldest; though from now on the chances of that happening diminished greatly and were largely forgotten in the intensity of Continuation Training.

There was much ground to cover. Basic infantry skills must be taught. A higher standard was now required from everyone, with a greater variety of weapons (or without them), tactics and over any terrain. All had to become extremely proficient at crafts that they may never have tried before: demolition, radio, advanced first-aid, mountaineering, abseiling, boating, skiing, swimming and diving; though in "B" Squadron some of these were postponed to allow rapid progress in jungle warfare. Parachuting, like jungle cookery, was regarded in the SAS as just another skill to be mastered. Then there was learning to live off the land, enemy land, and how to behave if you were caught: Combat Survival and Interrogation. A student had to be irrepressible to see anything light-hearted in this part of the course, which had to be essentially disagreeable to serve its life-saving purpose. It was not part of Selection but training.

A man was not therefore plunged into the final vexatious exercise without thorough instruction in arts and skills fundamental to this role of operating beyond the frontier. Some toadstools are edible; eat them. There is a vine in the jungle which when cut drips the purest water, and another, not dissimilar, which is poisonous. Rabbits and scaly anteaters are nutritious; right, first catch your scaly anteater, then what? Lillico is an expert: "If you're really on your uppers, cut the jugular and drink the blood, which puts pure energy into you (together with all the bacteria and viruses) and then eat the lights and liver raw. Now some officers are repelled by this, not done at public schools, but if they have to do it the sooner it's got over with the better, if you take my meaning? The rest must be cooked; no batman, so they've just got to learn." There was, of course, much else, notably mitigating the potentially lethal effects of exposure, hiding, laying false trails, evading or killing tracker dogs.

Then came the exercise: five days alone, inadequately clothed, without food, inexorably pursued by large numbers of troops from other units. Although ultimate capture was assured, it was important to do well and husband one's strength in the first phase. Apart from actual survival being at risk in really severe conditions, a starved and exhausted man would be less resistant to the continued physical and intense mental pressures of interrogation, in which to let slip the least information meant instant RTU. The experience is best illustrated by those who know it from both sides.

Mike Wingate-Gray: "The SAS are not trained as interrogators but it's very important for them to know what happens; they are more likely to be captured and have more to reveal than other soldiers so they are liable to be interrogated severely. Very unpleasant; deprivation, noise, light, silence, discomfort; even pain in those days before questions were asked in Parliament, because the Russians would undoubtedly use it, although our own skilled interrogators are convinced that brutality can be counter productive and subtlety pays much better. Frightened, helpless in a hostile environment and disoriented, you hang onto the thought that it's only an exercise, but even so you begin to think, where the hell am I? *Who* am I? Damn it I'll tell them and they'll stop it; but you don't because of your motivation, group psychology, ego, or whatever. If you can stand each successive stage, you can probably stand the next one, and you know that sometime they'll come to the end of their repertoire . . . Mind you, if the Russians pull out all the stops, they can probably break anyone, especially with modern drugs which put you out of control so that it's not you talking at all, they've taken over your subconscious and that's a horrible thought, isn't it? But even though you'd know it wasn't an exercise and that they need never stop, training helps because you learn how an interrogator's mind works; and ·if you can convince him he's *never* going to get anything out of you, he *may* let up."

Lawrence Smith: "I was involved in an exercise with an RAF aircrew who had no idea it was going to happen. Brought the aircraft down somewhere they weren't expecting and took the whole crew into custody; bags over their heads, driven about 200 miles in the back of a truck, cold, miserable, not a word spoken. At the Interrogation Centre they were put in a cell, bugged of course and with all the usual disorienting techniques, which is quite frightening; then when the bags were taken off after about ten hours they were surrounded by people in strange uniforms speaking what could be Russian, only the interrogators spoke English. They were kept awake, that's the big secret of interrogation; after about 72 hours everyone starts deteriorating and then the questions start being asked, first the nice kind chap and then the harsh one. By the end some of the crew literally didn't know where they were, thought they might have been in Russia despite knowing they'd come down on a British airfield. You can imagine letting things slip unintentionally but that's the idea of the course, to teach. From the subject's point of view, once you've done one you've done them all; a lot of exercises end with interrogation. You know you've got four or five cold, wet, tired, miserable days and switch your mind off; that's one of the techniques, mind over matter, and it does work. There are two schools of thought, whether to answer negatively or say nothing at all, remembering that the interrogator's first aim is to get you talking about anything, whatever it is you like, say football; then it becomes a psychological game for him to find out your weak points and work on them to break you. In ten days I think the body might break, but the mind certainly wouldn't break before the body; I've never got to such a state myself, but I do believe I could hold out.''

John Edwardes: ''There's only one answer and that's to say absolutely nothing; if you even reply 'Yes' to a perfectly innocent question they can put it on tape and use it for propaganda . . . The more sensitive you are, the worse; we persuaded one visitor to have a go and he convinced himself he was really being tortured by the Russians and completely broke down; took a whole bottle of whisky to get him straight.'' Mrs. John Edwardes: ''Everyone in the SAS goes a little odd after a bit; I suppose it's natural; John did.''

At last the twelve were in and John Woodhouse gave them their winged dagger badges. Friends of the SAS may wish that another symbol had been chosen. A dagger is traditionally a thug's weapon and does less than nothing to free the SAS from an image that they so bitterly resent, and which those who know them realize to be untrue. But to the initiates it meant much because they had joined a very exclusive club after paying an appropriately high entrance fee. The SAS was no longer mysterious, daunting and forbidding, but offered them their greatest opportunity for fulfilment. They felt welcome and secure in an environment of perpetual and sought-after insecurity.

The Regiment, having taken them to the threshold of hell, now demanded their all. The more they gave, the more they loved it, so that there was no longer any difficulty in identifying motivation; it was it. Ask anyone, from trooper to colonel, and he will tell you so quite simply, surprised that you need to ask. Fred Marafono, a gentle and intrepid warrior from Fiji, joined "B" Squadron soon after Penny and was put into 6 (Boat) Troop because he had grown up in canoes among the islands. Many years later, in the damp chill of a Northern Irish winter, still in 6 Troop but now sergeant of it, Marafono pinpointed the allegiance which evoked his enthusiastic acceptance of extreme hardship and danger in aid of a people so far from his home.

"The cause."

"And what is that? Law and order? Freedom? Democracy? Peace?"

"The Regiment."

Slightly chilling? Especially from one who can entertainingly discuss his cannibal ancestors of not so many generations back and spark a flash of savage but quickly-suppressed pleasure at the image of the IRA in a stewpot. Unease stems from wondering whether this loyalty is directed at anything but itself.

"What if you're ordered to do something you think would not be a credit to the Regiment?"

"I can always leave."

It was said with a merry laugh because the possibility was absurd; the Regiment, to which he had given his heart, existed only to do good, so if it were to do evil it would no longer be the Regiment and he would leave, even though his heart would break. Greater loyalties are scarcely mentioned, but only because the Regiment would be nothing if it did not subscribe to them. If a cynic is to sneer at such Boy Scout devotion he should reflect that it includes willing self-sacrifice to the point of death itself; though to understand fully is granted only to those who give themselves completely to the ideal of service. If he should, rashly, wish to rile the SAS, he should try calling them "The Special Air *Services*" as though they dispensed high-grade maintenance and piping-hot meals.

Next came specialist training, every man having to be either a signaller, linguist or, like Penny and Marafono, a medic. They did not make a vocation of it—one's priorities have to be nicely graded if one has to kill some people and cure others—but they studied intensively. This they needed to do, because the syllabus was formidable and far exceeded what is usually understood by first-aid. "Survival in different terrains, natural history and treatment of major endemic diseases; surgical emergencies such as maintenance of breathing in the unconscious by high tracheotomy, or completion of traumatic amputation; management of all types of injuries and wounds including treatment for shock and pain." All those were to be expected, but they also had to deal with "psychiatric casualties, dental care, ulcers, acute medical conditions, viral infections, paediatric emergencies, midwifery with complications, elementary pharmacology." There was a great deal more, slanted, of course, to likely SAS operating conditions; for instance, the treatment of blowpipe wounds.

Penny and Fred Marafono were greatly helped by a month in the casualty department of Paddington hospital where, providentially but sadly, some inhabitants of Notting Hill and Kilburn offered plentiful and varied opportunities to treat wounds resulting from armed and unarmed combat.

The last major obstacle for some individuals was the jungle. Most preferred it to the desert or anywhere else; it was cooler, kinder and they felt more secure and effective in it, but that depended entirely on their mastery of its ways which in turn derived from an affinity with it that led them to observe and side with nature rather than hopelessly to fight its immensity. Taught by "old Malayan Sergeants," the recruit soon learned to feel at home, unless he was handicapped by an instinctive aversion such as many people have for snakes and submarines. Such men are overwhelmed by the close confinement, where the very trees are hostile and seem to reach for them with arthritic, clutching hands. Indeed, the ubiquitous rotan, whose stalk becomes the universally valued cane, has at its forward end filaments several yards long, so fine as to be easily unnoticed but immensely strong and equipped with backward-pointing thorns with which it clings either to branches for support or the passing tenderfoot for sheer devilment. It is called "Wait-Awhile" because disengagement is not to be achieved by panic wrenching but delicately, prick by prick. The misfit stumbles blindly on he knows not whither, and is not to be convinced that there is any means of knowing. Wild and surely dangerous animals crash in the undergrowth or shriek from the tree-tops, serpents slither, clothes rot in the dank gloom, companions grate on jangled nerves; and if all that were not enough, the deadliest enemy of all, a human one, may be watching him from as close as five yards at any time. Strong men who have beaten Selection and all else have been floored by the forest; but Penny and Marafono loved it. Penny then stayed on in the East to take a Malay language course, which showed that he was fully seized with the SAS principle of always doing a little more.

Now, in the summer of 1964, adequate numbers had joined and "B" Squadron took its final shape. All its troopers were new and the rest of the recruits went to "A" and "D" in exchange for NCOs of all grades. Group training in patrols, troops and as a squadron superseded individual; though if each individual had not continued to strive for perfection with all his time, effort and creative thought, filling the unforgiving minute with "something constructive like demolition," the units would have stopped short of excellence.

Major Johnny Watts joined and set his mark on the Squadron. A non-deleter of expletives, he would bellow across the square, " 'Tanky,' you bastard, come and have a drink"; and it would not be long before another foreigner from "A" became reconciled to "B." But no one ever accused Watts of insincerity; the idea was laughable to men from whom he could not hide that he cared for them from the depths of his generous nature; whom he trained to be as tough and enterprising as befitted the best squadron there ever was—which they were in no doubt would be the case—and then could scarcely bear to commit them to the hazards against which he had done so. "Mother hen," says Penny; though that did not preclude a sharp peck when stimulation was indicated.

Discipline became superb, though its manifestations were esoteric rather than overt. "We might salute an officer once in the morning and that took care of him for the rest of the day," was the men's affectation; but they respected him none the less or he would not have been there at this stage. Even the young ones—Charlesworth, Saunt, Graham-Wigan, Pirie—had been awarded the subtle acknowledgement of acceptance "boss" rather than "sir." They in their turn had learnt that leadership in the SAS depended entirely on genuine esteem and that superficial forms counted for nothing. Badges of rank were not worn. The practise had started in the field for good operational reasons and then extended to base, both because there might still be stitch marks in an officer's shirt if he was captured and, as "Tanky" Smith pontificated, "If you need them you shouldn't have them, and if you don't need them don't wear them."

On the job, the commander commanded, without doubt though rarely without question. The only possible relationship between men who were chosen for their ability to think and act as individuals was easy familiarity within a framework of real if concealed discipline. High achievement though that was, it could look terrible. All ranks therefore put on an act to impress visitors, saluting and "siring" with tongue-in-cheek gusto for the Regiment's sake. With another of their mores, however, they did not dissemble; orders once given were remembered until the time came to act, however much later that might be. The sure and silent process often astonished those accustomed to NCOs haranguing squads at the last minute to drive home every detail.

The pace of training quickened, as Woodhouse and Watts would have ensured had they needed to. Reports were received from Borneo of increasing Indonesian aggression and SAS actions in which men had been killed. Finally, the sight of "D" Squadron arriving home at last, exhausted, created a powerful incentive in "B" to take its share and win its spurs. The restless atmosphere was just right for getting the most value from one of Woodhouse's important innovations, the Map Exercise, a Staff College-type exercise that he himself conducted in a classroom. Woodhouse had not attended Staff College because he could never summon up enough application to pass the entrance exam, rank and career formed no part of his ambition which was wholly devoted to his beloved Regiment and the success of its activities. He wrote the settings and narratives of fictional operations and the students in turn had to say what they would do at each stage and why. There was no staff solution, but every answer was discussed and developed by the whole class.

Firm, positive and quick decision-making based on constructive reasoning was, of course, the main aim. The art of logical disputation was also acquired so that what was known as a "Chinese Parliament"—implying a garrulous exchange of uncompromising assertions leading to flat contradictions and culminating in personal abuse—should be an informed debate from which the leader could select the substance, reassured that no option had been overlooked. Men learned how each others' minds worked, which could make their actions predictable when out of touch. The veterans' experience could be offered to the young; indeed, it could be imposed in the form of orders or Standard Operating Procedures, but now was the opportunity to question and analyse everything. Fresh thoughts from fresh minds were actively welcomed because the SAS was uncomfortably aware that even they could pursue an idea too far down one set of tramlines, so Woodhouse made his settings new and unexpected to encourage the habit of original as well as reasoned thought. Knowing they would soon be on active operations, the men of "B" Squadron had no difficulty imagining themselves in the paper situations and responded realistically, with feeling as well as reason. Enthusiasm for action was the first essential for success in it, and that they had to the full; smoothly flowing adrenaline also had its part to play, but uncontrolled excitement allied to emotion, whether fear, bravado, hatred or anything else, absolutely not. They had to learn to be cool, calculating and, when need be, deadly.

The Squadron packed its bergens in early October and went to Brunei for final jungle training in patrols and troops. The pace became hotter yet in line with the climate. The instructors worked hardest of all, preparing exercises at night and taking part all day. "It really was a round of ceaseless toil," says "Tanky" Smith; and appreciate their dynamic commander though they did, they yearned to get away from him on operational patrol. They were to have their wish, and it would be a great deal harder.

CHAPTER 8

"A LITTLE FURTHER"

"A" Squadron's Third Tour, June to October 1964

Major Peter de la Billière was not one of those who thought
Lillico a bit of a nut, but, like him, enjoyed the job and put all
his boundless energy into it with total dedication.

His thinking was free, imaginative and wide, yet under firm
objective control so that he could encompass broad visions and
small details simultaneously with each in its proper place. His
decisions were thus quite likely to be right; and the calm assurance with which he reached them inspired confidence, both in
his men for whatever he imposed on them, however hazardous,
and in the unenlightened whom he sought to lead into the way
of truth. He seldom raised his voice and became even quieter
when thwarted, but his steely determination was none the less
evident and could be disconcerting, especially to senior officers
before they saw the point.

When de la Billière first joined the Regiment in Malaya, that
independent cuss Lawrence Smith, upon whom the young tyro
was foisted to command the Troop that Smith had hitherto led
to his own entire satisfaction, astonished himself by accepting
the reversion with equanimity, even enthusiasm:

"We had this rapport; whatever he wanted to do—and he
always wanted to do something—I'd suddenly find it was also
what *I* wanted to do."

Now, as Squadron commander and Sergeant-Major, that dynamic relationship continued and developed, for there was plenty
to be done in Borneo; but since the next tour was months away
and neither could tolerate idleness, de la Billière connived with
Woodhouse for "A" Squadron to go to Aden, ostensibly for
training but really on the off-chance of action, which seemed
ever more imminent there.

The outcome was intensive patrolling among the wild and

hostile tribesmen of the wild and desolate Radfan Mountains, where the scorching, inescapable sun and waterless rock made the kindly tree canopy and gushing brooks of the Borneo "ulu" a tantalizing memory. Contacts were frequent during the four-week tour, and its highlight, the Battle of Shi'b Taym, was significant in the Regiment's history beyond the context of Aden.

Captain Robin Edwards and eight men of 3 Troop were caught in the open by a horde of at least fifty fanatical Arabs whose cherished aim was to kill them all at whatever cost to themselves. All day the attackers were kept at arm's length with the crucial support of RAF fighter-bombers, but at nightfall the Arabs closed in and the SAS broke out. The ensuing hand-to-hand mêlée compared in savage exhilaration with Rorke's Drift and a thousand last-ditch stands where only superb training and discipline give any hope of survival against teeming numbers. More than thirty Arabs died, but Edwards and Trooper Nick Warburton were killed too. The rest, with three of their number wounded and Arabs following them down the wadis, only survived a nightmare journey through the darkness by the skin of their teeth.

Was that just another day in the life of the SAS? At first sight yes, at least to Sergeant Alf Tasker who comments:

"It was a good day; we were fighting for our lives, weren't we?" to which, observing his listener's eyes to open wide and stare vacantly, he adds in explanation:

"When you're fighting for your life with a fifty-fifty chance you've got to enjoy it. Know what I mean?"

Not exactly, even yet; perhaps if given a little time.

Lance Corporal Paddy Baker, who was badly wounded in the leg and having dropped behind during the escape picked off several following Arabs and earned the Military Medal, strikes a faintly less enthusiastic note: "I much prefer fighting in the shade." But his preference was not consulted and the Regiment was to see a great deal more of South Arabia before Aden was finally abandoned.

de la Billière at base, however, was in no doubt that the day and night were the most agonizing of his life. Even his relief when seven exhausted figures limped into camp at dawn began to dissipate when he understood that they needed more than just a good breakfast to restore their well-being. Their strain was not eased by the Arabs exhibiting Edwards's and Warburton's heads in public, and their delayed shock was severe and prolonged, the memory of it becoming absorbed into "A" Squadron's corporate soul.

Borneo, however, was no place for introspection. In June 1964 the enemy was on the make with continuing company-sized raids into Western Sarawak as well as Sabah, aiming at best to establish bases in Malaysia and at least to unsettle the border tribes. That he could do the latter without achieving any military success had already been demonstrated and the implications were serious. Soekarno's whole adventure was an exercise in influencing hearts and minds, not only of the natives but of the world, by any means of which military aggression was just one, and the imperial powers' recent history had shown that it could succeed.

At yet another summit meeting, in Tokyo, Tunku Abdul Rahman asked bluntly when Indonesian forces would leave Malaysia so that discussion on what "Maphilindo" meant could begin. Soekarno replied that they had every right to be there because Malaysia did not exist. That was expected, but the Tunku's previous moderation paid him well in world opinion while Britain's resolve to support him was strengthened; though whether that support would survive the forthcoming general election which Labour was tipped to win remained uncertain, socialists tending not to be keen on colonial wars.

Life, however, is full of surprises; Denis Healey became Defence Secretary and prosecuted the war with, if anything, increased vigour. True, Labour's policy was to withdraw from Britain's residual empire east of Suez, but not dishonourably by abandoning allies in trouble; so the aim was best achieved by setting them straight quickly and then leaving them secure. Walker was delighted, the more so because Healey's grasp of military affairs was outstanding for a politician. With Healey at the top, Lord Mountbatten as Chief of Defence Staff and Admiral Begg as Commander-in-Chief Far East, Walker felt well backed and got on with his job.

Diplomatic and other measures were taken to convince all concerned that the British cause was good, that they intended to stay as long as they were wanted, that they *were* wanted and that they *could* stay. Should the Indonesians launch a massive assault on land, the Royal Navy and Royal Air Force could isolate Borneo from the rest of Indonesia—as Lillico advocated, for whether or not private soldiers have field marshals' batons in their knapsacks, SAS sergeants certainly do—and veiled threats were leaked as psychological warfare measures. But the essence of British policy was not to set Southeast Asia alight but the exact reverse; to contain the enemy's aggression with the least possible fighting and publicity. If that could be done the fewest people would be upset and most could sympathize with the British; the cost in lives and money would be kept low; the British Left would be less inclined to put a spoke in the wheel; and the method would be essentially civilized. So low-key was the British government's approach that today most Britons are either unaware or have forgotten that there was ever a war in Borneo. But in midsummer 1964, with a considerable and growing threat, that approach, however desirable, might or might not prove effective.

Soekarno too got on with his job, the fulfilling of a boast that Malaysia would be crushed before the sun rose on 1 January 1965. From that master of circumlocutory inexactitude such precision was out of character, and the date was as near Christmas with all its pitfalls as made no odds, but predictions must sometimes be made to inspire followers and there is no knowing what one can get away with until one tries; some people are pushovers and the British have a tempting appearance of being so, until actually pushed.

de la Billière's first aim was to restore morale along the border, where it had become dangerously low. The Muruts of Kabu and Saliliran were even found to be passively hostile. They were acting, at best, as double agents, so there was no certainty that incursions would be reported. SAS patrols themselves were in real danger. High intensity hearts and minds was therefore the order of the day, and it was arguable whether making friends in these circumstances was more or less perilous than fighting enemies.

The SAS must visit the villages personally for there to be any chance of success, whatever the risk. The latter could be mitigated by care and forethought, such as arriving unannounced, perhaps after walking in a stream to leave no tracks and sending one man tentatively ahead to check whether Indonesians were present. The usual chat would then follow, but it was sad to get a surly response and glean so little news. However, toothache and septic cuts compelled acceptance of relief and the medics were soon busy as of old. Work, such as cutting landing-points for payment, was put in hand; the village's urgent needs were signalled to base and small presents handed over; and in the evening the patrol vanished, hoping that the seed would germinate. Nevertheless, they would walk for as long as possible through the gathering darkness when even the natives found tracking difficult, and would move on at very first light for the same reason. Within a week the patrol would quietly reappear to take the next step on the road to friendship, having visited other villages in the interval though never daring to spend a night in one.

Even in the remote jungle there was no certainty of security. The patrols lived as though in enemy territory, at constant alertness with all cutting forbidden. The number of Border Scouts was increased to six or even eight for each patrol, to maintain touch with the villagers and report every scrap of information; they had therefore to know the patrol's position and intended movement, so betrayal was a possibility although it never happened.

So far so good; but only when the Muruts truly believed that the British could protect them would they give their full confidence and help. To this end, de la Billière hit on the idea of turning Step-Up exercises into psychological warfare spectaculars with the enthusiastic collaboration of the Gurkhas, the 2/7th until mid-July and then the 1/2nd under Lieutenant-Colonel John Clements.

"It was a great game," says de la Billière, "and we only cheated a little by making sure the Gurkhas and helicopters were at split-second readiness. 'Look,' we said to the Muruts, 'when you see any sign of the Indos, come and tell us straight away and we'll use our magic radio box to bring masses of soldiers in to clobber them.' Well that was a bit unconvincing at first so we said, 'Let's try it tomorrow; you pretend you've found some footprints, anywhere you like, and see what happens.' So along they came and told us there were signs where the tracks cross just south of Bukit Oojah; and this bit wasn't cheating because our patrols knew their areas intimately and landing-points with lateral tracks had been cut wherever tactically expedient, so within an hour or two a hundred Gurkhas bristling with weapons would be right on the spot and the locals' eyes boggled."

The Muruts were thus impressed that the British were more efficient than the Indonesians, as well as a good deal nicer; but the most telling effect was to the headman's prestige. That factor was crucial because had it just been a matter of troops arriving arbitrarily in his domains, his authority might have been shaken and his displeasure incurred. But as it was:

"I, the Pengulu of Kabu, Sakikilo, Sabaton and great dominions beyond the trees, called for soldiers and they came; I spoke and they descended from the skies; and when I wanted them to go, they left again. 'Saya yang ta-tinggi' ['I'm the greatest'].''

de la Billière took advantage of Wingate-Gray's presence and walked the length of the Pensiangan front to see it for himself, gingering everybody up and generating new ideas for pursuing excellence. The list was long:

To ensure efficient coordination with the infantry and other Intelligence agencies, the SAS should have Liaison NCOs at Battalion Headquarters, carefully chosen for their ability to advise senior officers tactfully. Paddy Baker filled this bill precisely, and not yet being fully fit after Shi'b Taym went to Pensiangan itself. The radio beacon Sarbe was a clear need; so too was a more efficient resupply organization, the precision of which was important to the patrols' planning and morale. de la Billière wrote to Brigadier Tuzo with considerably more asperity than is customary from a Major to such a senior officer, but the latter, wisely and tolerantly, let him get away with it and put matters right.

Ideas for hearts and minds tumbled forth. Crops were the natives' main concern so a farmer's bulletin should be produced to be read aloud. And even more important, a news sheet. The Regiment needed more Malay speakers, so courses must take priority. If the British were to open trading-posts near the border where Kalimantan natives could buy essentials like rice, which was known to be short, hearts and minds might be won as well as useful information gleaned. Budding entrepreneurs in the villages were fuelling inflation, which was both expensive and would spoil them for the future, so wages for services such as porterage and cutting landing-points should be fixed. Also, no presents should be given away without some quid pro quo. And so on, and so on.

Serious consideration was given to evacuating some of the wavering villages like Kabu, which Gerry had thankfully turned over to Sergeant Paddy Freaney with his patrol of "Mau Mau" Williams and George Shipley. The weather was bad, their resupply was late so their food ran out. When at last it came and they cached half, everything not in tins was eaten by termites; including 10,000 cigarettes that Williams had ordered at his own expense, the better to win hearts and minds while himself turning an honest penny. "Sakikilo was a very boozy place," says Freaney; "they were on a four-day blinder when we went there once, bodies sprawled everywhere." Perhaps that was not surprising with the future so menacing. Late in the month, signs of a large enemy force were found on the border, and those of a scouting party in the home "ladangs." Freaney organized a

Step-Up but nothing more happened. The atmosphere lightened a little at the end of July with friendships beginning to form, and the decision was taken not to evacuate, the SAS with their experience of the Long Pa Sia Bulge arguing that almost any natives, even fence-sitters, were better than none at all.

That other troublesome parish, Saliliran cum Talinbakus, was taken over from Lillico by "Gipsy" Smith, who went about restoring trust and confidence as his particular talents prompted, ordering a bicycle dynamo and headlamp by the next resupply. At the Haunted House, they might well have asked "Why no bicycle?," but SAS lore has it that a man in the field gets what he wants at once and questions come later; besides, they knew their "Gipsy."

Construction took five days and Smith became uneasy lest the Indonesians should hear of his patrol's immobility, but the Talinbakusians were so intrigued by the thing, whatever it was, that they did nothing to prevent its completion. A framework of jungle poles, a paddle wheel and water-guides of old boxes, a driving belt of air-drop webbing and a heavy flywheel carved from a tree-section proved on first testing to be too slow; but it was simple to add a small gearwheel and other refinements. The spare radio cable just reached the headman's house, and the 22 SAS hydro-electric generator went on stream to provide the only electric light in all the border to people who could only regard it as a miracle. Its rays first lit a memorable "tapai" party and then spread to all the country round about, where the supremacy of Talinbakus was acknowledged and a hearts and minds breakthrough achieved at one technological stroke.

Smith disappeared on his rounds without more delay. When he returned a week later the Muruts wanted something new, so he made them one of his stills from bergen-frame tubing and a biscuit-tin, which he had first researched and developed among the aborigines of Malaya. To a discriminating palate, "tapai" in its natural state is just tolerable if duty is the spur, though the Muruts rarely had enough of it; but this eye-opening, throat-closing poteen challenged even them, and socially progressive activists might reasonably have complained that, whatever they needed for their welfare, in was not that, even though there was a war on in which exceptional measures were sometimes in order. However, a benign providence conspired to achieve the aim without the drawbacks; for when Smith demonstrated that the fiery liquor could indeed be readily ignited, the Muruts became even less enthusiastic, and while they now possessed a second object of pride and prestige, they never mastered its operation.

Talinbakus had been selected for these favours because Saliliran was almost on the border, and Smith did not dare make other than fleeting visits there during July. Those were enough, however, to foster a particularly warm and effective relationship with the headman, Likinan, an exceptionally able leader who played a difficult political game with single-minded delicacy. Pressurized on one day by Smith and the next by Indonesians from Nantakor, little more than a mile away, only survival mattered. When Likinan invited the patrol to refreshments, it was a sore test of nerve to sit in the open sipping ''tapai'' through a straw and making small talk while expecting a bullet between the shoulders. Such fears were justifiable but proved groundless; even in the early days, Likinan promised that they would be safe as his guests, sending out a screen of hunters to ensure early warning of danger. As he became convinced that Saliliran's future lay with Malaysia, his village became a pleasure to visit and earned three stars in the SAS good food guide.

Nantakor was the dominating factor. In normal times it was like home to the Salilirans, for the two communities were closely interrelated; but now its inhabitants had been replaced by a platoon of 40 soldiers and the village turned into a strong defensive position. Saliliran's Border Scouts watched it constantly; barefooted, armed sometimes with shotguns which were consistent with their being hunters, and sometimes with just a cover story, such as having come to enquire after auntie's health, they bravely and effectively operated under Smith's orders. The area's vulnerability was such that he was ordered to cut a system of landing-points and tracks, for which he engaged the people of both villages.

All along the SAS front other patrols did the same job with the same dedication and initiative, though with different approaches and methods as circumstances and personalities dictated. Results were less encouraging in the Highlands, where there were many more villages close to the border with strong enemy forces just the other side. Although Step-Up exercises reassured the Kelabits while the troops were present, they remained nervous at other times, with justification, too; on 6 August, four landing-point cutters employed by the SAS were fallen upon and captured. This incident had to be acknowledged as an important reverse. The Kelabits demanded a permanent infantry presence, which was granted, and the SAS were gradually withdrawn to more useful places.

The mental and physical stress of defensive campaigning was no less for ''A'' Squadron than it had been for ''D'' and the incidence of sickness was higher than expected. When men had to be evacuated from patrol on medical grounds—''Medevac''— it was no cause for satisfaction; nor for shame either though the word carried a subtly different connotation to ''Casevac.'' de la Billière had bet Woodhouse that it would not happen in his Squadron, rashly because anyone can become ill and he had to pay up; he explained that since patrols had to move camp frequently a ''bed case'' could not stay in the same leafy bower long enough for a cure. Owing to his uncompromising insistence on taking paludrine and other prophylactic measures there were few tropical fevers, but exhaustion occurred and prolonged tiredness reduced resistance to various medical conditions.

This was a time when much thought was being given to limiting the weight of a man's pack to give him a better chance of survival in a hostile environment by lessening fatigue and improving alertness and agility. Foods with high calorific values were investigated, dehydrated the further to reduce weight, but even so the rations which could be carried in a 40- or even 50-pound pack were insufficient for a big man at full stretch; all right perhaps for an in-and-out offensive mission, but constant under-nourishment could impair health and ultimately defeat the object for which it had been introduced. Very well, this was no choir outing but the SAS on patrol, and as in so many ways they were pioneering a new technique for going always a little further, now achieving Woodhouse's goal of being able to operate for a fortnight with nothing but what they carried.

SHOOT-AND-SCOOT

The remote Third Division was being taken over by the Guards Independent Parachute Company, now trained in the SAS jungle role, and that was a relief; but the uninhabited Long Pa Sia Bulge with its unresolved problems was still very much on the SAS agenda and those now present in it were Sergeant Maurice Tudor and his 4 Troop. Three patrols covered the main ''ulus,'' the Berbulu, the Paling/Plandok, and the Moming, which was Tudor's own stamping-ground though he visited the others from time to time; they would have been thick on the ground in a populated district, but here every point in the border marches had to be inspected personally and revisited constantly so that there was never a respite from "going to and fro upon the earth and from walking up and down in it."

The Bulge thus became increasingly familiar, and by early August it was possible to be fairly certain that the enemy no longer made himself at home there. de la Billière even judged it prudent to withdraw Tudor for a Malay language course, the need for more linguists being pressing, and he was lifted out from Landing-Point 1 near the River Plandok on the 4th. Lance Corporal Roger Blackman, fastidious concerning eggs as may be remembered, now commanded a patrol for the first time. On the following morning he led them back eastward to the Moming, spending a further night on the way.

Trooper White was usually the lead scout, "Chalky" to his Army mates of course but his name was Billy and he preferred that. "A harum-scarum lad," as his brother John, now an SAS Sergeant, admits with approval, he had been RTU'd in Malaya for an over-exuberant "lark"; but he and the SAS were made for each other, and he clawed his way back. This was his first patrol in Borneo, but it had lasted a long time and he had well proved his fitness to lead the way.

Another trooper, young and newly-entered, was Jimmy Green, though that was not his real name. It is said of the SAS—indeed they say it too and delude themselves greatly—that security being so much a part of their lives, they have lost the ability to talk freely even when they safely may. But here was one man who might have originated the myth, and his anonimity must be respected.

The patrol still comprised four men without Tudor because they had a visitor from Australia. That country naturally kept a close eye on Confrontation and Woodhouse strove to enlist the help of her SAS Company, so far unsuccessfully. But it happened that one of their number on attachment to the British Army in Malaya met Woodhouse at a party and, like calling to like, jumped at the chance of trying his hand in Borneo. So here was Lieutenant Geoff Skardon, who had been with the patrol four weeks and was fully integrated, enjoying the life, companionship and indeed excitement at the possibility of a real enemy being behind every bush, though so far that had remained only a possibility.

On the evening of the 5th, however, the 1/2nd Goorkhas at

Long Pa Sia heard a faint rattle of musketry way up in the "ulu" Moming. Blackman was in dead ground though much closer and detected nothing; but having been ordered to check the main trade-route track parallel to the river he did so on the morning of the 6th, very slowly, very quietly and fully alert.

White led, down a slope, across a sunken creek and up to the low ridge along which ran the track, followed by Blackman, Skardon and Green. As they climbed they became involuntarily taut, sensing a subtle change in the atmosphere but instinctively rather than consciously. None of them having the experience of a Creighton or a Richardson, they only realized afterwards that the causes were not extra-sensory but palpable and could have been acted upon. Although absolutely quiet themselves, they heard no jungle hum, as though the insects too were listening apprehensively, and in the still air hung the trace of a scent that while not being distinctively human was not quite of the forest either.

Scarcely moving, White glided round a big tree and found himself standing over an Indonesian soldier who was kneeling and preparing his meal with soundless movements. White had no doubt what he had to do and did it instantly; without needing to raise his rifle he inserted the butt into his own shoulder and, twisting to his right, the muzzle into the "salt-cellar" above the collar-bone in the enemy's. The bullet stabbed downwards to emerge from the buttock and the man was dead; stone-dead like a statue, for his knees supported and balanced him and he knelt there yet, as though humbly before his god.

Blackman shouted "Get out!" as was his duty. Expecting the others to obey, he broke left with Green, both men slipping their bergens, when these impeded them as was customary; though the radio was lost too and that was unfortunate. White, however, stayed where he was, shooting. Seeing this, Skardon broke right but forward rather than back, first thinking that whatever White's target the patrol had the initiative and must keep it. Having dropped to the prone position and discarded his bergen too for greater freedom, Skardon saw the thick jungle along the ridge blaze with fire from at least a platoon of soldiers with White almost among them. The cover on the slope now proved to be horrifyingly sparse. He changed his aim to cover White's withdrawal, but it was already too late. He caught the words: "Geoff, Geoff, I'm hit!"

Oblivious of the Shoot-and-Scoot drill and of his own safety, Skardon ran to White, diving beside him and pulling him behind the big tree, which at least afforded protection from the closest enemy to the old front. Those to the flanks, however, had the pair still in view and poured in fire. They missed only through incompetence and because of the undergrowth, thin though it was. Skardon saw blood in huge quantities spurting under pressure from White's upper thigh and knew that a tourniquet must be applied within seconds. Expecting a hand-grenade at any moment, he grabbed White's collar and with all his strength dragged him a full ten yards to a shallow depression that looked as though it might offer some protection, but it did not. Their movement was seen. The firing continued to break down branches and thud into the earth around them, and with his hand still on his friend's shoulder, Skardon said:

"I think we've had it, Chalky."

"I know skipper, thanks for trying."

Skardon then saw White's wound, which was big enough to take his fist; the reason he could see it was because blood had stopped flowing, and the reason for that could only have been that White's heart too had stopped. Had it still been pumping it must have produced a pulsing flow however feeble, but that deduction did not strike Skardon, whose mind was busy assessing how best to get White to the cover of the sunken creek. He could not know whether Blackman and Green had got away, so he shouted to them for covering fire, without response. He said, "Come on 'Chalky,' I'm going to carry you," but there was no response from that quarter either; of course there wasn't, but Skardon was set on his plan. He swore angrily and slapped the insentient face, then half lifting poor "Chalky," staggered a few more yards to another slight hollow which, however, afforded no better protection. The intense fire was still singularly ill-directed, but the law of averages must surely be operating, unfavourably.

Four or five of the enemy broke cover on the far flank and ran down towards the creek, the only way of escape. Skardon again slapped White's face and scanned it searchingly, comprehending at last that he was witnessing the eternal mystery. Whether or not the body was clinically dead at that moment, Billy White was no longer of this world for anything Geoff Skardon could do about it.

Awakened, that most compelling of instincts, self-preservation, urged Skardon to instant flight. There was now no reason to subdue it. He rose, fired three aimed shots at the enemy group and without waiting to see the results sprinted for the creek. Leaping in he was hidden by the high banks, but now he must move some twenty yards downstream to where good cover lined the left bank before the enemy could cut him off in the stream. He was slowed up however, helplessly as in a nightmare, by a "wait-awhile" hooked lash that had seized him by the belt. Having no time to wait, he discarded the belt in an instant and pressed ahead. Speed and concealment vied for priority, though his reason told him that the check had eliminated his chances either way; but something, perhaps his shots, had delayed the enemy too. Skardon reached the thick jungle, scrambled up the bank and slipped into safety by what must have been the narrowest margin, later evidence showing that the enemy had indeed moved up the creek and taken his belt.

Meanwhile, Corporal Wally Poxon of the Plandok patrol had heard the battle. Reporting it to the Haunted House he was told to go straight to Landing-Point 1 and secure it for Blackman's possible return. Tudor, still in Brunei, flew "hot helicopter" to Long Pa Sia and guided a platoon of the 1/2nd Goorkhas to intercept a presumed enemy. They were all down on Landing-Point 2 by three in the afternoon and hurried to the trade route just short of the border, a smart manoeuvre which deserved success but failed by a hair's breadth, signs of the enemy's headlong retirement being clearly evident.

It was not until late the next morning that Blackman and Green arrived at Landing-Point 1. Skardon followed two hours later, the rendezvous drill not having worked as intended and he having had to navigate without map or compass which had gone with his belt; that he would succeed was predictable after his display of courage and resolution in the action, but it was hard and tortuous going, fraught with anxiety just the same.

The three survivors were flown out to Long Pa Sia to be debriefed and re-equipped, and sent back in with the Gurkhas the following morning. Most of the latter were deployed along the frontier in case some of the enemy were still at large, but the SAS led two sections back to the contact area where they found what they least expected. Apart from Skardon's belt being missing, nothing whatever had changed. There was the Indonesian, kneeling still with his uneaten food and unfired rifle before him; there were the bergens exactly where they had been dropped; there were the ambush positions of 30 enemies, littered with spent cartridges; and there was Billy White with the same dreadful wound that Ian Thomson would suffer, his femoral artery fully open to prove that he had died within minutes of being hit. Blackman was a young soldier then:

"Never experienced anything like that before; basha-up with a chap and get to know him intimately—nice chap; then next day wrap him in a poncho and bundle him into a helicopter; affects you more than you like to admit."

There was plenty of evidence to show that the Indonesians had been in ambush for some days, but their reason for opening fire the evening before the contact could only be surmised. Had they been trying to "bait" the ambush they would hardly have expected the Gurkhas to be so foolish as to march headlong down the track and would have been better placed at a border landing-point. It seemed like an accident, sprung perhaps by an animal, and that their commander took a chance that they had not been heard and stayed where he was. If so, his hopes would have been dashed when an apparent attack came in from the flank, and assuming that those dreadful Gurkhas had already flooded the area he legged it for the border as soon as the shooting was over. White had fired six rounds and if some of those had hit, which at five yards range was likely, the ensuing confusion might well have resulted in the kneeling corpse being overlooked.

An apparently insignificant brush in which both sides had disengaged as soon as possible was thus a tactical success for the British, the enemy having lost at least one man and recrossed the border without achieving his aim. White's death could therefore be justified, but when the SAS mulled it over in retrospect they were seized with terrible misgiving at what might have happened under the rules of Shoot-and-Scoot had he been less seriously wounded. True, he might not have been wounded at all had he scooted instantly after firing his first shot, in which case Skardon would not have been tempted to go forward. That indeed was what White and all of them had practised many times, so that the fact that he did not do so indicated that the option was not open to him, visible enemies being so close that to turn would have invited a certain bullet in the back and probably several.

White was wounded nevertheless. Skardon went to his aid in an act of high and selfless gallantry, which was enhanced rather than diminished by his deliberately contravening the rules, a hard thing for a disciplined soldier to do even though it was emphasized that SOPs were guidelines rather than binding orders. In doing so, he nearly ensured that two men were lost instead of one, which the rules were expressly designed to prevent. But had he scooted as they prescribed, White might have been alive for all the patrol would have known; and acting on that assumption, they could have returned for him ten minutes after the contact, the enemy having left. The rules, however, did not allow for that.

Throughout the Regiment, honour battled with expediency in innumerable Chinese Parliaments; considerable warmth was generated and no less a pundit than Sergeant-Major Lawrence Smith gave it as his view that "Shoot-and-Scoot was a perfectly correct SOP and that's what we taught the lads, but if it had been me and, say, Alf Tasker and one of our mates was missing, no way would we have paid any attention to the SOP." His word cannot be doubted, ill-disciplined though it was or perhaps because of that for there was no more loyal member of the Regiment than he; and one may wonder, daringly, whether Woodhouse's own legs would have carried him away had he been faced with the choice of following his own procedure or risking his own life.

The policy had been instituted to save life, both for its own sake and to preserve regimental morale; but now the question had squarely to be faced: whether the latter would be worse affected by leaving a possibly wounded man to die or be captured by a savage foe, or by losing more lives trying to save him. Woodhouse, deeply concerned at the possible backfiring of his principle, now understood that the reason he had not specified the action to be taken was because he had subconsciously assumed that a missing man would automatically be accorded a priority second only to the immediate aim of the mission; with good justification too, both Richardson and Woodiwiss having returned to the scenes of their contacts as soon as circumstances permitted and survived. A mere assumption was not much help to a young patrol commander seeking loyally to obey his orders, and Woodhouse's first reaction was to write to de la Billière:

"I believe troops will welcome, and morale demands, an order that if a man is known to have fallen the patrol will remain in the close vicinity until either they see for certain that he is dead or they recover him alive. I think we should expect to fight to the death for this."

As usual, however, he invited discussion and acknowledged that such an order might send men into danger uselessly, while it failed to cater for the many possible variations on the theme which a commander might face, each demanding a different reaction. The apparently simple aim of saving life was thus shown to be highly complex, and indeed the modified instruction which emerged still failed to bring about the early rescue of Lillico and Thomson six months later (see Chapter 1). Only after that was a satisfactory procedure adopted, which is best not detailed lest it help a future jungle enemy.

BOOTS, DMS, MODIFIED

Three days after Billy White's death, Poxon's patrol found an inscription on a tree near the border: "Go no further, winged soldiers of England." The point was elegantly made and well taken; but SAS business being always to go a little further, Captain Ray England (regarding himself as personally addressed) and his winged soldiers Corporal Spike Hoe and Lance Corporal Bill Condie were already engaged in changing the tread-pattern of their directly-moulded boot-soles from standard British Army to Indonesian with that express purpose. To find somewhere in the Haunted House sufficiently secluded to prevent a casual enquiry as to what all this was in aid of was not easy, but it had to be done; even if no answer was vouchsafed, an accurate deduction that cross-border operations were at last beginning would not be difficult. The absolute secrecy demanded by the mission could only be achieved by not telling anyone who did not need to know, and those who did were very few indeed.

To keep a secret on which one's life may depend is not hard, especially in the SAS where secrecy is the norm and friends do not take umbrage when a barrier of silence descends between them; and now an extra constraint was imposed from above that the whole enterprise must remain permanently *sub rosa*.

General Walker had obtained permission to operate a country with which the British were nominally at peace by his reasoned moderation as well as importunity. He had no wish to invade Indonesia and turn Confrontation into war, but merely to unbalance the enemy by intermittent shallow raids and make him feel too insecure to mount offensive operations in his turn. Thus Malaysia would be defended without being fought over; the clandestine communists would be discouraged from rising; and the Indonesians would eventually acknowledge that they could not succeed. Even so, the political and military risks were considerable and much honour is due to those who supported the policy; particularly Defence Secretary Healey who took the final decision and responsibility, seeing clearly that it offered a real chance not just of containing Confrontation but of winning it, and with minimum casualties to British forces and civilians on both sides. These offensive operations were codenamed "Claret."

If the secret could be kept from all but the enemy, the hope was that he would keep it too, not wishing to advertise his own reserves. It followed that all encounters must indeed be reverses for him and not for the British because the Indonesians would certainly exploit the latter exultantly. Professional efficiency thus became doubly imperative, and only the most jungle-experienced troops would be used after intensive planning and rehearsal. As for the SAS patrols that would undertake the preliminary reconnaissance in totally unfamiliar terrain, their aim must be leave no evidence of their presence, and any unavoidable traces must be demonstrably deniable. Having already been warned by Woodhouse to prepare for cross-border operations, enterprising spirits like Lillico had envisaged landing by, say, submarine at, say, Pontianak and doing something constructive like blowing up the supply depot. That would have been a perfectly valid SAS activity in war, but this was Confrontation, and the indulgence only allowed penetration of 3,000 yards. Although paltry in comparison, it offered considerable scope nevertheless, and it was quite exciting too when it actually came to doing it.

England's objective was the River Sembakung, southeast of Labang which, supplying as it did a considerable number of troops at bases along the Salilir nearly to Kabu, must surely be vulnerable to interdiction. The patrol would watch the river for a week to assess the traffic's density and regularity, find good ambush positions for the infantry, and return with a general picture of the topography and pattern of native habitation and movement. The 1/2nd Goorkhas would then follow with a strike, so Lieutenant (Queen's Gurkha Officer) Manbahadur Ale was sent as the patrol's fourth member.

Secrecy, security, self-sufficiency and deniability were England's watch-words in making his plan, which began with what each man was to carry and where, in minute detail. In his hand he would carry his self-loading rifle with full magazine. On his person would be his escape compass, 100 Malay dollars sewn into his clothing for soliciting help in emergency, field dressings, morphine, plasters, torch, notebook and pencil, map (never to be marked with his true position, but a fictitious track entirely in Sabah to imply a genuine navigational error), loo-paper, matches, knife, watch, and wrist compass for those lucky enough to own one. On his belt would be his compass, "parang," two full magazines, water-bottle, mug, sterilizing tablets, two days' rations in his mess tin, spoon, cooking stove with hexamine fuel tablets, more matches, paludrine, wire saw, insect repellent, rifle cleaning kit and a hand grenade.

The bergen's contents varied from man to man. Hoe was the signaller, carrying the radio with its spare battery, aerial and codes, and the Sarbe, which had at last been issued. Those were heavy items, so most of his food was shared around the others, leaving him with his spare shirt, trousers, socks, boots, poncho, sleeping-bag of parachute silk, nylon cord for contingencies, and book for beguiling the hours when not on observation duty, though not during the eleven-hour nights when the escape would have been most welcome; a candle on a sharpened stake conveniently positioned at the hammock-side was a luxury of the past, for no lights or stake-sharpening would be permitted now. Condie's extra load was the medical pack, containing surgical scissors, forceps, thermometer, syringe and needles, scalpel blades, suture needles and thread, extra morphine syrettes, sterile water, assorted plasters and bandages, and a comprehensive pharmacy. England and Manbahadur took the binoculars, camera, and two large water-bags. The latter were carried empty; on passing a stream all would replenish their personal bottles and drink their fill—and more, for one can never have too much in the tropics, while too little causes heatstroke which can kill as readily as hypothermia. A night-stop near a stream would not be safe and it was then that plenty of water was needed for brewing, soaking dehydrated foods, cooking and washing-up. The supply was carried up in one load and the water-point never used again.

Rations were keenly debated and whittled down, for it would surely be acceptable to lose weight for a maximum of twelve days rather than carry an incapacitating and tiring load. England further reduced the weight by specifying the daily allowances for two men rather than one, thus saving containers: two Oxo cubes, 1oz; two oatmeal blocks, 2oz; one tin of sardines, 4½oz; one packet of biscuits, 3oz; two tins of cheese, 3oz; salt, 1oz; two dehydrated meat blocks, 12oz; four vitamin tablets; sugar, 2½oz; milk cube, 2oz; and, of course, tea, ¼oz, without which no Briton can face his future. The total was 16 ounces a day per man giving 2,000 calories instead of the 3,600 they really needed.

England then looked at the standard operating procedures, trying to foresee everything that might differ from an ordinary border patrol. Remaining undetected was paramount so they would move very slowly and for only twenty minutes before a halt to ensure they missed no unnatural signs. The lead scout would change every hour to maintain alertness. On stopping for the night the main meal of the day would first be cooked and eaten; often curried, for little individual preferences were permitted to add relish to the taste and comfort to the soul. Also before dark so that no lights need be shown, the evening signal was drafted by England to be coded and tapped out in Morse code by Hoe; this generally obsolete method allowed the use of high-frequency with its much longer range than ultra-high frequency voice. Daylight time must also be allowed for receiving any messages from base and perhaps replying to them. No restrictions were placed on the volume of signalling, the risk of interception by the enemy being considered slight. Indeed, it was mandatory to send at least two signals a day and if any were missed the emergency organization would slot into gear; three, and the patrol must return to the border.

The meal washed up, the radio dismantled and all stowed as though for moving, the ponchos were to be produced only just before the light failed. England had even contrived to save weight here by extending the idea of shared rations to the same pairs sharing bashas; he with Hoe and Condie with Manbahadur, so that with only one poncho each they could all have one over and one under. While doing all this, no unnecessary noise would be made and weapons must always be within arm's reach; but now, finally, there would be absolute quiet, immediate readiness and intense listening because it is a cardinal principle of conflict unchanging through the ages that one is most vulnerable at dusk and dawn.

Long before daybreak, therefore, before even the first glimmer of light, everyone would have activated his natural alarm mechanism—which is accentuated by SAS training—and be sitting on his packed bergen, facing outwards with weapon cradled. Breakfast, tea with half a tin of sardines and a biscuit, would either be taken at full light or after the first hour's march. All rubbish was to be carried at least that distance before being buried below the reach of pig-snouts (to de la Billière's disapproval even so, had he known; nothing, in his experience, ever being beyond the reach of pig-snouts). The camp site was to be left immaculate with every leaf in place and never visited again unless used as the patrol rendezvous for emergencies. Lunch was a brew of Oxo, the rest of the biscuits and one tin of cheese each.

Any locals met were only to be shot in self-defence as the ultimate resort; it would be much better to make friends with them, but better still to use every artifice to avoid meeting them at all for then the operation would be compromised and must be cancelled. On detecting anything suspicious, each man would melt sideways and freeze; if soldiers or locals passed apparently unsuspecting, the line of march would be changed, but if one of the patrol was seen by an enemy, he would at once fire a double-tap; the other three would follow suit whether or not they could see a target, and without an instant's delay scoot in pairs for the patrol rendezvous. The missing man drill remained much the same as before, there not having been time to assess the lessons of Billy White, but it was emphasized that the most incriminating piece of evidence to leave on the wrong side of the border would be a man, dead or alive.

England trained his men for a week until de la Billière was satisfied. On 13 August they flew to a landing-point near Bantul and were met by the resident patrol, commanded by Jimmy Catterall. Then they marched together to the border for two days, living on their hosts to save rations. A border rendezvous was jointly established so that both could be certain of finding the place again after the patrol or in emergency.

On the 15th they symbolically donned their boots DMS and crossed the great divide, feeling small and lonely in a big and hostile world; except for England, who was possessed by a sense of transcendental serenity. He knew precisely how this had been engendered. During the preparations the atmosphere had been electric, not only at the Haunted House but up to General Headquarters itself and perhaps beyond. The risks were great, but the mission must on no account fail, otherwise all cross-border operations might be revoked by a nervous high authority. If that should happen, it was inconceivable how else the campaign might be won. It is therefore understandable that England had been seized with vivid foreboding of utter catastrophe, including his own death. Being an experienced soldier, he knew this was more than normal pre-operation nerves and realized, sadly rather than fearfully, that it must be accepted as fact; so, breathing a silent farewell to his wife Dorothy and baby son, he stepped out to meet his destiny. Immediately, all the grinding stress dissolved and flowed away through his modified boot-soles, though the premonition remained.

It was most extraordinary. Far from finding himself in a state of saintly resignation, he had never felt more positively and joyfully alive. Expecting to be ambushed at any moment, his perceptions were at their keenest; navigating in unknown country, his eye made sense of ridges and spurs revealed by infrequent glimpses so that he took the right ones to avoid descending into valleys and climbing up again unnecessarily, and all the while he remained aware of the jungle scene which he thought had never looked more beautiful. Poor Manbahadur, however, in a severely practical mood, gazed at his compass despairingly. They headed in every direction but the right one, and he wondered how he would later lead his Company through this labyrinth.

Progress was oh so slow, one and a half miles a day, but at that speed they moved almost soundlessly, left few tracks, observed minutely, reassessed their situation at leisure as it developed, ran little risk of blundering into trouble and were well poised to react smartly if they did. Cutting their path had, of course, to be a last expedient, and they did not need to; the forest had been undisturbed and dense shade from huge trees left the floor mostly clear. Scrub grew thickly where deadfalls had admitted light, but there animal tracks abounded; like the soldiers, animals preferred high ground for travelling, but also leading part-hunter, part-hunted lives shunned the crests where one only walked if one had nothing to fear. So much game implied few human hunters and there were no signs of any.

They made three night-stops on slopes between ridge and stream, where they were hard put to find flat ground to sleep on and were therefore uncomfortable; but that was expected and no setbacks occurred. Then, on the afternoon of the 18th, there quite suddenly down a steep 300-foot slope was the Sembakung. So much imagination and anticipation had been concentrated upon this river that it had assumed a mystical significance, like the sacred Alph, and England in his exalted mood was quite taken aback to find it just like any other: 70 feet across with a wide shingle beach on the near side and rather muddy. He had to acknowledge that fortune had favoured them, and this was confirmed when after very little searching they spotted halfway down the slope the upturned roots of a great tree which had fallen outwards but retained a toe-hold. It offered a perfect nest where they would be invisible from below and, with a little help from nature, from above too for the slope was thickly wooded.

On scrambling down they found that all the ledge lacked was a wide view of the river. But again, as though intended, a smaller tree-root a little further down presented itself as an ideal observation post. They did not take long to settle in because they remained at instant readiness to move as though they were still marching, with nothing unpacked but what was in use at the moment. Each pair manned the OP for half a day in turn. Unremitting alertness, though a strain, was stimulated by the activities of the locals; some fished, and this was evidently a good spot with traps and nets being raised and reset regularly; others journeyed up and down, sometimes paddling their narrow boats, sometimes walking on the flat beach, and sometimes when going upstream combining the two, the passengers leaving the boat to relieve the strain on the paddlers. But two whole days passed before the patrol first saw what they had come for, soldiers. Even then there were only two; they paddled a boat with a bearded civilian, clearly a foreigner, and some boxes that might just possibly have been military stores. At last there was something to radio home about.

Interest intensified, only to dwindle as days slipped by with nothing more to revive it so that it had to be maintained by conscious will, as did all aspects of morale in the micro-world of the upturned tree-root. Of the two pairs, England and Hoe were old friends, who spoke little except of the day's events because they had already discussed most topics of mutual interest exhaustively; they knew more of each other's private lives than would perhaps have altogether pleased their respective wives, and their personal habits evoked no friction. England read his book through several times to his vocational profit, it being a Malay dictionary with phrases; but he came to wish he had brought something like *War and Peace* instead, together with some sweets to suck while reading it and subdue the distracting insistence of hunger. Hoe's wife Janet sent him a record request on "Forces Favourites," which the Haunted House relayed. Although the radio was ill-suited to music, he improved the resonance of the earphones with his tin mug.

Manbahadur and Condie, on the other hand, found that both being hill tribesmen, from the Himalaya and Grampians respectively, was not a close enough bond when deciding a delicate matter such as which part of a broken biscuit was the larger; and it is only the pompous who cannot admit to have ever been so childish. They needed to laugh, but whereas Condie could crawl to the other basha for a chuckle—"Why can't you bloody officers stick together?"—Manbahadur had to contain himself until back with his own kind in the mess at Pensiangan.

England was on watch when two soldiers walked along the beach and stopped, looked up straight into his eyes and kept on looking. Shooting monkeys is good sport and the men may have thought they had found one, or they might have heard the swarms of flies which buzzed with loathsome zest around the only spot the patrol could use as a latrine that was both invisible and accessible on the slope. There were no monkeys and the men moved on, showing no sign of having been alerted. That was only partly reassuring because to betray that one is aware of something potentially dangerous can trigger a pre-emptive strike, and England had to judge whether the patrol had been compromised and should retire. He decided to stay, and then spent an uneasy 24 hours wondering whether by doing so he had invited the disaster which his orders specified must be avoided at all costs.

The next day, the 23rd, all was shown to be well by six carefree soldiers paddling lazily downstream; and that was the surprisingly unremarkable highlight of the patrol when there was every reason to expect a constant flow of personnel and logistics. On the 25th, it was time to leave, and the final task was to descend to the beach and take photographs up and down the river from the water's edge. With extreme caution they managed to do so without being detected and were astonished to see the roofs of villages in both directions no more than 400 yards away in whose hunting areas they must have been. Their luck seemed amazing, yet their infinite capacity for taking pains had perhaps contributed even more to their concealment.

Then came their worse experience, completely unexpectedly; undernourished and unexercised they were as weak as invalids and could hardly begin to climb the bluff, wondering in a moment of real alarm whether they could haul themselves to the top. But such a challenge had only to be recognized for the mind-over-matter switch to make; the immediate hurdle was surmounted, creaking joints became lubricated, and with light bergens and a more direct route observed on the way in they reached the border rendezvous after only one night-stop. Catterall's patrol were there just as they should have been, and having their priorities exactly right spread a repast before the pilgrims that their shrunken stomachs could scarcely contain.

Thus did they enter the underworld in expectation of high drama, carrying in their bergens the hopes and fears of mighty men; but they saw only a few minor devils and escaped their clutches with so little difficulty that the impression may be given of leaden anticlimax. Not so; relief in high places that such missions were practicable ensured their continuance and expanding scope, while the SAS had proved their techniques to be on the right lines and returned with a useful if negative report which at least saved the Gurkhas an unnecessary journey and freed them for some more profitable enterprise elsewhere.

STRIKE AT NANTAKOR

The policy of cross-border strikes having been decided, a start had to be made. Nantakor was selected as the most suitable place within the 3,000 yard limit, for two reasons. First, the enemy platoon there was most unsettling to the Salilirans; and, secondly, so much was known about the place and its defences through the efforts of "Gipsy" Smith's Border Scouts, Headman Likinan and others that the attacking commander would start with every advantage.

Why send an infantry force which would be lucky not to incur casualties when aircraft were available to take Nantakor off the map in a few minutes without opposition? Simply, because Denis Healey in accepting the former as a calculated risk had strictly disallowed the latter for compelling reasons, despite the airmen's eagerness to play their part. In the first place, such escalation would directly contravene Britain's muted policy; and in the second, civilians might get hurt which it now became another cardinal principle to avoid, except for self-defence in extremis. Long experience had taught that soldiers fighting each other, though a nuisance, need cause little general ill-feeling; but that one unnecessary civilian casualty can generate hate and opposition in a whole community where none existed before. Britain had no quarrel with the Kalimantan natives, but every reason to solicit at least their passive acceptance of her soldiers on their soil. Most weapons could be aimed selectively, but an air strike into jungle was partially blind; it was not therefore to be used even if the chance of civilians being present was slight. There must be no possibility whatever, and since that could never be guaranteed, there were never any air strikes in Borneo. Contrast Vietnam now getting into its indiscriminating and bloody stride, whereby friends were lost and new enemies created.

Major Digby Willoughby's "A" Company of the 1/2nd Goorkhas, whose Assault Platoon was commanded by Manbahadur Ale, were chosen for the task. Willoughby had been responsible for the follow-up after Long Jawai and exacted heavy retribution for that disaster, but this time the plan, the execution and above all the initiative were to be his. The plan derived mostly from "Gipsy" Smith's Intelligence: the layout of the enemy camp with its outlying machine-guns, the fact that the main cross-border tracks were mined, and many details beside. Its execution relied on Smith's landing-points (tactically sited just far enough from the border not to give the show away and of sufficient capacity to pass the whole Company through in the shortest time); on his being the man on the spot and, most of all, on his Border Scouts, who led Willoughby all the way.

Smith himself was not allowed to go and nor was there any point, he having stuck to the rules with an effort and refrained from visiting Nantakor previously. The story of the battle is therefore out of place here, except to record that when the advance was checked by a troublesome machine-gun, Manbahadur's platoon overran it from a flank in a spirited action. The operation was a complete success; the enemy commander and five of his men were killed, and the rest fled down the tributary to their Company base at Lumbis. Nantakor camp suffered the immemorial fate of being razed to the ground, and the Indonesian propaganda machine, usually so strident, breathed not a word.

Best of all, the effect on the nearby border villagers was one of unconfined joy. The Salilirans nipped smartly over to Nantakor and salvaged all they could, and then became scared that the enemy might retaliate; but they were reassured with a Step-Up from another unit of the 1/2nd, nothing happened, and soon the immediate area was Arcadian again. SAS patrols moved freely where they pleased, slept in villages without apprehension, and even—just occasionally and, of course, solely in the line of duty—got drunk, secure both personally and in the knowledge that any incursion would certainly be detected and reported. The price was four Gurkha soldiers wounded. A small statistic perhaps and incommensurate with the gains, but it is no fun being wounded.

OPERATION "VIPER"

There being no hearts and minds to be won in the Long Pa Sia Bulge and no local help for the three overstretched patrols in detecting incursions, logic suggested a way of making at least some use of this grave disadvantage. If explosive ambushes were to be laid on the enemy's most likely entry routes, he might both be endangered and unwittingly reveal his presence. The Gurkhas could then instantly deploy to cut him off.

England was given the task of detailed planning and organization, and he naturally brought in his Troop Sergeant "Gipsy" Smith, whose speciality this was. Claymore mines were the centerpieces; dished canisters holding 900 steel shot and firing in cones up and down the track:

"Deadly," says Smith; "Wherever you were within fifty feet you collected about thirty balls; we put them up trees to avoid the undergrowth and filled in the gaps with grenades, all wired together to trigger at the same moment. The big problem was the detonator cord, which was white and stood out a mile, so we stuck moss onto it with black glue and when we came back later the moss had actually grown and the cords looked so like creepers that even the Border Scouts couldn't spot them."

Success needed a keen imagination which could predict the enemy's actions and reactions and induce him to destroy himself; a ghoulish art, yet performed with impersonal professionalism. Positions were chosen where the enemy would be disinclined to leave the track by reason of some natural obstacle, such as a steep slope, and where it was leafy enough to conceal the weapons but open enough to permit their full blast. The layouts were planned in precise detail to include as many enemy as possible in the killing areas and then ensure that they were all killed. Triggers needed much thought, sited so that animals were less likely to activate them than men; and Smith, having heard of the enemy's notice to "go no further," used one of his own—"Sabah, Keep Out!"—deliberately brusque so as to rile an Indonesian into knocking it down. Exact drawings were made with copies for base, showing in addition to the hardware the procedures for arming and disarming.

Painstaking slowness was the hallmark of laying. When at

last it was done, "Gipsy" would stand with outstretched arm like the artist he was, critically studying the subtleties of light and colour in relation to his composition; only a masterpiece would deceive men trained to read danger into the least abnormality. Then he would be left alone in the lethal zone to make the final connections, knowing that in due course he must return for the even more hazardous task of taking it all away. No fewer than nine of these Groves of Baal were created, a considerable undertaking.

Arming Day was 1 October, after which Smith and his patrol sat at the centre of his web waiting for the flies. He was ready to distinguish a detonated ambush—"Stingray" from "Snakepit," "Tapeworm" from "Big Wheel," "Black Beauty" from "Scotch Egg"—both by its bearing and its individual explosive signal that he had added for the purpose. Time passed stressfully, particularly because the other two SAS patrols had been withdrawn so that early warning in the Bulge now depended entirely upon "Viper." Professional fulfilment insistently demanded that the enemy should come and be torn to shreds.

"Thar she blows!"

"Pork Scent" without a doubt. A signal was made; the Gurkhas deployed; helicopters dropped noisy battle-simulators to drive the enemy in their direction; and the SAS returned cautiously to the ambush site with queasy expectancy. But all they found for their satisfaction were strewed branches, charred bark, lacerated leaves, and a meal of devilled pork from what little remained of the luckless animal. And that was all that "Viper" produced during "A" Squadron's tour. Perhaps the enemy had heard of it and been deterred, though it seems more likely that after his earlier abortive attempts he had no intention of coming anyway, thus enhancing the significance of the encounters in which three SAS men had been killed.

Smith was at first disappointed and then, as he considered the implications, pleased: "It meant that nobody had come through, and because the ambushes were really there to find out what was happening, it was just as good as clobbering people."

CROSS-BORDER

Cross-border operations having been proved possible and politically acceptable, meaning that no one who might object had heard of them, continued and developed because the enemy's overall behaviour was seriously aggressive. Checked at one point he tried again at another, more assiduously in Western Sarawak than in Sabah, and even made two descents into mainland Malaya. Disastrous failures though these were, it was clear that he must be firmly deterred from continuing such adventures, or hearts and minds on which the integrity of Malaysia ultimately depended might waver.

Second across was Corporal Wally Poxon's patrol, who went to the Three Camps on the River Pa Raya and made a more leisurely and thorough inspection than Woodiwiss could do. But they also had to contend with the uncompromising isolation of such operations; a man developed glandular fever from a septic cut and could have been taken home, for he could still totter, but completed the course instead for nine days. That has to be the SAS attitude to their chosen way of life or their boast that they go always a little further would be arrogant and meaningless.

Sergeant Lawson followed the track used for the Billy White ambush to Long Tapadong and found, together with useful military information, that sleeping bags of parachute silk were miserably inadequate at 5,000 feet. Sleep was just possible until one in the morning after which the four men huddled together to share what warmth they generated. Three patrols reconnoitred the Highlands area, Catterall's sighting 45 armed men, and their findings were later exploited by the 2/6th Gurkhas. Sergeant Saunders went to Nantakor and found it still ruined and empty.

Although England had seen so little activity during his patrol, the main Selalir/Sembakung river must have been of primary importance to the enemy, and much more had to be found out about it. He was not supplying his forward units by air or that would have been apparent, and no one in his senses would use porterage for bulky loads when boats on a navigable river were available, unless for a very good reason. There was as yet no such reason, though the British aimed to provide one, and the stretch of river near Labang was an admirable place to watch.

Accordingly, Sergeant Maurice Tudor took his patrol to a point not far from England's tree and settled down to watch. On the second day he felt ill and ran a temperature which, on the third, shot up to 104°F. Tudor was totally incapacitated with lepto-spirosis. He could not move; he could not even think through the raging fever, blazing headache and griping stomach pains, while vomiting and coughing blood drained him of strength too until he was left with so little that life was barely sustained and death drew near, perceptible to them all.

SAS rules prescribed "Immediate Medevac," but since that was out of the question the patrol stayed where they were, counting the boats and again being surprised by the apparent absence of military traffic, while Trooper Russell the medic discharged his dismaying responsibility. He succeeded, just, with the aid of chloramphenicol, Tudor's unfaltering will to live, and medical advice by radio; though coded messages tapped out in Morse did not convey the patient's true extremity, which de la Billière was later appalled to discover.

After twelve days on the river bank, Tudor could just drag himself to his feet and with the support of his companions began the painful, halting, three-day march to the border landing-point and base, where de la Billière took one look at the haggard face and wasted limbs and hurried him to hospital. He recovered, so all was well that ended well, and the patrol having been "uneventful" the illness was largely forgotten. Only the demonstrative affection of these two fast friends add any colour to the story:

Tudor: "I felt quite sick."

de la Billière: "You nearly died, I'm glad you didn't."

As Tudor's patrol came out, Captain Arish Turle led in another, a little further upstream. He had the same aim of building up the river picture, but in contrast his stay was short. On the second day, a dog sniffed its way into the observation post and yelped when it saw the men. Appeasement was attempted—"Sh, Fido, there's a good dog; have a biscuit?"—but to no avail for it leapt away bristling and tumbled helter-skelter down the slope. The dog rejoined its master who now appeared on the towpath and looked up intently. Then he moved on, not apparently alerted.

Next day the sudden appearance of two locals on the patrol's little track between the camp and observation post could have been quite innocent too, though momentarily terrifying. The intruders seemed equally scared at first, but Turle managed to detain them for a conversation in jungle Malay which became relaxed and friendly, if not entirely sincere. The SAS were unhappily lost, he said, and would be most grateful to be put on the track to Bantul, but they were frightened of meeting Indonesian soldiers so were there any about? None this side of Lumbis came the equally specious reply; Turle knowing perfectly well that the nearest garrison was much nearer, only two miles upstream at Labang.

The men said they were hunting, but although they might reasonably have been investigating the spot where their friend's dog had behaved strangely, they had no dog themselves and carried no traps, spears or blowpipes, only "parangs" which are not hunting weapons. When they left in the direction of Labang, studiously unhurriedly as it seemed to Turle, he decided to leave too. That was in any case obligatory on being discovered by anyone; and it was also prudent, as Sergeant Paddy Freaney's shaggy dog story would illustrate.

Freaney's patrol, which included Hoe on his second cross-border venture, started on the same day as Turle's, but was allowed longer to observe the river without distraction. Again there were no soldiers but plenty of boats, and scrutiny of the visible parts of their cargoes led at last to the simple deduction that the enemy was using local transport and labour for his supplies.

Then came the dog, standing in the bow of one of two boats being paddled up from Labang and quivering with excitement at something it detected in the bush some 25 yards short of the patrol. The crews, clearly a hunting party, caught the excitement and turned for the shore, the dog leaping the last two yards and sprinting for his quarry. It was a wild boar. The SAS knew that because with a grunt and a squeal the massive brute hurtled directly into the observation post with the dog snapping at its heels. Right behind them raced a hunter who had made astonishingly good time up the slope and burst into view with a tally-ho and stabbing-spear at the high port.

The company thus precipitately assembled was ill-adjusted to social intercourse and dispersed with similar dispatch. The boar and dog pressed on regardless of the patrol's convenience, while the man froze in mid-stride, his eyes wide and white with terror. Then he spun round and tore downhill to his boat, which he boarded without waiting for his friends and paddled downstream as one possessed. Freaney was shaking his head and wondering whether all this had really happened when another man approached, circumspectly this time and clearly in order to see what had caused the flurry. Compromised already, Freaney used all his Irish charm to make friends and influence the newcomer favourably; but when circumstances require one to materialize suddenly and unexpectedly at very close range, it is hard not to appear more like a malevolent djinn than a fairy godmother. The man hastily excused himself, murmuring like the White Rabbit that he was already late for an appointment and must be getting along.

An element of humour has been detected in this action-packed sequence when viewing it from afar; but Freaney was the man on the spot and far from wanting to laugh, his mind concentrated on the pressing need to get off it. The overriding consideration was that the first boatman would reach Labang and its garrison in something under ten minutes at his present rate of striking. The patrol therefore left promptly, but then moved excruciatingly slowly so as to leave no tracks, stopping to listen every half hour in case the enemy should try and cut them off. It was a hard decision. The alternative, which was much more to Freaney's inclination, was to go like the wind and hope to outpace either movement. Indeed, they had only covered 1,200 yards in two hours when the enemy stormed the observation post with a great deal of explosive noise, and Freaney wished they were much further away. But he had been right, for there were no tracks for the enemy to follow and the patrol was unmolested.

de la Billière, always trying to keep a jump ahead and never being short of ideas, suggested that since the locals were clearly reporting SAS patrols to the enemy—and there was evidence that they had been threatened with dire consequences if they did not—it should be practicable to stage-manage the Freaney type of incident so that he would find not an abandoned position but a whole troop of SAS or even a company of Gurkhas. As for the river traffic, they could not shoot the boatmen but there was nothing to prevent SAS stopping them and destroying the stores; indeed, that might be a very good way of inducing an enemy response at a time and place of SAS choosing. The time would come to try these proposals, but tactical expediency now dictated that the area around Labang should be rested temporarily.

"A" Squadron's last excursion of the tour was also their first offensive one. The current policy of SAS reconnaissance and infantry strikes was undoubtedly the best division of labour, but cloak without dagger became irksome to those trained as hitmen. Just this once they were allowed off the hook to sharpen up both morale and expertise. The mission had, of course, to suit the overall plan, and nowhere would a small-scale deterrent strike do more good than near Pa Fani just outside the Bulge. Captain Dunseath led ten men of 3 Troop, and Squadron Sergeant-Major Lawrence Smith went along too, as he often did when a project seemed interesting; they stayed a week but nothing eventuated except stomach upsets, caused by substituting small dried fish for the usual sardines.

Lawrence Smith has not so far been mentioned on this tour because he had been doing something interesting in the First Division of Sarawak. The SAS repertoire includes raising and training irregular forces in almost any circumstances; Major Muir Walker, in a change of appointment from the British Embassy in Djakarta, was charged with creating a team of 40 selected Border Scouts for cross-border operations. It was a task for which the warlike Ibans were eminently suited, having done little else in their entire tribal history until comparatively recently. They would be far better at penetrating undetected and surviving in the jungle if things went wrong than the best-trained foreigners, and were keen for a front-line opportunity of defending their country.

Training began in the early summer of 1964. A close bond developed between the highly motivated SAS and the equally enthusiastic warriors, simple yet intelligent, charming, hardworking and incomparably sincere. Sergeant Pruang, the chief, and Nibau, his No. 2, were both headmen of their home longhouses and strong characters. Jogong was a jungle operator and a tracker beyond compare even among his peers. Krusin was the intellectual, speaking Cantonese, English and Malay as well as his native Land Dyak, of which tribe there was a leavening among the preponderant Ibans. Soon, however, it became evident that decisive leadership and military discipline were not their strong points, but since, without them, otherwise brave men would rather too readily invoke bird-watching taboos in favour of "tidak apa" ("swing it till Monday"), much of the training was devoted to developing those qualities.

Major Walker decided in July 1964 that some of the team were ready for their first mission. He sent them on a shallow incursion to watch a river and ambush an enemy boat, but none came. Several similar attempts were made in August. At the fifth attempt, they achieved their first success, ambushing a track, killing two Indonesians, and returning in triumph with—a head.

This was a poser, revealing that the long-suppressed headhunting urge had resurfaced with the appearance of a legitimate enemy. Forcefully, too, as the SAS soon realized, a head being highly prized as a battle trophy, which a man had to win in fair fight before he could tattoo his forefinger. To tell the Ibans they must not do it might blunt their enthusiasm or make them angry and uncooperative. ''Why on earth not?'' they would ask; ''the chap's dead anyway and it's part of our religion. If you kill someone in battle you *must* cut off his head and drink his blood because that makes him part of you so he can't haunt you, *and* you get his courage. Besides, it's kind to him because it frees his spirit, which would otherwise be trapped in his body, and we always do it with proper religious observances, like Holy Communion.'' That comparison may seem inexact, but refuting it was not easy; many of the team knew what they were talking about, being practising Christians as well as animists so as to obtain the greatest possible protection against all the changes and chances of this mortal life.

Why then did it matter? Was instinctive revulsion a good reason for trying to stop it or should that be suppressed as one had to do when eating ''jarit''? Honesty had also to concede that the effect on the enemy would undoubtedly be to enhance his alarm and despondency which was the main purpose of these raids. All the same it stuck, as it were, in the gullet, and could be guaranteed to do so to a much greater degree in the world beyond Borneo, indeed outside the team itself, which could not be expected to understand the local ethic. The practise was therefore banned, with stern edict and pious, if fragile, hope.

October 1964 drew to its close and ''B'' Squadron was already in Borneo, completing its training and eager to step forward. The turnover was gradual and during it Lieutenant-Colonel John Woodhouse went on his last operational patrol before leaving the SAS and the Army at the end of the year. Sadness was evident then, despite the boisterous fun enjoyed at a hail and farewell party for those of the two Squadrons not in the jungle. No one could fully believe that the man they all regarded as the father of the modern Regiment would soon be gone.

''A'' Squadron had again earned General Walker's commendation, and de la Billière took the Squadron to Singapore en route for home. There transport was delayed for a week, as his Sergeant-Major, Lawrence Smith, clearly remembers: ''The delay didn't worry us because Singapore was a marvellous place to spent our accumulated pay and have a marvellous time; but then he said, 'I know! We'll do some parachute training.' Well

I mean, really, after a hard four-month tour! So I said, 'You must be joking!' But parachuting we went; quite enjoyed it actually and glad not to have spent the money, but oh dear, what a man!''

CHAPTER 9

THREAT TO KUCHING

"B" Squadron's First Tour, November 1964 to February 1965

Major Johnny Watts hoped that his new Squadron would be spared a major enemy incursion before the men had settled into the rhythm and mastered the anxieties of operational life, in which every activity would be more difficult than it had been in training. Medics thoroughly versed in the theory of tooth-extraction found that much practise was needed to perfect their skill, their patients submitting, poor devils, "faute de mieux." Signallers who had qualified well in Wales often took several hours to contact base, for incomprehensible and infuriating reasons that yielded only gradually to the fine tuning of conditioned instinct: the set was damp, the basha-site was masked by hills, hissing rain and an uncomfortable slope inhibited precise work or the aerial would be better laid out in another direction. But when at last the crackle came, "Pass your message," and frustration was swallowed up in exultation, the weighty text was probably at this time, "Nothing to report," and just as well. "They learnt on the job," says Watts, "fast."

Watts walked the SAS frontage as his predecessors had done, but chiefly to assess his men's problems and reactions to uncompromising reality. He found one or two weak links, men who had surmounted every selection and training hurdle whose harshness they now justified by falling at the very last. He also resolved the odd clash of personalities that could seriously impair a patrol's effectiveness, raw nerve-endings agonizingly scraping together despite genuine efforts to sheath them. Sergeant Jimmy Daubney, "a barbary little NCO, first class," could not get on with one of his men who was quickly removed, but went on to prove himself an excellent soldier too.

Apart from those few cases, Watts was greatly heartened by the potential and performance of his Squadron and urged them

152

ever onward with his usual colourful emphasis; but, at the same time, he adopted a private policy of careful "pacing," trying only to give them tasks within their growing abilities so that they would not outrun their strength or suffer some grievous blow to morale. He was only to be allowed a single year with them and conceived it his duty to hand over truly seasoned warriors with plenty of fire left in their bellies.

To begin with, therefore, cross-border patrols were few. Sergeant "Darkie" Davidson investigated the Long Tapadong track again and found no sign of the enemy, a significant improvement after Billy White. At Nantakor, however, the enemy had returned, so the Salilirans' carefree holiday was over for the time being and SAS patrols along the Pensiangan front had to resume their wary existence. Daubney's beat was the important Bantul area through which the River Pensiangan flows south across the border to become the Sembakung and leads to Labang, where the enemy garrison had been reinforced; an incursion was suspected and a company of Gurkhas took up an ambush position on the river just over the border, guided by Daubney. When the force had settled down comfortably, some locals who had watched them dropped in for a chat and whatever might be going in the way of goodies, which they got; and leaving with expressions of great goodwill went straight and told the Indonesians, who came stealthily up the far bank and poured a heavy fire into the position.

The Gurkhas were well concealed and none was hit, neither was there an incursion, but Daubney noted two useful lessons. One, that ambush as a tactic can only succeed if surprise is nothing short of absolute; and the other, that to use boats (which he had done) when there was even a chance of the enemy lurking on the thickly wooded banks would, despite their convenience, be "very, very untactical," as one of his team, Norman Hartill, put it; worse even than walking on a border track.

On the home front the weather was thoroughly depressing, with constant drenching rain which slowed movement and delayed air resupply. Improvisation and endurance were thus demanded and just what the Squadron needed to set the seal on its training. Kabu was re-roofed as a gift from the Army. Watts put the work in hand because he was told to, while wondering whether it might be overdoing generosity to the point of engendering odious comparisons in less favoured villages and a habit of grasping acquisitiveness rather than genuine liking and collaboration; but Kabu was still not really happy, and its strategic position could make it critical.

"Tanky" Smith took over the "Viper" ambushes from his namesake "Gipsy" and was professionally impressed as they inspected them together. Using "Gipsy's" detailed instructions, without which they would have been helpless, they would start by identifying, say, a distinctive tree and approaching it from a given direction. Then they would walk perhaps fifty yards on another line and dig up a buried wire that was not dangerous but led to a forked stick from which the detonator was so many feet on such and such a bearing. "Gipsy" would then disarm the ambush and show every component to "Tanky," who would accept responsibility when he was satisfied and set it all up again.

There were no signs of compromise, but Indonesian patrols had again come over and left more of their notices—"Winged soldiers beware!"—which they evidently thought rather good. "Tanky's" patrol was given an escort of Gurkhas for their servicing rounds in future. At an ambush, the Gurkhas would guard both approaches while Smith and Ted Stafford went in to do the job. Mike Seale, the signaller, on his first operation, stayed outside with earphones on, exchanging Morse-key taps with the operator at base to hold the line open in case of accidents. It was, he says, "trembly," for even if nothing had been disturbed—one ambush had been partly blown by a falling tree leaving the rest extremely dangerous—explosives could become unstable in such damp conditions and once, despite all precautions, a detonator burst in Smith's hand.

The wound was most painful; frightening, too, because he was also holding a tin of pig-repellent which was injected forcibly into his bloodstream. The tin had announced its contents as deadly poison which was on no account even to be touched, but Smith survived to declare later: "Let that be a lesson not to believe everything you read on tins." Seale called for a helicopter, Smith was "casevac-ed" and "Darkie" Davidson, another constructive demolitionist, relieved him later.

Jim Penny, that fugitive from bullshit, found none when he was sent with Dave Abbott to join the Cross-Border Scouts, now commanded by Major John Edwardes previously of "A" Squadron. Edwardes had returned to Borneo for a task that would fully exercise his talents for adventure, initiative and snake-collecting.

"It was a laugh a minute with him," says Penny, though one's sense of humour needed to be robust. "He'd suddenly pick up a scorpion and throw it at you; grabbed snakes by the neck and got them to bite his handkerchief, which he then tied round the head with a neat knot. The Ibans wouldn't go near his bergen.

"It was all recce that time. We were supposed to take the scouts so far and then push them off on the job, but it didn't work; great little guys, always cheery and far better than us in the jungle, but we never knew what they got up to and they didn't achieve much, so halfway through the tour John Edwardes decided we'd stay with them all the time."

That was Edwardes's way; no one knew so no one grieved, while he suffered no flicker of conscience nor fear for his career, which mattered little to him anyway so long as the task was accomplished.

By mid-December 1964 "B" Squadron had been spared a major test, but now felt able to take one on. The work had been hard with Watts himself working harder than any, both to operate his patrols—a job demanding ceaseless exertion accompanied by nagging anxiety—and to nurse them along as well. The idea of a restorative evening off occurred to him with growing insistence, though he suppressed it as impossible to gratify. But on the 16th, circumstances combined to allow a break without detriment to duty, indeed to its advancement. He therefore vanished from the Haunted House to pursue his excellent aim, and minutes later a personal message arrived from General Walker demanding his attendance at 7 o'clock in the morning.

A search was instituted, but the SAS are not easy to find when they decide to get lost. It was only when billowing white mist floated in the still dark valleys below pinky sunlit ridges, the dawn chorus of insects, birds and monkeys shrilled in Watts's head with more than usual resonance—for the jungle dominates Brunei even around the capital—and the deadline drew perilously near that a well-loved commander reappeared, contented certainly, and potentially restored though in the slightly longer term. His loyal band set about him in their rough, kindly way with a cold shower, brisk massage, stimulating potions, crisply starched uniform, and delivered him at the appointed hour, the convincing image of a spry and receptive officer.

"This is absolutely Top Secret," the General said; "cut your throat if you breathe a word." Watts did not so breathe, but concentrated with negligible difficulty on what was clearly going to concern him directly. It was nothing less than the likely fulfilment of Walker's long-held belief that the Indonesians were planning a major thrust. Intelligence had reported at least a division of their best troops massing opposite the First Division of Sarawak while their main parachute force was at readiness, putting Kuching itself at risk. General Panggabean, commanding in Kalimantan, and Colonel Supargo, his Director of Operations, were efficient professional officers with successful combat experience against the Dutch, and the political atmosphere in Djakarta pointed to some such initiative, the Left faction being dominant and Soekarno in a state of more than ordinarily excited fantasy.

General Walker had asked for reinforcements and got them; not as many as the threat warranted, but they marked Britain's resolve to uphold her friends and her honour. The Royal Navy and Royal Air Force were also strengthened, not very much but with disproportionate publicity, and all this happened in time to act as a deterrent instead of the more usual last-ditch, last-minute defence.

Walker told Watts that he intended to enhance the deterrent effect by mounting "Claret" strikes against the enemy's preparations to an increased depth of 10,000 yards; not as a preemptive offensive nor even with the expectation of causing serious disruption, but as psychological rapier-thrusts to make Supargo think defensively and take his mind off other things. The first essential was thorough reconnaissance of the enemy's border territory by the SAS, so Watts had been booked on the next flight to Kuching where he was to confer with the Brigadier, West Brigade, assess the task and report back to the General. He left, still without a word.

The 400 miles to Kuching in a slow aircraft was refreshing. Brigadier Bill Cheyne of West Brigade welcomed the SAS to serve under him; if, that is, they agreed with his orders, since their unorthodox command structure allowed them to appeal directly to the General if they did not. But Woodhouse had prudently entertained Cheyne at Hereford before his posting to Borneo, so he understood the relationship; and the SAS, finding him to be a good guy by their lights—short, bouncy, radiating energy, above all professional—strove to please him.

Cheyne's command was crucial to the outcome of Confrontation and a splendid one for a dedicated soldier. His three infantry battalions faced several times their own strength along a

150-mile front, and no Briton can ask fairer than that; nor is there usually much point in asking, given Britain's habitual parsimony in defence. Cheyne could lose the war at a stroke; but he could also defend his territory so thoroughly that its people would hardly know there was a war on, while he presided over a vigorous campaign across the border which would exercise all his leadership, daring and finesse, his troops' enterprise, skill and courage, and be professionally fulfilling for all. Morale was high in Walker's army, and its attitude to the threat, eager and confident.

The First Division was as different as could be from the Sabah front. The original Sarawak, it was now more densely populated and cleared of jungle than anywhere else in Borneo. Many of its people were Chinese, whose hard work stimulated the economy but a proportion of whom were infected by the communism of their spiritual motherland and thus posed a major latent threat. The land being mostly flat and extensively cultivated, with a road running the length of the division with branches to places like Tebedu, there was nothing to prevent the enemy deploying large formations which would have only 25 miles to traverse from the frontier to Kuching. Although some stretches of the border were marked by ridges, these were not difficult to cross, while in others one could march on wide trade-route tracks without even climbing.

There was much to find out, more than could possibly be achieved by one Squadron in a short time, but at least nearly its whole strength could be devoted to the task. Ever since "A" Squadron's first tour the infantry had here taken care of border surveillance with hearts and minds, working from their jungle forts close up to the frontier, and constantly patrolling the area with greater numbers and higher frequency than the SAS could ever have managed. That being so, Watts realized that infantry cooperation would be essential to SAS success on several counts. Firstly, nasty accidents could occur on the way to and from the border without very careful joint planning. Secondly, previous SAS cross-border patrols had each been sponsored there and back by another, responsible for securing the crossing-point and for sending them off fresh and with full packs and bellies; why not therefore try and persuade the infantry to undertake this duty, thereby achieving greater safety from friend and foe alike and freeing all SAS patrols for the main task?

Thirdly, cooperation for cooperation's sake could not be taken for granted; some infantry officers, but particularly those of the

Gurkhas, by no means conceded that the SAS could achieve any more than their own men. That was as might be, but the SAS had been tasked to find targets for the infantry to attack and might well have to lead them there. Thus, it behoved the SAS to observe the enemy through infantry eyes; it behoved the infantry to make clear what they wanted and give every facility; and it behoved both not to argue over who was the greatest but develop the sort of companionship that alone would achieve high success. Watts therefore visited all the commanding officers to make friends as well as to learn the lie of the land and set up the scheme. Then he agreed final details with Cheyne, asked for a headquarters and accommodation to be found in Kuching, and flew back to Brunei in clear-sighted though pensive mood.

"It was a tall order; we were an untried Squadron being asked to do more and go further than the other two, and in far more difficult country; but I was most grateful to Peter de la Billière for all the typically thorough work he'd done on cross-border ops. When I'd come out on a visit during his tour, I joined the sponsor patrol which saw off Maurice Tudor the time he got ill so that was a help. Anyway I went to Walter Walker and reported, 'Everything's fine, we can do it'—actually there was no goddamned option—and then to Harry Tuzo and told him, 'Hey! You're losing your Squadron.' He hit the roof. Typical of Walker, never told anybody anything except personally, good for security I suppose."

The Gurkha Independent Parachute Company, now trained to augment the SAS, relieved "B" Squadron in the north. As each patrol came out, Watts sent it south, leaving only the "Viper" team and one or two others. Daubney's patrol, staging through an up-country airstrip, arrived by chance just before General Walker himself and were hustled behind a hut by local officialdom as being no fit objects for a discriminating and potentially critical eye and nose. But the General had already spotted them from his helicopter, for they were undeniably conspicuous, and, Hartill relates, "He got out and made a bee-line for us, asked who we were and what we'd been doing, listened to what we told him and *then* went to meet the officers. A really nice fellow."

A soldier's general; and an effective one too, for 1965 had come and Malaysia was far from crushed.

Lieutenant-Colonel John Woodhouse left the Army in the New Year for other activities, and Mike Wingate-Gray took over 22

SAS. General Walker thanked Woodhouse for his great contribution to the Borneo campaign and the border peoples, "among whom you and your men are worshipped." And he added: "You enjoy a unique, unchallenged reputation as an expert in counter-guerilla warfare and it is my hope, shared by many others, that the powers that be will recognize this and continue to employ you in this sphere."

The General tried hard to persuade the powers that be that they could not afford to lose Woodhouse. His advocacy was ineffective, perhaps because he too was a man who did his duty as he saw it, without fear, favour or affection; a fine moral principle but one that is often too disturbing for establishments to live with. When the Hereford Headquarters was to be inspected by the local General, Woodhouse used to order, in print, that no special arrangements, rehearsals, kit-polishing or anything else were to precede it. The great man would be shown the Regiment that Woodhouse loved as it really was. He must be made to see that it was good without frills or hard selling, which, if he was a good General, would repel rather than impress him; but he could think little or nothing of Woodhouse personally for all the latter would do to push himself.

Yet—or perhaps because he understood himself and his friend so well—he told Johnny Watts in a farewell message, "Work hard to be a General," while knowing perfectly well that Watts would not take the smallest designing step to that end. He would not have known how to begin and did not want to know, abhorring the very thought of promotion politics like all in the Regiment and perhaps a little more; but regiments need generals for their advancement and survival, and Woodhouse saw that Watts could make the grade on merit alone if at least he did not go out of his way to alienate his seniors other than in the course of duty.

Woodhouse's premature retirement was a greater setback to both himself and the Army than either admitted; but as to his main labour, the same inexorable law of cause and effect operated to reward him unequivocally. The Regiment under him had never been better. More than that, he had implanted it with the seeds of its own regeneration so that it was to become better still, and as it did so his own renown grew within it until, alone among that band of "finger-poking" brothers, he never has a finger poked at him.

Kuching was an attractive small town of 50,000 people who went about their peacetime occupations without a thought forf the threat that reared up against them. The Army had not been given wartime powers of requisition so it was hard to find ideal accommodation for a Squadron of SAS at short notice. The place actually rented was not, in Watts's view, ideal. "A long upper room," he says—and although usually a master of direct language this memory is so painful that he has to recall it in hesitant steps—"built over a *bar*; a *girlie* bar; it was a *brothel*, god dammit, a screaming brothel!" He stormed the verandahs of power, declaiming against lack of security and moral hazard to the innocents in his care, but even so there was no alternative for several weeks. The only mitigation was his planned operational intensity, which would allow the men very little time and excess energy in Kuching.

Watts and his operations officer Wilf Charlesworth worked very hard. Pressure was on them for quick results, but there would be nothing headlong or slapdash about their methods; the more difficult the task the more carefully did the SAS prepare for it. This one being dangerous as well as difficult, the same intensive briefing, rehearsal and minute attention to detail was imposed on every patrol as had been on England's first one. Most dangerous and difficult of all, but with the highest priority, was the area of border closest to Kuching, between Stass and Tringgus. Intelligence indicated that the enemy was building up his forces here by way of the River Koemba and its tributaries, though with the usual poor maps the SAS had to go there before they discovered the full extent of the problems. The task was purely reconnaissance, of the enemy, the locals and topography; all signs of a patrol's presence must be concealed and offensive action was not allowed.

Parts of the border here were marked by hills up to 1,600 feet, but swathes of lowland ran between them which were sometimes cultivated and thickly populated by Borneo standards. The weather was very wet when the first three patrols took the plunge on 29 December, and Captain Angus Graham-Wigan had a most miserable time, sitting in the rain on Gunong Jagoi for a fortnight watching a track along which nobody came. That was too long to be static except for some special reason, Watts decided; it was bad for the circulation, digestion, muscles and morale.

Corporal Joe Little passed over Jagoi and down into the plain beyond to watch the main track between Babang and Stass, which the enemy had previously used for incursions; but he never reached it because concealment was impossible in such open country with many locals working in the "ladangs." He prowled around for a week where the terrain permitted and came away with much topographical information and the distinct impression that the enemy did not patrol the area regularly.

The third patrol of the initial wave was "Tanky" Smith's. He had returned from hospital with some pieces of detonator still in his hand, but not where they mattered. His old team of Seale and Stafford was brought up to strength by Paddy Byrnes. They approached the little plain from the north, where a border ridge covered with good primary jungle ran east and west parallel to the Separan tributary on which stood the village of Kaik. As soon as the patrol descended, they too were frustrated by ubiquitous "ladang" dotted with toiling peasants, and then by impenetrable swamp as they tried to approach the river. Nevertheless, they confirmed the enemy's presence by his tracks right up to the border and his practise of firing mortars sporadically, though at what targets was unclear.

The first pieces of the jigsaw were thus placed on the table. To be sure, Watts was forced to conclude that the Kaik/Babang plain was unsuitable for the present type of patrolling, but that was useful information in itself and there were plenty of other places where the SAS could profitably go.

Watts next sent a patrol to the south of Gunong Brunei where the Koemba itself swings east close to the border. Bennett was the commander, a trooper still but that is no obstacle to leadership in the SAS if a man is up to the job. The place proved more promising than any so far, the ground between ridge and river being real "ulu" with steep hills, primary jungle and rocky streams where men could move, hide and leave no traces, though enemy patrols had done so. Pressing on downhill, Bennett made the remarkable discovery of a high rock containing a group of caves that were quite clearly used as shelters by travellers both civilian and military. One hundred yards on through a belt of bamboo was a veritable motorway of a track running east and west and presumably connecting Seluas with Siding. The patrol crossed it very carefully. Feeling cut off and vulnerable, they inched their way another 300 yards through swamp to the river, which was navigable to small craft.

Returning to the cave-rock they climbed to the top. Now knowing what they were looking for, they saw the line of the

main track curving southeast outside the river bend to Siding
and also a left fork leading over the border. The area thus had
exciting possibilities for ambushing both track and river from
excellent cover. Bennett therefore settled down to observe the
pattern of movement; but he could stay no longer than a few
days because the all-pervading damp gradually devitalized the
radio. One routine call was missed and they tried cooking the
set over a hexamine stove; two, and the Squadron commander
started clucking; three, and they came out according to the rules.

Smith's and Little's patrols were turned round quickly and sent
in again. Smith went over Bukit Knuckle (so called because it
resembled a clenched fist), but was foiled again by swarms of
locals harvesting sugar-cane, though he did find a track with
footprints that might have been soldiers'. Little tried opposite
Tringgus and watched the track along which the enemy had
raided that place in earlier days. The cover was good here and
promised well for future operations, but this time the patrol saw
only locals and had to return early because their radio too succumbed to the damp. This was just not good enough, Watts
complained, and the operational research team at Hereford applied itself urgently to waterproofing the sets.

Sergeant Dave Haley led his first cross-border patrol to another likely incursion track between Gunong Jagoi and Gunong
Brunei and watched it for a week despite the predominantly
open country with "ladangs," longhouses and many locals.
Then one of the patrol became tensely aware of a man close to
him and their eyes met simultaneously. Unlike Freaney's encounter this was a slow-motion, hushed affair. The man was
squatting motionless, intent as it turned out on stalking a honey-
bear, and so remained until after a brief conversation by whispering and sign language on the lines of "Good hunting, we be
of one blood, thou and I" (Kipling—*The Jungle Book*) when
they all softly went their separate ways.

Watts experimented with the idea of sending three patrols over
the border together, parting for their separate missions and rejoining before coming back. They would be more detectable
than four men but safer when in company; and also when apart,
because one patrol could be ordered to support another in emergency. None knew where the others were going, however, a
sensible precaution with sinister overtones. The infantry liked
the plan because it demanded fewer sponsor platoons. The SAS

greatly appreciated the infantry, who carried their bergens and shielded them from the harsh world with a trace of awe that rude, soldierly disparagement could not altogether disguise; marching erect with loose shoulders and light tread they felt like kings, or, moods being changeable, sacrificial victims.

Such was the case on the foothills of Gunong Brunei as twelve SAS men strode upwards surrounded by 40 soldiers of a famous British Regiment. The slope steepened, the heat intensified, humid air wheezed into heaving breasts and, with bowed backs and drenching sweat, some of the sponsors could no longer bear their extra loads. The SAS first retrieved their own bergens and then, pitying the poor fellows, relieved them of theirs too and continued with powerful, buoyant steps to the border crest. There they crossed and vanished, leaving those of the infantry still present silent upon a peak in Borneo.

The three patrols marched together until well into enemy territory, established a rendezvous and separated. Bennett had been allowed only one day at base before being included in Corporal Thompson's patrol to show him the way to the cave-rock, which afforded a wonderful observation post; they manned it in pairs, the two off duty being in the lying-up position some distance behind in thick jungle. A succession of locals passed both ashore and afloat. After some days a second track on the far bank of the river seemed to be indicated by the appearance of a soldier in uniform who strode up and down gesticulating, his manner suggesting either mental derangement or an officer giving orders. The latter was proved to be the case by eight armed men rising from obscurity, shouldering their packs and moving off westwards. Scarcely had they gone when three more came and sat down to rest at the same spot.

Almost immediately again the watchers' growing interest was sharply heightened by a murmur of voices at the cave-mouths directly below. In straining to see who was there, they dislodged a boulder; it toppled only slowly at first, but evading their grasping fingers bounded and rebounded down the cliff face in hideous dissonance that ended at long last with a sickening thud and a silence so absolute that it seemed to embrace all Borneo. The two men crept soundlessly back to the LUP and froze there with the others, every sense alert. Nothing ensued and Thompson boldly resumed the watch, hoping that those below had assumed the rock fall to be natural. His decision was justified by the absence of a search, but there was no more enemy activity for the rest of the patrol either.

Daubney's experience was less satisfying. He and his men were only a mile or so downriver from Thompson, but wherever they probed there was either insufficient cover or their feet sank into the soft mud of drying swamp to leave tracks like dinosaurs'. They saw just a few locals and no soldiers, but painstakingly recorded a great deal of topography. The outcome of these two patrols was a detailed knowledge of this stretch of the Koemba which "D" Squadron later exploited; in Thompson's beat of course, not Daubney's.

The third of the three patrols was Corporal Bigglestone's, due west along the Gunong Brunei ridge. Watts had accepted that the track between Babang and Stass was impracticable for unobserved reconnaissance and ambush, but the route remained important. He wanted to see if it was approachable beyond Babang, where it led to the enemy's known base at Seluas on the Koemba. It seemed to be, for although the patrol did not actually reach the track, they could see that their fine, jungle-covered ridge extended to it. They were not disturbed as they investigated and mapped the area.

The three patrols reassembled at their secret rendezvous as planned, warily lest the enemy should have found signs of their earlier presence. Then they marched by a different route to the border where they were met by the same platoon of the famous regiment. But what a change! Regiments do not become famous by good fortune but by their reaction to adversity, and while limping back to their jungle fort, those men had determined to retrieve their honour at whatever cost. It was not just on their leaders' orders, but by the tooth-gritting will of each man that they spent every waking hour bashing the jungle and themselves remorselessly. Now, after ten days, here they were again, tall, grinning, rippling muscles glistening with healthy sweat, bearing crates of beer and other luxuries, and ready to carry not only bergens but the SAS too had they so wished. It was a good homecoming.

Bigglestone's report that the Seluas to Babang track could be approached unobserved was just what Brigadier Cheyne wanted to hear. Knowing that this key area contained at least a company of Indonesian troops, he decided on a "Claret" strike, obtaining General Walker's approval as he had to do. Two Gurkha platoons were guided in by Bigglestone's patrol, but the operation was not a success. The infantry carried only five days' rations and needed a precise objective in order to waste no time searching, but Bigglestone had not been able to find a good ambush position, so the attempt was premature. Still, those and other lessons had to be learnt, so the exercise was useful.

So much for the first-priority area immediately opposite Kuching; on the whole a poor one for offensive operations, but much information had been collected of great value should a threat be mounted from there, though at a price which Watts observed with some concern.

"Bill Cheyne really put the pressure on us; that was his job of course, very good guy, loved the SAS and reckoned we could get him the info he wanted, but he wasn't accountable for the Squadron's welfare and long term morale and my poor blokes were getting knackered. On any one day I'd have five or six patrols over there, another five or six going or coming, and four or five de-briefing, resting, or being briefed for the next job. They'd be lucky to get three days off, and instead of building up their strength with wholesome food the silly bastards spent their time boozing downstairs and got weaker still; lost weight, came out in sores and ulcers and were less resistant to disease. And you couldn't abort a patrol just because someone got sick; had to bloody well sweat it out and hope he could walk by the time you were due to return, and if he couldn't you'd have to go on half of what little rations you had left until he could."

Now, in late January and February 1965, the Brigadier wanted to know about cross-border areas to the northwest; particularly the River Koemba at Poeri, where it seemed from the map that the enemy's main line of communication could be threatened, forcing him to divert troops to guard it. Detailed reconnaissance would be needed first, for nothing was known of the 6–8,000 yards between border ridge and river, except that air reconnaissance photographs showed most of it to be thickly wooded; that at least was promising, but what of the ground beneath?

The answer, anywhere near the river, was impassable swamp. Three patrols entered it and although they accepted defeat only when the water reached their necks, none reached the bank; but bootprints and mortar-fire showed that enemy patrols were active. Another indication of their presence was gathered by Sergeant Dick Cooper as he watched a track being cut by locals, gaining the impression that the enemy had employed them to do so. Watts then sent Haley farther downstream to the 10,000-yard limit. He too found signs of the enemy but no approach to the river. The lower Koemba was thus revealed as one of those challenges which the SAS delighted to surmount, for it was clearly vital to the enemy and the Brigadier was determined to exploit any opportunity that persistent probing might reveal.

The next river used by the enemy for access to the border was the Sentimo tributary with its own tributaries. Daubney and Thompson took their patrols to the vicinity of what was subsequently found to be Babang Baba. They too were hindered by swamps, even more extensive than those on the Koemba but shallower so that they were at least negotiable. This area too became the objective of many British visitors.

A point struck Watts forcibly; to carry a casualty through dry jungle was difficult enough but in swamp it might be impossible. Only a helicopter gave hope of survival, and he pleaded successfully for an emergency procedure to ensure a quick response should a sortie be approved at high level. Although none of his men needed such a rescue, Lillico soon would.

North now to the last stretch of border before the sea, drained on the enemy's side by the Rivers Bemban and Sempayang. It was particularly important here to prevent the enemy feeling secure on the high Pueh Range, whence he might sweep down across the narrow strip of Sarawak to the coast. Furthermore, Lundu, a pretty market town and port, harboured more than its fair share of clandestine communists who were known to be supported and encouraged by a constant flow of cross-border subversives.

Bigglestone was sent to find a place called Batu Hitam (Black Rock). He found it, an ordinary Land Dyak longhouse set among green "wet-padi ladangs," but he had been led to expect an enemy camp, of which there was no sign despite the country being so open. Moreover, he met a field worker to their mutual embarrassment and made the best of it by asking questions, though to little advantage. The man was terrified. He swore that there were no troops in Batu Hitam; there were no police in Batu Hitam; there was not even any food in Batu Hitam because they had run out and the rice would not be harvested until April. So please, please would Bigglestone *not* go to Batu Hitam where there was nothing whatever to interest him. The more the man protested the more sceptical Bigglestone became, and he left Batu Hitam with a large question-mark over it for his successors to resolve, he too being the first of many.

The River Sempayang was navigable to Sawah, and from there a main track ran on up the dwindling upper reaches until it turned due north over a spur of the Pueh Range and down to Bemban on the river of that name where there was thought to be an enemy garrison. The jungle-covered spur afforded a concealed and dry approach to the track, which two patrols led by Graham-Wigan and "Tanky" Smith found to be regularly used by the enemy, revealing bootprints, military litter and, finally, two armed soldiers in person, casual and very tempting.

Graham-Wigan's stay was curtailed by a chance encounter with locals, so hard to avoid as others had discovered, but he was eager to revisit the Bemban track, and Watts let him. This time he took Sergeant Jimmy Hughes's patrol which included Fred Marafono, and they watched undisturbed for ten days seeing many locals and another pair of soldiers. That small number would have been disappointing had it not been for all the signs of vastly greater usage, and Graham-Wigan returned seething with ideas for a large-scale ambush. Sadly for him it was now mid-February and "B" Squadron's time was up, but the thought persisted in their minds for implementing the next time round if nobody else forestalled them. In the meantime, the Bemban track became a household word in the SAS, along with the Koemba, Sentimo and Batu Hitam.

Why the Bemban garrison had to be supplied by track from Sawah when it had its own river was explained by Captain Alec Saunt and Sergeant Cooper, who took their patrols to the lower reaches where they found it to be only just navigable. Ten miles further up at Bemban it was therefore unlikely to have been any use, and although they did a comprehensive topographical survey they saw nobody.

John Edwardes and his Cross-Border Scouts also operated in this general area, looking for a camp "somewhere beyond the Bemban" and that was all he had to go on. Numbers were therefore needed and his method was to take about 30 men across, set up his base camp in some wild and unfrequented spot and send Penny and Abbott patrolling with the scouts. It was hard, slogging, unrewarding work and Edwardes needed all his ebullience to keep the team cheerful; drenching monsoon rains flooded the valley to a great width, and the country being new to the scouts they often floundered through swamp for days without knowing when they would hit dry ground again. By the end of "B" Squadron's tour they had found only indications of a camp, evidently used for jungle training by the many tracks criss-crossing the area, but not the camp itself. Never mind, the truth would be revealed by persistence, and the SAS were not short of that.

Having accorded first priority to the enemy forces supplied through the Koemba river system, Brigadier Cheyne now became concerned with those dependant on the important Sekayan, whose headwaters shared a watershed with the Koemba's and flowed parallel to the border in the opposite direction, supporting several garrisons and outposts.

Balai Karangan was the enemy's main base on the Sekayan, and being just within the 10,000-yard limit, Cheyne mooted an SAS patrol there. Watts was keen enough in principle, though when air photos revealed a dismaying pattern of cultivated land studded with longhouses all the way from the border, he demurred, gently at first; but when Cheyne persisted, he took the distasteful course of opposing a respected senior and appearing fainthearted as he did so:

"It was suicide and I wouldn't do it. Furthermore, I didn't have to; that's the great thing about SAS command and control. I could have gone straight to Walter Walker."

That was not necessary, the two commanders worked together too well to split on such an issue, and a compromise was reached. Seven miles east of Balai Karangan was the village of Jerik—not quite Jericho, nor was it planned to demolish it with a trumpet-blast—and the same distance on, Segoemen, the main track between them running over a wooded spur of the border ridge as at Bemban and presenting an equally attractive objective. Two patrols were chosen, Haley's and Little's; they passed over, and all the trumpets sounded for them on the other side, a fitting salutation for pilgrims.

First, however, they carried out their missions successfully. The patrols split and Little found an 80-man camp, unoccupied but indicating that soldiers were no strangers in those parts, while Haley located the track on which military bootprints led him to the same conclusion. He earmarked a good ambush site for future use and settled down to watch, dividing his men between an observation post near the track and a lying-up position on the spur to the rear.

At noon on the second day the unhurried tempo of civilian traffic changed abruptly to one of urgency and stress, when ten men passed at high speed heading west toward Jerik. The first seven were unarmed and dressed as civilians, but the other three wore khaki and carried shotguns, the last man sporting a bushy moustache like a traditional sergeant's and confirming that impression by shouting orders to his squad. They were presumably the Indonesian equivalent of Border Scouts, and although quickly out of sight they had performed the useful service of stimulating the watchers to intense alertness. In less than ten minutes an apparently endless column of regular soldiers in jungle-green arrived from the direction of Jerik, hunched and purposeful with weapons at the ready as though their objective, whatever that might be—and a frisson of alarm suggested one—was not far away.

Five men passed the observation post, and evidently feeling no need to be silent were heard to leave the track and start climbing the spur east of the patrol; others did the same to the west and the two groups maintained touch by shouting, while yet more spaced themselves along the track and faced north. The two SAS crawled quickly and quietly back to the lying-up point, but not a moment too soon and possibly too late, for even as they told Haley their news, shots rang out from east and west, south whence they had come and, shockingly, north where they must go. It was a moment for savage self-control; the shots, coolly assessed, were probably signals to pinpoint and coordinate the enemy groups, but Haley too could use them to advantage.

He set off northeast-wards as fast as was consistent with reasonable silence, deducing that his inward track must have been found and followed for the enemy to have been able to mount such a set-piece attack. The shots to the north and east grew louder—were they indeed signals? or decoys?—but Haley steered between them, adjusting his course as they moved, until with agonizing slowness they fell away, first to the flanks and then the rear, to form by evening a straggling line at ever increasing distance.

"Dave Haley had a dreadful fright," says Watts, and being Watts so, vicariously, did he. That was his Squadron's last patrol and he shed his burden of responsibility with exquisite relief. Honour had been satisfied; half-trained recruits had accomplished a task which the veterans of "D" Squadron, now arrived, faced with a slight gulp as demanding all their own experience and skill. It had been done without casualties, which was near to Watt's heart. His "pacing" policy had succeeded too, the men's loss of body-weight being by no means reflected in their morale but decidedly the reverse, for to initial enthusiasm was added confidence in their proved ability. They were tired, of course, and so was he, utterly; but Woodiwiss already had several of "D" Squadron's patrols in Kalimantan, and Watts took his second evening off in four months, this time with no sequel but the sleep of the just.

CHAPTER 10

"LICENSED TO KILL"

"D" Squadron's Third Tour, February to May 1965

Major Roger Woodiwiss arrived before his Squadron. After discussing matters with the weary Watts, he applied his fresh mind to the still irksome matter of accommodation.

Watts had eventually managed to move "B" Squadron out of the brothel in Kuching; the change could only be a vast improvement to them, but Woodiwiss took one look at the bare warehouse, which was all that had been found to house the élite of the Army, and refused to put his own men into it. That was easy enough to say but administrative regulations tend to be inflexible; proper quarters could only be built if the war was expected to last seven years, which was not the case—happily, although it was a very nice war. So while engaging authority from the front Woodiwiss executed a surprise flanking movement, putting his people into hotels to the great uplift of their morale and the corresponding impairment of the chief obstructing functionary's when he received the bills. The outcome was interesting; a Chinese family of, unremarkably, about 25 souls were quite content to leave their big house and live in hovels, while using their native enterprise and three months advance rent to start building a new and better dwelling, so all parties prospered.

Woodiwiss also retrieved the few patrols remaining in the north and continued at first with the same task as Watts; reconnaissance and plenty of it. "D" Squadron was much refreshed after their gruelling time eight months before, but now the Borneo scene had greatly changed with cross-border patrols the norm instead of occasionally by accident. The jungle on the far side might look the same as on this, but it felt very different. Woodiwiss was quite content for each of his patrols to have at least one mission whose aim demanded keeping out of trouble rather than stirring it up.

Now, to tell the story of a battalion which marches and fights as a unit is very different from conveying a true impression of an SAS Squadron's activities, split as it is into some sixteen four-man patrols doing different things in different places. The general trend and highlights must and will be recorded, but to include every patrol would mean a schedule of bald outlines. This would inevitably be dull because although it was the actual achievement of each that added its mite to the sum of the campaign, the main interest lies in the manner of the doing, the margin of success or failure and, above all the hearts and minds of the doers on whom all else depended. The ambience of mortal combat or the threat of it is barely tolerable tension, to which the veteran may be seasoned but is never immune, under which constructive thought leading to correct and decisive action is a high achievement; but that is not readily comprehended from a relaxing armchair unless we can become acquainted with a comparatively few men and feel them to be as real as ourselves.

So one patrol's story will be told in more detail than the others' to serve as an example for all, yet not a pattern because each commander confronted his different problems in his own way. Which then to choose? Not one led by a hero, for there are none in the SAS; and not necessarily the most successful, for that would imply a judgement which it would be impossible, invidious and indeed imprudent for an outsider to make. The choice will be of one with an eventful story which, by great good fortune, has been told by no fewer than three of the four men.

Don Large was a well built six-foot four inches and well entitled to be called "Lofty," a gentle giant from the Cotswolds in contrast to all the Tynesiders and Scots, but with the same passionate yearning for adventure which had led him to Korea with the Gloucestershire Regiment at the age of twenty. There he had fought in the great battle at Imjin River in which countless thousands of Chinese soldiers advanced and were mown down, until a pitiful remnant of the Gloucesters was surrounded. He was captured with two bullet wounds in his shoulder, which were never treated during his two years as a prisoner; neither was his capture reported, the Chinese not being concerned with such niceties as the Geneva Convention. They did, however, try to brainwash him with communism so as to send him home qualified in subversive techniques. Yet, young as he was, Large saw the fallacies without difficulty, recognizing communism not as a new kind of fraternity but old-fashioned domination of the many by the few and inherently evil, both in its aims and methods. His arm becoming paralysed, he was repatriated as a useless soldier; another four years were then sliced out of his young life while surgeons rebuilt his body until, at last, he was fit again, for the SAS too. Throughout this ordeal, his mind remained unblemished by hate, fear or trauma.

Large's team comprised Paddy Millikin, a gifted signaller from Southern Ireland; John Allison, who had unintentionally crossed the border before with Richardson, Allen and Condon; and Pete Scholey, a bright and breezy lad from Brighton, on his first tour. They were one of the first threesome of patrols across the border, to explore the watershed between the Koemba and Sekayan, which might offer a good jungle-covered approach if it led to anywhere in particular. It did not; instead, the going was so rugged that Large found himself on a plateau from which further progress was blocked by 800-foot cliffs, so sheer as to be impassable even for men who hated admitting defeat above all things.

They wandered around the plateau for several days, trying to find a way down on the enemy's side. The patrol became thoroughly depressed by failure and, in Large's case, by hunger too. The officers' current obsession with keeping the weight of bergens down to 50lb, even to the extent of having them weighed at the very moment of departure and ruthlessly ordering the least excess to be removed, was anathema to Large. His great frame needed vastly more than that, and since he could easily carry another ten pounds he took pains in future to circumvent the rule unobtrusively. On this occasion his suffering was slightly mitigated by meeting another frustrated patrol, in which a man who was trying to give up cigarettes and had come without any was seduced by Large's offer of his in return for a few spoonfuls of rice.

Large's patrol, which had been told by base that there were no friendly forces in the area, arrived first at the border landing-point to secure it for the other two. He approached it with the usual extreme caution, and just as well for at precisely that moment the leading file of a Scots Guards platoon also stepped into the clearing. "When you see something in the jungle it's through your rifle-sight," Large explains, his trained reaction being to aim the weapon even as the eye turned and to slip the safety-catch off too. Such instant readiness at least permitted a moment for identification before the other party was equally alert, and white faces with familiar uniforms were enough to halt escalation at the preliminary stage of severe palpitations.

Worse, however, followed. One does not stand around in the open in such circumstances, so both units melted into defensive positions to await the next SAS patrol, led by Corporal "Old Joe" Lock. His lead scout was a Fijian called Takavesi, who glided warily out of the jungle just as a party of Border Scouts, attached to the Guards but unexpected by their masters, did the same opposite him. A large brown man confronted small brown men; Takavesi was the faster on aim and the scene was photographed onto the watchers' memories, the exposure being brief because the picture would change one way or another in much less than a second; but Large was quicker even than that and showed himself to Takavesi, whereupon all present froze for a space before breathing again. Sergeant Spence's patrol returned without incident.

The same three patrols returned to the area for their next mission, which had a wider brief. Spence further explored the watershed ridge, hoping to find a way down the cliffs and a lateral track which must surely exist somewhere between the Koemba and Sekayan; but he was thwarted again and the ridge was discarded for future operations. Lock went directly to Badat, the first village on the southern, Sekayan, side where for ten days he watched local life pursue its peaceful course. There being no sign of the enemy and it now being permitted to contact natives judiciously, he learnt that soldiers were based near to the border, at Sidut and further downriver at Kapala Pasang. This information tallied with what Ray England had discovered as long ago as 1963 (Chapter 3), and soon proved to be still true.

Large did the same on the Koemba side. His village was Kapoet, which was not at all easy of access across the Pawan tributary, where he noted a fish-trap as a nagivational mark, and on through much exhausting "belukar." His patrol hid their bergens and went forward to observe Kapoet. What they saw was indeterminate; some men in green trousers which might or might not have been uniform, but there was nothing positively military about their behaviour nor any sign of a weapon. Hoping for something more definite, Large peered through his binoculars, losing track of time; that was his first mistake. Then, back at the Pawan, he wrongly identified a fish-trap as *the* fish-trap; so his in-built personal gyro was now programmed with the wrong datum and they missed the bergens. It grew dark; it rained; it poured; they were dog-tired; and there was nothing to do but sit on their wet hunkers for eleven hours without shelter or food. They did not touch their emergency rations because their predicament was not yet an emergency, but merely the most miserable night they had ever spent.

" 'Lofty' was maddening," says Scholey; "he'd been in that Chinese camp and you just couldn't get him to gripe."

In the morning they stretched their numb and aching limbs, found the right fish-trap with some difficulty and eventually sighted the bergens; but their trials were not over, for Large's always seemed to come in pairs. Standard operating procedure required them to watch concealed for half an hour before approaching the bergens, after which the surrounding area had to be searched, or "cleared." Large and Scholey went off to do that, while Allison and Millikin prepared the ravenously awaited breakfast which, of course, included last night's supper. The day was already well advanced when the two men started the search, and it took another hour for them to realize that they were lost, again. Concern then combined with utter exhaustion to demand their last ounce of mind over matter. They hooted like owls, but to no avail, and changed their position before doing so again. Not until a further hour and a half had passed did they hear a faint answering call.

Insufficient daylight then remained for useful work, neither were Large and Scholey in any sort of shape for it. Even the next morning they were scarcely restored, and Large decreed a day off: "We're all knackered and if anyone wants to take us on it'd be a walkover; we're not moving till we've had a good day's rest."

" 'Lofty' was good like that," says Scholey; "sort of unorthodox."

Further north along the border three patrols headed by Squadron Sergeant-Major Bob Turnbull started together over Gunong Brunei. They continued the investigation of the Seluas to Babang track and the River Koemba en route to Siding. One patrol had a very near miss with an enemy party, smelling cooking, hearing voices and finding them to be only twenty yards away. Further probing revealed more of the enemy's habits in this important central area.

The first of "D" Squadron's attempts to reach the lower Koemba was made by Captain Gilbert Connor and Sergeant Townsend where the Separan joins from the east. They so nearly succeeded that they heard diesel-engined launches on the river, offering tantalizing targets. The swamp beat them as it had their precursors, but each successive failure served only to enhance the will to succeed of everyone from the Brigadier downwards, and this part of the Koemba became a watery embodiment of "a little further."

Somebody also had to go to Batu Hitam and this task was given to Sergeant Alf Gerry accompanied by Corporal Mallett. There was nothing there of course, as a hunting party they met were at pains to tell them with the same emphasis that their fellow villagers had used to Bigglestone. But these natives were most friendly, discussing the still unripe crops, the wet weather, why they were no longer allowed to trade at Lundu in Sarawak which they had done from time immemorial, and comparing their weapons, which were of great mutual interest; particularly, to the SAS, the Dyaks' two muzzle-loading flintlocks in perfect condition, one engraved Tower 1863. But there were no Indonesian soldiers, absolutely not, despite continuing Intelligence reports of a camp in the district. The mystery deepened, Batu Hitam came to mean the camp rather than the village and determination to find it intensified.

The southern half of the front, supplied on the enemy's side by the River Sekayan, had now to be given attention, which was why Lillico set out to observe it midway between Sentas and the main base of Balai Karangan. He failed, with honour but a failure it was. No other patrols followed his, and three weeks later signs of unusual activity began to be noticed near the village of Plaman Mapu, two miles into Sarawak behind Gunong Rawan, and continued to rumble.

DOCUMENTS

There followed an operation whose nature bordered on the cloak-and-dagger, a useful reminder when studying the straightforward if enterprising soldiering of the Borneo campaign that the repertoire of the SAS is almost unlimited except by scale, the truly impossible, and honour. Woodiwiss was asked by a certain authority to obtain certain documents from a certain individual who was known to visit a certain hut near Sidut; the man would be useful too but the papers were what mattered.

Captain Jonathan Mackay-Lewis was assigned the task, which was made interesting by the need for precise execution and the hut being inexactly located some distance beyond the Perditin tributary. He therefore took his patrol across the border for a preliminary reconnaissance. They found a good fording point on the Perditin but, the river being wider than expected, Mackay-Lewis refrained from crossing lest they be seen and the objective compromised. And that was just as well because on the way back they saw a uniformed figure scurrying through the jungle and soon afterwards advancing mortar-bombs encouraged their swift transit of the border.

Twelve days later Mackay-Lewis took Spence's patrol as well as his own, and such was the documents' importance that 9 Company, 1st Scots Guards was sent to see them safely across the river, both ways. Three local guides were recruited to lead them to the hut, an indication of the Kalimantan people's attitude to the enemy. With so many men, speed became the essence of surprise, and a base was established just short of the Perditin by evening on the first day; the SAS crossed after dark, accompanied by two sections of guardsmen to secure the crossing point and ambush the track leading to the hut against pursuit on their return.

After a catlike approach the patrols spent the last part of the night lurking within 40 yards of the hut. At the first glimmer of light, they crept forward again, so cautiously that they noticed a trip-wire attached to a mortar-bomb and negotiated it safely; then they split to surround the hut and move in for the snatch, but it was not to be quite the copy-book operation they would have liked. The occupants woke with the dawn and started to move about; that might not have been insurmountable but just then a boy emerged and came boldly down the track, possibly to lift the trip-wire as part of his daily routine. He saw the SAS and shouted. A man on the verandah seized a weapon and was shot dead before he could use it. The SAS charged in, firing, and three or four men ran out behind to be swallowed by the jungle before even the SAS could aim and fire, illustrating that in such country prisoners must be taken instantaneously or not at all. The men were unarmed and partially undressed so there was hope that they had not taken the precious documents.

The assault was speedily concluded; a grenade was thrown into the hut, another man emerged, dying, and then the SAS were inside. There were rifles, ammunition, grenades, equipment of all sorts and, thank goodness, papers; the guides were able to identify the first man killed as the snatch target, so there was nothing more to be done. About turn, double march; the Guards' ambush made no mistake, the river crossing and final retirement across the border were accomplished without interruption, concluding the first successful aggressive operation by the SAS in enemy territory. Mackay-Lewis's sponsors were pleased, but never told him what the documents revealed; neither could he read them, being in Chinese.

Two patrols went over at the southernmost stretch of the border. Connor's was to continue Haley's investigation of the track between Jerik and Segoemen where he surprised an enemy patrol which fled, summoning reinforcements whose arrival was again revealed by signal shots. Connor, a nonchalant officer, did not retire immediately but sent what Woodiwiss describes as a half-baked contact report with no subsequent indication that he was all right; so that when he eventually breezed into Kuching he was "gripped" by an infuriated Squadron commander. "I was very pleased to see him and all that, but . . ." Sergeant Townsend's search area was east of Segoemen, which he found to be occupied by the enemy, both by meeting some locals and by hearing shots from that direction; the patrol was a model in gleaning useful information without incident.

To end this mainly reconnaissance phase of the campaign six SAS patrols were deployed simultaneously to watch the central front between Stass and Tringgus while the local infantry battalion handed over to another which had not been to Borneo before, Intelligence indicating that the enemy knew of the move and might be preparing to exploit it. The SAS did not like the task which tied up nearly half the Squadron defensively and severely curtailed their more adventurous programme, but it was important and had to be done.

Turnbull's patrol was one of the six and with him was Kevin Walsh on his second mission, the first having been with Lillico and harrowing enough but this was quite exceptionally unpleasant. When they had just crossed the border it chanced that a friendly aircraft roared close overhead from behind and was instantly engaged, ineffectively, by an enemy heavy machine-gun not 50 yards dead in front into whose field of fire they would certainly have blundered. Their deliverance seemed miraculous, but whatever kindly fate had fixed it now exacted a heavy fee. The aircraft reported the gun, the two SAS patrols on either flank took bearings of the noise and did the same, and so did Turnbull together with his own position which was of course

Above: primary jungle in contrast to secondary jungle (belukar), a cleared area reverting to forest. Landing-points can be seen at right. Below left: hard going through belukar. Below right: expecting trouble, in light order with belt and weapon only; bergen cached.

Left: wrong. Bunched and exposed. One burst from near the camera could wipe out the whole patrol. Below: right. The distance between them is constantly adjusted so that the man in front is only just visible. Above: George Stainforth (left), who for many months commanded the isolated patrol at Long Jawai in the Third Division of Sarawak, and Eddie Lillico; 1953.

Above: a jungle village. Right: semi-nomadic Punans in the Third Division of Sarawak, with SAS boots and clothing hanging out to dry. Below left: a medic at work. (*Soldier*).

Above: Major John Edwardes, GM, in characteristic pose. He commanded 'A' Squadron in 1963 and Cross-Border Scouts during 1964–66. Below: part of 1 Troop, spruced up. Back row, left to right: 'Mau Mau' Williams, Bill Condie, 'Lofty' Winmill, George Shipley, Bob Zeeman and Alec Kilgour. Front row, left to right: 'Geordie' McGaun, 'Gipsy' Smith, Ray England, 'Paddy' Freaney and 'Spike' Hoe.

The Three Camps operation. Top: the second of the three camps discovered by Sergeant 'Smokey' Richardson, belonging to the TNKU guerrillas and showing signs of general sloppiness. Middle: probably the camp where Trooper James Condon was murdered. Bottom: hole in the forest.

Above: any fool can be uncomfortable. Even in a swamp, it is possible to sleep dry and cosy, but these bashas are too complex for quick dismantling if an enemy is thought to be near. Below: this basha is rigged for a hammock, which is just visible. Few signs of occupation need be left in the morning if nothing is cut and care taken not to bruise leaves, snap twigs or make rope-marks on the trees. Finally, footprints would be obliterated and leaves spread naturally.

Below: the vulnerability to enemy ambush of a helicopter and its passengers at a border landing-point may be imagined.

Sergeant 'Gipsy' Smith's hydro-electric generator at Talinbakus, Sabah.
Top: construction. Middle: teething troubles. Bottom: on stream.

Above: breakfast in the Haunted House, Brunei, 1964. Majors de la Billière (left), commanding 'A' Squadron, and Johnny Watts, 'B'. Right: Iban Border Scout. The tattooing is largely religious and the crucifix wholly so, signifying a double insurance against the hazards of jungle life. The high brow and fine features, however, give the lie to any assumption of primitiveness, other than by environment. Below left: Trooper Billy White, 'a harum-scarum lad' (left), killed in action in the Long Pa Sia Bulge, 6 August 1964. Below right: a slim George Shipley at the end of a Borneo tour; the result of 2,000 calories a day instead of 3,600.

Left: boating could be convenient and at times delightful, but 'very, very untactical' if an enemy were to be on the bank. Below: the other side of the picture. This boat on the River Siglayan in eastern Sabah is passing an SAS OP to deliver a load of stores to an enemy camp upriver. Two hours later when it returned, all six soldiers on board were killed; the civilian helmsman was spared, unhurt. The story is not told in the text.

Right: swamp (photograph taken in Malaya).

Special Air Service: the Army's Borneo strategy depended entirely on the skill and daring of RAF and Navy helicopter crews, the SAS making particularly challenging demands of them.

Right: longhouse (with hot tin roof) in Indonesian Borneo. Below: George Shipley (left) and Bill Condie looking apprehensive.

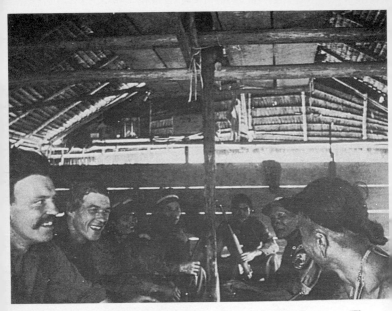

Above: joint planning session. SAS and Cross-Border Scouts on 'The Island'. Below left: Captain Malcolm McGillivray and Sergeant Nibau. Below right: Corporal 'Rob' Roberts and Trooper Franks returning to 'The Island'.

Above: the wrong side of the river; looking back over the Bemban from Gunong Kalimantan. Below: how they crossed the Bemban.

Above: the enemy camp on the River Bemban at which George Shipley in Bill Condie's patrol found himself staring up a hillside completely cleared of undergrowth. Surrounded by a firing ditch and reinforced parapet with benches on which to keep watch in comfort were machine-gun dugouts, a mortar pit, a radio aerial ready for hoisting, basha frames needing only ponchos to keep out the rain and what could only have been a pair of parallel bars. 'Keep-fit fanatics, the Indos', says Shipley; curiously, the SAS themselves not being backward in that regard. Left: a fulfilled Cross-Border Scout (Iban).

nearly identical to the enemy's, but his was the only signal which did not get through; and it was evening.

The Royal Artillery gunners behind the border were delighted to be given such a precisely located target and opened fire with their 105mm and big 5.5-inch weapons, keeping it up at intervals all night. Ear-splitting explosions far nastier than the crack of discharge, lurid flashes around and above, splinters tearing through the foliage, branches and whole trees crashing down, the hopelessness of moving in the dark knowing it might be straight into the next burst, the agony of trying to keep calm and transmit a message which for whatever local anomaly or other reason could not be heard, and the pointless irony of being killed by one's friends unknowingly, all combined to lower their spirits to the point where they could only remind themselves that while there was life there was hope, but not much. Walsh had reason to wonder whether his SAS career would continue in the downward progression of tribulation with which it had started to an early end, but after many active years, this night proved to be his most disagreeable recollection.

Large's patrol was deployed too, without Millikin who was in hospital for an emergency appendectomy, but for once nothing went wrong. The infantry turnover was completed without interference and the new battalion, the 3rd Royal Australian Regiment, signalled the old eastern Commonwealth's decision to join Britain in thwarting Soekarno.

The decisive period began with Major-General Walter Walker's relief by Major-General George Lea as Director of Operations. This event was hard luck on the former because it was he who had launched the offensive policy in principle and achieved the means for implementing it: political backing, reinforcements, the initiation of cross-border operations, and, above all, bringing his troops to such a pitch of professional excellence and morale that Lea was amazed and delighted when he met them.

Walker had successfully defended Malaysian Borneo, but left under a cloud nevertheless; mainly because of his efforts as Major-General, the Brigade of Gurkhas, in trying to save them from the economic axe. His bitterness at that threat was not founded just on sentiment but on a lifetime's experience of their enormous value to Britain, culminating right here in Borneo, where he put them in the forefront of the battle and they well repaid his trust. He was allowed to creep home without the knighthood which precedent should have accorded him, despite the enthusiastic backing of important people such as Healey, Mountbatten and Begg without whose help he might even have been retired.

Walker said on leaving: ''It is true that we have imposed the present lull on Soekarno and that the Borneo frontier is under our control. I don't think the Indonesians will risk all-out war, but I am sure they will increase the scale, tempo and intensity of raids and terrorism, and it will be a major tragedy if a complacent mood that the crisis is passing develops. We must not underrate the Indonesian soldier, who is tough and well trained, and the threat of the Clandestine Communist Organization though now controlled could explode if a large-scale Indonesian incursion succeeded in setting up a puppet régime in a pocket area.''

Lea paid good heed to that, but the front did indeed seem quiet when he took over on 12 March. True, the enemy had recently raided mainland Malaysia again, which revealed his unrelenting mood, but in Borneo there was nothing except continuing reports of strange if minor happenings around Plaman Mapu. These were not accorded much importance, perhaps partly in consequence of the turnover at Headquarters and partly because the 2nd Battalion, the Parachute Regiment were only now taking over the area and had not yet been in Borneo; though it remains odd that Brigadier Cheyne and his experienced staff at West Brigade did not prick up their ears.

Lea let the organization continue to function as before while he mastered his intricate and demanding job, which was both military and political with responsibilities to many authorities and councils. He had to woo those departments and interests whose cooperation was vital but would only be given wholeheartedly if they trusted him. Lea was extremely good at that; relaxing his victim with transparent honesty which was never belied, and then stimulating him with irrepressible enthusiasm and energy. The same qualities also pleased the troops, whom he visited constantly in and out of the jungle. They agreed that he too was a soldier's general.

Lea having commanded 22 SAS during its period of greatest achievement in Malaya, the Regiment welcomed him warmly. They liked him, and as the man for whom they would work they knew he understood their capabilities, limitations, methods and outlook as well as liking them in his turn. Liking them so much, in fact, that he felt it necessary to suppress his urge to visit

Lillico and Thomson in hospital lest it be thought that his first act was one of favouritism.

Wingate-Gray was in Borneo, opportunely, to make Lea welcome, promise faithful service, and to ensure being present when policy was formulated. He was also there because the SAS task was expanding and the available units with it, the British Squadron commander being fully occupied operating his own patrols in the cross-border role. Three independent parachute companies were watching the border in the less sensitive areas, a half squadron of New Zealand SAS were training in Brunei to take the field in April and the Australian 1 SAS Squadron would do the same in May. A small SAS theatre headquarters had therefore been set up on Labuan Island near the Director of Operations with either Wingate-Gray or his second in command John Slim always there in charge.

As soon as Wingate-Gray thought he could get away with it, he tackled the General and his Principal Staff Officer Colonel Anthony Farrar-Hockley on whether the SAS might take offensive action. Reconnaissance was all very well if the resulting information was put to good use, but the aim was to find precise and worthwhile targets for the infantry and it was not at all clear what those should be. To attack a defended enemy base like Nantakor was now considered a wrong interpretation of the hyper-secret "Claret" philosophy; the inevitable casualties would give the show away, and more than a few were not acceptable in any case. In addition, to catch the enemy in ambush needed more detailed knowledge of his habits and consequently more reconnaissance. But in the meantime he was not being hit at all, which would surely encourage him to further aggression; besides, the SAS badly wanted to fulfil the function for which they were so highly trained, indeed they might get into bad habits if they were always made to run away.

Lea understood his man perfectly and chuckled, but he took the point too. Knowing the quality of the SAS, he calculated the risk as small that they would leave attributable evidence of their presence in enemy territory; particularly their own dead bodies, not perhaps being fully apprised of how nearly Lillico's and Thomson's bodies had come to being so left. Indonesian bodies would be all right, unless of course the enemy complained publicly; a few SAS pinpricks would usefully test his reactions in that regard, as well as keep him on his toes and looking inward. The order was made; reconnaissance was still the main aim and offensive action was only to be taken during the last two days of a patrol against those targets which offered a realistic chance of complete success.

The first opportunity came in April and was grasped by Corporal Marley Carter and his patrol of Ayres, Dicker and Tapstaff. Carter had been on the Lillico patrol, a reverse to the Squadron, however gallant, that needed rather badly to be offset by undeniable success.

Acting on information received—from Bennett, Daubney and Thompson of "B" Squadron—they went to the cave-rock area on the River Koemba south of Gunong Brunei. First, to investigate two apparently newly-built huts that had appeared on aerial photographs and then to watch the river. They found the huts to be old and of no importance, but local craft passed constantly on the water. Many of these carried soldiers and obviously military stores mainly in the direction of Siding, which made Carter think that the enemy must maintain his base there mainly by river; indeed, it was hard to see from the map how else he could do it. He might therefore be considerably embarrassed by a pinprick, which a four-man patrol could apply as effectively as a company of infantry because neither could expect more than one small boat as a target.

Accordingly, on the morning of the sixth day of noting every detail, Carter selected a boat being paddled downstream from Siding by three soldiers in uniform, their weapons readily to hand in the bottom of the boat but not readily enough. At a comfortable range Carter shot the centre man, who slumped dead in the boat. The other two were flung overboard by the immense thrust of SLR bullets from the rest of the patrol; one never resurfaced, but the third man swam a few strokes before being killed by grenades thrown into the water beside him. The boat drifted languidly with the current, turning slowly in an expanding pool of pink water. The patrol withdrew, and that was that.

Few patrols found such suitable targets, but reconnaissance continued with great intensity in April though that aspect can only be recorded in the barest outline, regrettably. Particularly sad is that I have no mandate to tell the New Zealand and Australian SAS stories.

Patrols went to Bemban and built up evidence that the garrison there was supplied by the track from Sawah rather than by water, though the camp believed to be somewhere beyond the river had yet to be found. The camp at Batu Hitam also eluded them yet again, even when a man defected from there, led Turnbull to the border and pointed out the precise route. Irritation was not too strong a word for SAS feelings towards Batu Hitam. They tried to reach the Koemba near Poeri and their appetites were whetted by the sound of large powered craft on the river and signs of some heavy construction work, but the swamp beat them every time.

Large renewed his quest for the enemy at Kapoet, but it began to seem as though this tour would offer him nothing but a succession of brick walls.

Millikin rejoined from hospital and exercised hard to get fit quickly; but Allison was lost to the patrol and Woodiwiss sent for Large to tell him:

"I've got a replacement for you," and shouted, "Walsh!"

"There was an answering bellow from outside," says Large, "and in came this horrible little man, an object of degradation after a night out with the Navy in Kuching. I was in a state of shock for ten minutes. When I told the other NCOs, they said nothing would induce them to go into the jungle with him or any of my lot, far less all three of them together."

Appearances, however, can mislead. Kevin Walsh was certainly little, a good foot shorter than Large. With his boxer's face set squat on powerful shoulders, he undoubtedly presented the image of one with whom it would be unwise to trifle; but that is a requirement rather than a sin in the SAS. A second glance would have shown the eyes twinkling humorously with much more behind them than Large, reeling, had had time to observe.

Large tried a new route to Kapoet and it proved a nightmare, strewn with thorns attached to unyielding undergrowth and broken only by high cliffs with deep ravines. They reached the village nevertheless and saw signs of the enemy on tracks, but never found his camp despite unremitting patrolling. Tired and dispirited after nine days on the other side, they returned to the border landing-point where the first part of their accustomed double misfortune befell; no helicopter was available. They were ordered by radio to walk 2,000 yards down a specified track to the nearest infantry fort where they would be expected, but having done so their greeting from the officer in charge was:

"Who the hell are you and how did you get here?" and when they told him his face turned ashen. "My God! We've got am-

bushes out all over the area—well not on that track of course—
I mean nobody'd want to walk down there would they? It's
mined.''

But they survived yet again, and the mission served at least
one useful purpose in showing that Kevin Walsh was one of
those whose effectiveness increased in adversity. Indeed, Large
began to wonder whether his little team was not really rather
good whatever his colleagues might say, even capable of achieving something out of the ordinary if only fortune would, if not
smile, at least stop frowning quite so loweringly; though he,
being himself, did not yet fully realize that the strongest justification for this notion was the liking and trust they had learnt
to accord him personally.

Sergeant ''Blinky'' Townsend's objective was Kapala Pasang on
the upper Sekayan, long since known as an enemy forward base.
His aims were to find the camp and a good ambush position
overlooking the river. He achieved both objectives, the only
difficulty being that the village was on the near bank and the
camp on the far so that it was almost impossible to watch the
latter without being spotted by locals. Surprisingly, these were
neither welcoming nor scared but just not interested, vouchsaf-
ing little information of value so Townsend boldly stayed to find
out more for himself. The river traffic was sparse and apparently
all civilian. The camp was mostly hidden by trees and no more
would be revealed without crossing the river, which was out of
the question, but the enemy did not do so either and apparently
left the sensitive area to the border unpatrolled. Then, on the
second day of watching when sticking their necks out trying to
see more, the patrol was spotted by the enemy who opened fire.
Townsend quietly withdrew.

Brigadier Cheyne concluded that to ambush the river would
be unprofitable for lack of targets and to attack the camp on the
far side impracticable; but Kapala Pasang was close to the border with a good jungle-covered approach and if it were possible
to lure the enemy out of his camp and into an ambush the aim
of the ''Claret'' policy would be furthered.

A company of the Scots Guards was detailed, and while they
were getting into position Townsend found a local who was
much more forthcoming than his previous contacts. Apparently,
at the camp were Major Harim and eighteen Javanese soldiers
whom the villagers heartily detested for taking their food, shooting their pigs and being generally arrogant and unpleasant. But

brave though they were at browbeating the natives they hardly ever ventured out of the camp, and were supplied by track because they were frightened of using the river.

This confirmed Townsend's own deductions so, in order to instil some life into the enemy, he asked his friend to go home and spread the word that he had seen a very small British patrol that could easily be destroyed. Scared of what Major Harim might do to him, the man refused; the enemy made no move in the ensuing two days, and when Townsend took his patrol back to the river opposite the camp, its occupants were relaxed and obviously unaware of any threat.

His task was clear though uncongenial; he shot two unarmed soldiers who appeared on the far bank, expecting a hornet's nest about his ears and a hazardous dash back to and through the Guards' ambush, but the enemy cowered behind his defences and the enterprise just fizzled out in anticlimax. Nevertheless, a main purpose of "Claret" being to lower enemy morale, it was useful to know that the Kapala Pasang garrison's was already at rock bottom.

One hundred and fifty first-class Indonesian troops supported by two more companies attacked Plaman Mapu before dawn on the 27 April, after giving four weeks warning that they might do so; not the village either but the forward base of "B" Company, 2 Para, and with the clear intention of seizing it because wave after wave came in with dedicated courage. The greater part of the Company was out looking for the enemy in the jungle according to Walker's doctrine, and an understrength platoon of what Lea calls, with high approbation, cooks and bottlewashers held the position by the narrowest of margins in the classic British outpost style, fighting hand to hand in the very weapon-pits. Company Sergeant-Major Williams, Distinguished Conduct Medal, inspired his men with unbreakable fortitude though blinded in one eye halfway through the fight. Over thirty Indonesian casualties were inflicted for two British killed and eight wounded.

The SAS played no part in this, neither had they been watching the border during the warning period as they had for the Australians' take-over in March. Only Lillico had ever been there, though whether there was any connection in the enemy's mind between that incident on Gunong Rawan and his selection of Plaman Mapu just behind it as the objective of his major adventure can only be guessed, but is no less interesting for that.

General Lea on the other hand was much concerned. "Had we been turned out of Plaman Mapu," he says, "our little faces would have been very, very red." If the enemy could so nearly succeed with just a company what might he not do with a battalion or even a brigade which he had available? Lea flew there at once and ordered all jungle forts to be moved to higher ground when that would improve their security, though not so far from the villages as to leave the locals feeling unprotected. Increased vigilance hardly needed to be emphasized, particularly to 2 Para who now had an axe to grind and decisively defeated an enemy thrust at Mongkus in May without letting him get anywhere near the place. But although effective defences were vital Lea was sure that "Claret" should be the fulcrum of his strategy, deterring aggression and persuading the enemy, gradually maybe but surely and finally, that Malaysia was uncrushable.

The best way of applying that principle tactically, however, was not immediately clear. The ideal target was undoubtedly an enemy raiding force before it struck, but since such forces were assembled in the rear areas and spent the minimum time near the border we should be lucky to get timely enough warning. Additional targets must be selected, the most promising being routine enemy movements on tracks or rivers wherever Intelligence indicated and topography suited, so Lea's policy became the art of the possible.

"Claret" began slowly because success was its essence and defeat over the border would be altogether disastrous; every factor had to be just right before a raid was attempted, not least the quality, acclimatization and training of the battalion concerned. The first infantry success in the First Division was not achieved until May and meanwhile the SAS had the field to themselves, often going where even the best trained infantry would have found it difficult.

"They did a useful job," says Farrar-Hockley; though he added, valuing them more for the information they collected, "but it was pretty small beer you know."

Small in scale it may have been, but evidence will be produced that the enemy did not like it.

THE NELSON TOUCH

Captain Robin Letts was a diffident and shortsighted young officer who loved books, balancing on knife-edges between life and death, music, and winning; he had been across the border under training with Bigglestone to Batu Hitam and with Lillico to Gunong Rawan, but only now commanded his own patrol for the first time. Corporal "Taff" Springles provided the experience as well as being both signaller and medic. The team was completed by Trooper Brown, another Welshman; and Pete Hogg, also a new entry, who had made his way from an upbringing in India by the unusual route of the Royal Electrical and Mechanical Engineers. It takes all sorts to make an SAS Regiment.

Berjongkong and Achan were known enemy forward bases, probably supplied up the River Sentimo and its tributaries. Daubney and Thompson of "B" Squadron had already visited the area, but negotiating great areas of unmapped swamp had occupied most of their time. Letts would now make use of their pioneering effort to find out more about the enemy's lines of communication, 9,000 yards in from the border. The patrol made good headway at first through flat, primary jungle, before hitting the swamp at about halfway, which slowed them down, not entirely because wading was difficult but because it was noisy.

Sleeping above a swamp was, however, decidedly difficult to any but proboscis monkeys, who are born to it. The technique involved selecting two trees the right distance apart, hanging your bergen on one, getting your hammock out and slinging it, climbing the first tree to the lowest branch, changing into dry clothes, wringing out the sodden ones and hanging them out to dry, sliding down into the hammock and resting snugly over the watery waste. One false move meant a mighty splash, a silent I'm-all-right-Jack guffaw from your companions and night-long misery.

On the morning of the seventh day they heard an outboard motorboat far ahead, which was both exciting and a useful check that their navigation coincided with Daubney's. Then they came to a twelve-foot wide stream, which they took for one of the many tributaries draining the swamp into the main Sentimo, where the motorboat must be. This was obviously the place to establish a base for the reconnaissance proper, fortune providing a dry little island 40 yards back from the stream on which to do so. Letts and Hogg left their bergens with Springles and Brown and went on a preliminary inspection, walking in the stream so as to leave no tracks and sometimes even swimming because it was surprisingly deep. Some 200 yards downstream they spotted the nose, eyes and horns of what looked like a ferocious wild beast but proved to be a domestic water-buffalo wallowing luxuriously in a bed of soft, warm mud. That indicated a village, which voices soon confirmed; in fact, Babang Baha though the name would have meant nothing to Letts. He decided to bring the whole patrol down for a thorough reconnaissance the next day, and retraced his steps. While pushing against the current, however, a thought struck him; the stream was quite free of the usual submerged roots, jammed logs and low branches. Closer observation then revealed what older jungle hands would have noticed at once, that someone, the Sentimo Conservancy Board or whoever, had been hard at work keeping the channel clear and quite recently too. Immediately, walking in the fairway was no longer seen to be prudent but suicidal.

Having completed the journey through the trees, Letts set a two-man watch on the stream at an admirable spot for the purpose, where it described a loop from the inside of which the view was clear for 60 yards to the left and 30 to the right. Towards evening two boats with two armed soldiers in each did indeed pass from right to left heading downstream. Letts and Hogg cowered behind large-leaved water-plants and were not seen; but it was an extremely close-quarters affair with the boats seeming huge, much longer than the stream's width. Every sound down to the paddlers' breathing was clearly audible as they steered their craft forcibly round the tight curves.

The boats disappeared round the next bend, and Letts, marvelling at the sight of an enemy wondrously delivered into his hand, went straight back to the LUP and signalled for permission to engage should the chance recur.

Left alone, Hogg gazed after the vanished boats. Then his back hair bristled with mortal fear, because he heard the splash of more paddles behind him and knew that his head was clearly visible. Crouching down with as smooth a movement as he could manage, he twisted round and prepared to sell his life dearly, grimly for he did not doubt that sold it would be; but these two crews unconcernedly followed where their leaders had safely gone without apparent suspicion.

No approval to attack having come by the morning, Letts, blind as a bat without his glasses, took a leaf from Nelson's book and resolved to engage the enemy just the same; closely too, there was no other way. Piecing together the evidence, he had to assume that the apparently insignificant stream was the waterway to Achan, and that the most likely purpose of the boat convoy was to embark men or stores at a staging-point on the

Sentimo proper and ferry them back upstream. It also seemed probable that the staging-point was at the village they had discovered, so that the enemy's reaction to an engagement would be swift.

At first light, Letts made his dispositions around the loop, which was ideal for ambush as well as observation. He had noted how the boatmen had to work hard with their paddles in order to round it, backing, filling, and fending off the shore, the manoeuvre demanding all their attention; and how when a boat had passed, it was lost to view from those behind, denying the enemy mutual support and augmenting his confusion on being surprised. Letts placed himself at the top of the loop with Springles to his right and Brown to his left, ready to engage boats coming from either direction. But because that was most likely to happen from the left, Babang Baba, Hogg was positioned on that side and a little back from the bank, to give warning of any attempt by the enemy's rear crews to rush the ambush from the flank and to hold them up. The ambush would be sprung when the first boat had rounded the bend and came opposite the man on the far side.

They might have had to wait for days; in the event, their suspense lasted only two and a half hours, but even that seemed unbearably long. It is said that a man in ambush is a dangerous hunted animal, which is superficially paradoxical since he is the hunter and would seem to have all the advantages; but in practise it is true because he is about to call down the enemy's wrath onto his head by his own act. In the jungle he will never know whether those he can see are all there, or how the survivors of his first and perhaps only volley will react, but he can be quite certain that that volley will alert the whole military district and that he will be hunted remorselessly until he is out of it, perhaps with a casualty to carry. Letts and his three men expected to face eight enemies in four boats, acceptable odds in the circumstances but considerable none the less, and afterwards they would have to traverse 9,000 yards of very hostile territory. Thus their aim, which was to kill as many enemy soldiers as possible in order to further the General's "Claret" strategy, underwent a subtle change in their own minds and became to kill as many enemy soldiers as possible to prevent the enemy killing them. Steely, fierce, pitiless, but with hate as well as softness eradicated from their thoughts which were concentrated on professional execution of the task, and tense with animal fear which could not be wholly suppressed, they were dangerous indeed.

At eight-fifteen on the morning of 28 April a boat nosed into view from the left, and when its length was revealed Brown saw that it contained three soldiers, not two. A second boat followed a length behind, also with three men. Each man in the patrol observed acutely all he could through his cover, assessing how best to kill the enemy and readying himself for the fight. In each boat only the front two men paddled and the third acted as sentry, alert with his weapon cradled, so there must be no mistakes.

As the first boat came abreast Brown and the paddlers forced her into the bend, he shrank down; he must on no account be seen yet. Before he judged it safe to raise his head again, the second boat, inexpertly handled, nudged the bank precisely where he was so that if he had been disposed to be helpful he could have reached out an arm and pushed her off. Preoccupied with seamanship her crew failed to see him, and when she too passed into the bend Brown saw a third boat approaching, well into the straight. If the plan worked as intended, this would be his.

The leading boat rounded the top of the curve with dreadful slowness. But finally her bow reached Springles, the second boat glided past Letts, and the time for action had come. To let live, and live? Rubbish! He stood up to shoot. His target was the sentry in the stern, but it was the bowman who reacted first, dropping his paddle and seizing his gun with such astonishing speed that Letts was in mortal danger. Disaster threatened the whole enterprise as he wrenched his body and point of aim through what was a wide arc at that absurdly short range. But Springles also saw the weapon come up and fired first, hurling the man into the water, and saving his officer by a hair's breadth. Now the two of them faced five alert enemies and only killing mattered. Letts swung his SLR back to the rear man and hit him squarely in the chest so that he leant against the gunwale and then slowly, his head and torso arching limply backwards, slipped fluidly over it.

By engaging Lett's target Springles had to neglect his own, a mere eight feet distant. When he looked back, the boat's crew had flipped her over like a kayak and were nowhere to be seen, a feat which—later—evoked his admiration. He fired ten rounds rapid at where they might have been and waited for heads to appear. Letts's boat, rocked by violence, was a poor platform for a gunner, but the remaining man steadied himself on aim and Letts was again in peril; he sprang sideways to spoil the shot, before firing and hitting the soldier, who fell forward in the boat. Letts looked downstream and saw the third boat being engaged by Brown, but then his eye caught sight of the man he had just shot raising himself from the bottom of the boat. He shot him again, twice, and this time he died; a brave man if he knew what he was doing.

In the micro time-scale of the engagement, all this took an age, and during it another brave and very quick-witted man from Springles's overturned boat achieved a kneeling position on the near bank and had taken aim at the preoccupied Letts when Springles again intervened and shot him with not an instant to spare. The man slid back into the water dead, but left his weapon on the land. At once, another man scrambled ashore and reached for it, an act of barely credible courage when he might have remained hidden under the bank in the water. He too died.

Brown had gone into action with the first shot of the sprung ambush. He had no choice of target because his boat was heading straight for him at 40 yards range. He first shot the bowman, who was thrown dramatically into the air and over the side, thus clearing his view of the second man, who was also raised by the shot but spun into the water. That exposed the man in the stern who, poor wretch, must have known what was coming to him, and it came.

Hogg, covering the enemy's rear, spotted the bows of a fourth boat emerging from the downstream bend and juddering to a halt as, he imagined, her crew seized the shore and hugged it for dear life; he fired at where they should have been, but they were able to haul their boat backwards out of sight. The action was over; there was no one left to shoot at.

The silence was stunning to deafened ears, and the scene grim. Four bodies floated in the reddening stream, one face upward and wide-eyed, drifting slowly; a fifth sprawled on the bank at Springles's feet; and two more lay crumpled in the boats, which had become their coffins. One man from Springles's boat escaped; they heard him splashing and crashing wildly through the jungle swamp.

Four months later, a newly-joined young officer in "A" Squadron, Mike Wilkes, happened upon the place, which disconcerted him:

"You could sense the ferocity just by the debris even after all that time; when a heavy SLR bullet goes through a tree it doesn't make a clean hole but shatters the wood into tiny fibres as though it were explosive, and the top of a two-inch sapling is wrenched off leaving a stump like a shaving-brush. Imagine one going into you. Salutory.''

The time, incredibly, still lacked a minute to eight-twenty when Letts raised his voice for the first and only time during the patrol to order retirement. Then they were all back at the LUP for their bergens, ready-packed, and away without wasting a second. Having so far to go Letts decided on speed rather than concealment as their best policy for survival, and, with SAS fitness serving the powerful instincts of the hunted, they really moved. One and a half hours later the enemy mortared the ambush position and presumably set out to chase them, but with few tracks to follow in the swamp and not knowing what size force he was up against, probably greatly overestimating it when he saw the carnage, he was most unlikely to achieve half their speed. By evening Letts and his men had nearly reached the border, a distance which had taken them six days to cover before.

Basha'd down, Springles set up the radio with pleasurable anticipation as the bearer of good news, but was forestalled by base with the urgent message that permission to attack had been granted. The Nelson touch was thus vindicated, and the light relief welcomed after they had recovered from their astonishment and reminded themselves that this authority had still been outstanding.

In the morning they were frightened by barking dogs, imagining themselves to be the quarry, but nothing ensued and after a slow and cautious last leg they crossed the border safely, found a gap in the tree canopy and asked to be winched out. It being evening they expected to have to wait the night and were pleasantly surprised when a helicopter homed onto their Sarbe. All, that is, except a disgruntled Hogg who had just cooked a specially generous and tasty curry which had to be buried quickly; and when his turn came to go aloft he was further irked by a vine coiling itself around his neck and threatening to hang him, downwards. But the four of them enjoyed an even better dinner in the ''Green Dragon'' at Hereford some months later when Letts was awarded the Military Cross for what was undoubtedly a classic of its kind. He transferred to the Australian SAS soon afterwards so as not to miss the Vietnam War which, even without Springles as his right-hand man, he survived.

Roger Woodiwiss flew home urgently, deeply worried for his wife who was gravely ill in childbirth—the risk business not being exclusive to the SAS—and distressed at having to leave his men at this active time. John Slim, his second in command, was in Borneo so continuity was maintained until Glyn Williams, the Adjutant at Hereford and already earmarked to relieve Woodiwiss, arrived out on 4 May and assumed command of "D" Squadron. Peg Woodiwiss and her baby surmounted their challenge staunchly and returned safely to base.

LARGE OF THE KOEMBA

Patrols continued up and down the front, and one of Woodiwiss's last acts had been to tell Large that his next objective would be the Koemba near Poeri. No fewer than six attempts to reach it had been foiled by swamp, but such was its importance that there was no question of accepting defeat. This would be "D" Squadron's last chance before their tour ended and was just the challenge that Large and his men needed, especially since nobody truly expected them to succeed. Even Brigadier Cheyne, who was most anxious that they should and took a keen interest in the planning, told them he doubted whether there was a way through the swamp; but such pessimism together with their own unsatisfying tour so far served only to tune their resolution to the pitch where failure was entirely discounted. The mission was to establish the pattern of river traffic and then, having obtained permission, to engage a suitable target.

Large approached the task well aware that he would do no better than the rest unless he built on their achievements with painstaking thoroughness in planning as well as determination in execution, qualities in which he was trained but also possessed naturally and enjoyed using. First, he extracted every last jot of information from their patrol reports and minutely interrogated any of their writers not on patrol, notably "Old Joe" Lock who had only just returned after penetrating nearer to the river than anyone else. They told him chiefly where there was swamp, that is to say everywhere they had been, which was useful negative information because some approaches had not yet been tried.

To that Large could add the positive evidence of air photographs which, although unable to show the ground or the limits of the swamp, did pick out contours, rivers broad enough not to be hidden by the tree canopy, and the nature of the growth whether primary jungle, "ladang" or anything between. The pictures were particularly informative to Large as a qualified Air

Photo Reader, and assisted by Staff Sergeant Watson of Brigade Headquarters, whose interpretive skill was little short of artistry, he added considerable detail to his largely featureless map. He did so with dots and smudges which would seem accidental to anyone else but were strictly disallowed just the same.

Pondering his handiwork Large's eye for country was attracted by two features which, taken in combination, might just possibly indicate a dry route to the river. The border ridge was low, 250 feet at its highest, and from it ran a just perceptible spur which became indistinguishable, even to Watson, 1,000 yards from the river but pointed directly into the big loop west of Poeri. What more likely than that the loop was actually caused by the spur? He would not walk along it because that would be dangerous and unnecessarily far, but aim to meet it in the loop; the plan seemed to offer an exciting chance, but it was still only a chance. He made one stipulation to Woodiwiss, which was readily agreed and would prove crucial; whereas earlier patrols had been directed to precise points on the river, he should be allowed complete freedom to select his own in the light of what he discovered.

On 9 May the patrol made their last-minute preparations, test-firing their SLRs and returning them to the armoury at headquarters where a final briefing was held. Then they packed their bergens with meticulous, unhurried concentration and returned to their house in the Kuching suburbs for a large meal and sleep, or at least rest. Large was tense; of course he was; had he not been, he would have stood little chance of reaching the Koemba.

Early the next morning a Land Rover and trailer arrived with the weapons and bergens and took them to the airport for onward passage to Lundu in a Twin Pioneer. But as soon as Pete Scholey was handed an SLR, he knew it was not his own, and from being the life and soul of the team with a never-ending flow of good-humoured chat, he started, as Large puts it, "to honk a good deal." After all, his weapon was part of himself, his very lifeline on which he had lavished the tender care of a mother, noticing and striving to eradicate the least blemish. It was useless to tell him that this one was identical and that the armoury would never issue an imperfect weapon. His deep instinct rejected the alien, ill-omened foundling; and remembering that he had been offered a fortnight's rest, after spending longer on patrol than anyone in the Squadron except Large, and being distinctly skinny, and having responded classically, "Not bloody likely," he now regretted his too hasty zeal.

Scholey's honking was directed to hurtling back to Kuching in the Land Rover; but the aircraft could not wait so he jumped in and stripped the offending rifle to its smallest component, found nothing wrong and reassembled it, the 20-minute flight providing ample time for one so expert. Large told him he could test-fire it at Lundu, but that was not to be either; the Pioneer taxied to a helicopter whose rotor was already turning and whose schedule was so tight that no delay was permissible, inevitably because although more aircraft were now available there were still barely enough. After another short flight they were put down at the border landing-point, where honking was unavailing and distracting since the only firing from now on would be in earnest. Marching through enemy-held jungle would demand all Scholey's attention, so he forgot his anxiety and got on with the job.

Scholey was number two in the patrol after Large, his normal position when they were in the first degree of readiness. Behind him, in the safest place, marched the signaller, Paddy Millikin. He was a true son of the elfin bogs, none too tidy about the basha, and his mien was strange to the Englishmen for he seemed to live in four dimensions, the last of which they could not share. A growing religious conviction played a part in this, but he was fey too. He knew for certain that he would die young and said so without emotion, though only in the haunted isolation and intimacy of jungle nights on patrol when spirits demanded that truth be spoken. But Millikin was an outstanding signaller, and it was perhaps his having a foot in the other world that enabled him to conjure messages from beyond when others could twiddle knobs indefinitely and be vouchsafed only wails and groans. Large prized him for this skill, which he could not match.

Kevin Walsh was a reassuring rearguard; tough, down to earth, extremely proficient after six years in the Parachute Regiment before his SAS training, and possessing a sense of duty that was highly developed though well hidden until it mattered. To liken him or Scholey to Dopey of the Seven Dwarfs would be impertinent, were it not that a puckish fate was to let fly with a succession of mischievous side-swipes which one or other of them, more sinned against than sinning, invariably stopped. Off to work they went; not with a heigh-ho but settling quickly into the operational regime of total, dogged vigilance and concentration, up and down the low hills in helpful primary forest.

On the second day Large heard that most distinct and revealing jungle sound, chopping. His arm went up in a smoothly deliberate but commanding gesture and all froze. Then he slipped off his bergen and went forward to investigate, a huge man yet he vanished with less rustle than a snake. At twenty yards from his objective Large saw what he needed to know, soldiers building bashas. There were only a few in his field of vision, but his ears indicated many more, perhaps a whole platoon. It was a disturbing discovery though not so much for the immediate present; rejoining the others he led them on a detour, avoiding easy walking places where visibility was good, though where the undergrowth was thick they risked making noise or leaving tracks so their utmost skill was called into play. They were undetected so far as they could tell, but it was a troubling feature of jungle warfare that one never knew if one was being followed or headed off. Whatever happened from now on, the enemy platoon would be a lurking factor in Large's mind.

The next day they crossed a well-marked track, probably the main route between Poeri and Achan. On the fourth day they came to another, which ran parallel to the river and was so straight that Large was sure it had been cut specially for shooting along, as well as for rapid deployment of cut-off forces against intruders such as themselves. They slipped across, again apparently unnoticed, and headed into the loop of the river to test Large's gamble that there they would hit the tail of the spur and walk dry-shod to the bank. They hit swamp.

It seemed limitless in every direction except the north whence they had come. At first the swamp was knee-deep, then up to their waists and finally to Large's chest and Walsh's and Scholey's necks; the latter observing with a naturalist's interest, slimy things crawling with legs upon the slimy sea and being greatly magnified by their extreme closeness to his eye. When even greater depths were reached, they turned back to probe elsewhere. The disappointment called for a conscious effort of resolution, which they made. But, as with many obstacles that seem insuperable, the swamp revealed weaknesses that they learned to exploit; every now and then they came to an island strewn with palm leaves that looked sodden but cracked like pistol-shots if trodden on, but at least they offered somewhere to rest or spend a night. Large used them as bases for his next probe, which he did in light order with one man. The other two—one of whom was always Millikin with his precious radio—were left to look after the bergens.

The direction of search was west for they had always been to the east of the spur, if there was a spur. Large was frightened, and not ashamed to admit it afterwards; movement could not but be noisy what with the difficulty of maintaining balance, the swishing of the water as they moved, and these ubiquitous leaves which even when floating crackled as they were pushed aside however gently; the danger of breaking an ankle in a submerged root was ever-present; and their trail was involuntarily blazed by persistent lines in the surface scum.

"I got this feeling that just in front there was somebody with a damn great machine-gun saying, 'Let him come another five yards and I'll blow his belt buckle through his backbone.' It was quite an experience making a blasted noise like that and not being able to help it."

Scholey's thoughts ran on similar lines and once when it was his turn to follow he whispered,

"I hope we're the goodies."

"Huh?" Large could not hear the words and was in any case preoccupied with feeling each footstep, watching his map and compass, mentally calculating time and distance, peering into the threatening shadows, and being scared. Scoley was lying well back, correctly, so Large beckoned him to close and deliver his no doubt pressing message.

"I hope we're the goodies."

Large had managed to switch barely half his consciousness to his companion and that half was both bemused and displeased;

"What the hell are you talking about?"

"Goodies always get away with it, but if we're the baddies we're going to finish floating arse up on top of this lot."

Large stared for a moment yet, then shook with noiseless laughter. His tension dissolved, and he learnt as every good leader does that having imbued his followers with strength they can return it to him in fuller measure than he gave it out, often when he has little left and needs it most.

"Worth his weight in gold just for that, Pete was," says Large gratefully.

Night came and they bedded down on a mud island. Each patrol commander had his own tenets; Large was a no-hammock, low-profile man so, wet through already, they lay cocooned in moisture beneath their ponchos and hoped for better things tomorrow. The next day they continued to flounder westwards, sinuously as the varying depth of water dictated, but not a suspicion of high ground did they find. Every now and again they were tantalized by the noise of boat-engines—heavy diesels, not just outboards—but the nearer they drew to the river, the deeper became the swamp.

After another night in the slough of despond, Large led northeast out of the swamp in the off-chance of finding a trace of the spur, but there was none. The air photos had indicated that it petered out long before reaching the river, and peter out it evidently did. What then to do, where now to go? Over breakfast on dry ground they held a Chinese Parliament.

Some said this and some said that, arguing their cases forcefully as was their SAS privilege. But none said—though being ordinary men, as they are always at pains to emphasize, each thought what ordinary men would think in the circumstances—that they would be fully justified in returning to base with its hot showers, dry clothes, plentiful food, ambrosial beer, slumberous nights and blessed relief from stress. Had not everyone from the Brigadier downwards already anticipated their failure and condoned it?

Scholey came to terms with the SAS that day. No one had asked him to join but he had overcome all the hurdles and done so; perhaps for adventure, perhaps to prove something to himself, perhaps for other half-stated reasons. But here he was in it: an outfit that prided itself on daring, winning and going a little further: entrusted with a task which demanded all those—except that as they could already hear the diesels there was very little further to go and he thought their precept should be to keep going a little longer. So what was the use of him, and what would he prove other than that he was a big-time humbug, if he chucked in at any stage short of absolute impossibility? It was good to get that off his chest for his interest revived, while fear and fatigue retreated.

Resolved, *nem. con.*, to press on downstream in the hope of finding a causeway to the river. Back they went into the swamp, heartened by the diesels drawing ever closer, and by the water through which they waded rising and falling gently with the boats' washes. Large took them as close to the mainstream as he dared; where the water-level came above his waist after which he would be ineffective as a soldier, knowing full well—though Walsh and Scholey thought he forgot—that those two shorties were incapacitated already. Just then a big boat passed, maddeningly close but still invisible, her slow-revving engine chugging throatily and the water hissing past her sides. The wash reached them first as a low trough, warning of a considerable crest to come which surged up to Large's chest, Millikin's neck and Scholey's mouth; while Walsh took a deep breath and vanished, only his rifle being visible above the mere like King Arthur's sword Excalibur. Re-exposed, he barely had time to splutter, ''Bloody hell!'' before again being engulfed, and finally surfacing after the third wave swore a dreadful oath that the Indonesians should smart for this.

They found their holy grail when they least expected it, indeed they had taken a tack away from the river. Not only was the land dry, it rose a good 30 feet above the swamp, the spur beyond a doubt. Large merely thanked his lucky stars, but his young followers revered him as a walking miracle. They passed through a narrow belt of jungle, and were then amazed for the second time to find themselves standing on the edge of a rubber plantation gazing through regular rows of straight, spindly tree-trunks at a broad and sunlit bend of the Koemba. It was a case of setting out to do something, doing it, and then being astonished at having done it.

After concentrating for so long on just getting there, Large took a moment to remind himself that this was just the first rung of the ladder and they must now step smoothly onto the next. A quick inspection of the rubber showed that the plantation was being rested, but fresh tracks were also evident and Large felt that the sooner they got into an observation post the better for their safety and the execution of their task. Where? To their right was rubber and littler cover near the bank. The obvious place was to the left, where the tip of the jungle-covered spur nudged the river-bend; so obvious, however, that if the enemy had but an inkling of their presence, it was just where he would search. One place he would surely never look lay right in front. A single spreading forest tree stood on the ten-foot high river-bank which tumbled down to the near side into a wide ditch. There was scrub enough here to give cover both to lookouts on the bank and those off watch below. The snag lay in this small haven being quite isolated, so that to leave it in a hurry would mean crossing completely open ground and then negotiating the rubber whose cover was little better. If the enemy appeared on the land behind them, they would have to take to the river, and Scholey could not swim. Nevertheless, that is where Large took them, trusting that if the enemy considered it at all he would not be able to imagine anyone being so stupid.

As a picnic-place it was ideal; shady, comfortable, picturesque and dry. Dry! Water in millions of gallons lay before them, yet not a drop could they drink; Walsh, who had cursed it only hours before, now prayed for it, and more positively but just as ineffectively tried lowering a bottle on a string. As an observation post far inside enemy territory, however, the position was not relaxing. The river was 40 yards wide, fast-flowing towards them from in front and curving downstream to their right. One man could see everything on the water with just his eyes above the parapet so the rest stayed hidden in the ditch at instant readiness; but one of them had always to watch the land behind, and it was that threat which made their adrenaline run cold.

More pleasantly exciting was their first visible launch, which came down river from Poeri during the afternoon. At least 40 feet long with two uniformed soldiers in charge and a crew of six locals, she carried a large cargo amidships hidden under a tarpaulin. She made an ideal target, painful for the enemy to lose and defenceless after the soldiers had been killed. Large, fidgety about the patrol's insecurity, would have liked to sink her and go while the going was still good, but duty easily restrained him. Firstly, he had not asked permission to engage; secondly, they had come primarily to reconnoitre and one boat did not make a pattern of movement; and thirdly, the attack must be faultlessly executed, which meant taking time for observation, planning and rehearsal.

The launch swung into the bend, revealing the Indonesian ensign at her stern though the patrol recorded it as just a red and white flag; they had been fighting the Indonesians for two years but not in places where colours flew. Watching her, Large gave thought to his plan. His strategic aim was to make the enemy fear for his line of communication, and his tactical option was either to kill as many soldiers as possible or to destroy a boat with her cargo. He preferred the second, which might well discourage the civilian boating community, owners and crews, from lending their support to the enemy, and hurt the latter's morale as well. Another consideration, not mentioned but transparent just the same, was that he would just as soon not kill a lot of people if there was another way to do the job.

Having established a maritime strategy that would have been warmly endorsed by Their Lordships of the Admiralty, Large turned his attention to tactics and adopted a well-tried principle from the time of Trafalgar: that "raking" the enemy from astern was far more effective than engaging his "broadside." In the latter case, if the target were full of soldiers the first volley would bring all the survivors to the gunwale in a row and the patrol would instantly be outnumbered; while bullets aimed at the hull would go in one side and out the other with no sinking effect, hitting vital parts like the engine only by chance. But to make use of the river-bend and wait until the stern was exposed would reverse these drawbacks and add advantages: soldiers would by no means rush to the narrow transom for that would be suicidal; each bullet plunging downwards along the length of the craft could well strike a disabling component, and if not would punch a hole in the bottom; shooting would be very accurate with no crossing movement; the enemy would be surprised by an attack from astern; the civilian crew would be less at risk; and if a boat heading upstream were stopped she would drift back and stay within decisive range.

Large explained his plan to the men, inviting questions and ensuring that they understood. Then he practised them at closing up to their firing positions, which he would order only after the target had passed and begun to turn so there must be no question of muddle: from left to right Walsh, Millikin, Scholey, three yards apart. Large would stand on the lower ground at their feet to direct the battle if necessary and add his own fire-power as events dictated. He would also watch up and down river for other enemy boats coming within range, and, most important of all, for interference from behind At the order "Stop" Millikin and Walsh would go first, snatch their bergens, and race twenty yards back into the rubber while being covered by Large and Scholey; then vice versa. That they did not practise.

Towards evening they ate their main meal of meat-blocks, raw and horrible because Large allowed no cooking. After dark he filled his water-bag, a brand-new one which he cherished and had not been easy to acquire. He allowed two bashas to be rigged in the ditch and the four men rested undisturbed, soothed a little by the powerful lap and gurgle of the river.

The next day proved that Brigadier Cheyne was right in wanting to know more about the Koemba. It started with a palpitation when a canoe paddled by two uniformed soldiers came downstream and headed purposefully straight towards them. They stood to, alert for attack from any direction because the boat might well be a diversion for a force ashore. Walsh's water-bottle hung over the bank on its string and had to stay there while the boat came so close as to be almost out of sight beneath them, but its crew were concerned only with their objective which was to haul up their fish-trap, empty the wriggling contents, reset it, and paddle away.

Civilian traffic continued at intervals throughout the day, and so easy was it to hear even a hand-propelled boat that not even one head was needed above the parapet and they relied on ears alone. A military supply launch with three soldiers, five locals and bulk stores came up in the morning, and Large mentally tested his plan against her, successfully. But he was far from expecting the little ship which glided majestically into view during the afternoon, a luxury motor-yacht by the look of her and all of 45 feet long. Sunlight flashed from her polished brightwork, her gleaming white side reflected a whipped-cream bow wave as she sliced through the calm water against the jungle background, and she made a holiday brochure picture of the most romantic and tempting kind.

Large was tempted. At the stern was the red and white flag, which had gained in significance because only those boats with soldiers on board had flown it so far. Amidships a superstructure built up to a small bridge whose canopy shaded its occupants so that Large could not make them out. On a short mast above the bridge flew another banner, this one having a strange device that strongly suggested to his practised eye the sort which very senior officers display to boost their egos and inspire awe.

"We'll have this one," Large whispered to the three men crouching out of view at his feet. Never mind that he lacked permission, the opportunity could not be expected to recur and success would deal a blow to enemy morale at high level where it would do most harm.

As the yacht drew near, however, doubt intruded; her crew were not in uniform and if the VIP turned out to be a civil administrator the destruction of his flagship would cause hideous embarrassment to many, from the Secretary of Defence right down to Large. Particularly Large. He wished he could identify the shadowy figures on the bridge, and at last, as the yacht swept past with a subdued roar fifteen yards away, one of them stepped out into the sunshine. Large gasped; it was a raven-haired girl with a trim figure in a daring white dress, and the travel brochure was complete. His left hand trailed at his side ready to beckon his warriors into battle, but now he turned the palm towards them and hissed, with knightly chivalry:

"There's a bloody woman!"

"We're not shooting them, no way."

(Large had been right in his first assessment. The banner on the motor-yacht had belonged to Colonel Moerdani of the Indonesian Parachute Regiment; and that is certain because twelve years later he visited the London Headquarters of the SAS as a general and said so. Walsh and Scholey, by then respected sergeants, met Moerdani and they all got on famously, as old enemies tend to do. Moerdani thanked them for his life and they were glad they had let him pass because he seemed a kindly, bouncy little chap. He told them he had known that the SAS were in the area, but failed to convince them because much could have been done to thwart them such as alerting the launches and patrolling the riverbank; those measures came afterwards.)

Scarcely twenty minutes later there followed a 40-foot launch with a hard, open-sided canopy beneath which seven relaxed soldiers entirely belied their Colonel's assertion, a perfect target that offered a good chance of killing all the men and sinking the boat as well; though that would have meant a last-minute change of plan which is usually unwise. It was late in the day too for getting well clear by nightfall. Confident that more good targets would present themselves Large now had no justification for disobeying orders; but his men, keyed-up with itching fingers in the ditch, accepted his decision restlessly.

In principle, though, the pattern of traffic was established, the time for action had come, and Large sent a message worded:

"Request double-O licence," partly because it was short and partly because he was in the mood for pleasantry.

"Not understood," came the answer in a flash, and indeed all experience shows that shafts of wit in such circumstances will inevitably bury themselves in the thick hide of some uncomprehending numskull; one who in 1965 had presumably never heard of 007 James Bond, if that is credible.

"Cancel."

"Cancel what?"

Oh for Christ's sake! Prolonged signalling was anathema to Large, who feared the enemy might listen and take bearings.

"Start again. Request permission to engage opportunity target."

"Roger."

First thing in the morning the reply came, "Approved." The second thing that came was the canoe with the two soldiers for their breakfast fish. Large was momentarily tempted to take the two men back to base as prisoners, but decided that to sink a launch would hurt the enemy's morale far more. Just such a target now headed downriver and the patrol tensed and made ready. But—there always seemed to be a but—this launch was only 30 feet long and it seemed a pity and less effective to take a sprat when they could have a whale; besides, no soldiers were visible and with the fast current under her she might, if lucky, escape. Large signed his decision down the bank, hoping his inactivity would prove masterly; but the men in the ditch, aroused and deflated for the third time and starved of a view, did not think so. They muttered; and Walsh, bolder than the others, did so articulately:

"What the bloody hell's he waiting for, the fucking *Ark Royal*?"

But Large just smiled and called them up to have a look at the retiring boat; he did not worry that he had a mutiny on his hands, the men were his body and soul and all four now knew it.

The next five hours passed slowly just the same; some of the local boats had soldiers in them, but small craft were no longer interesting. Then the sun vanished behind a cloud so black that the river was in twilight darkness. Drenching rain fell so heavily, raising such a spume above the surface that Large could barely see 100 yards, and so noisily that he reckoned the crack of a rifle would either be lost altogether or mistaken for the thunder which crashed savagely in wild abandon. He himself heard the muted sound of a diesel engine only just before the launch herself came mistily into his view after a couple of watery blinks. The scene was set and fitting for the dark deed about to be wrought. This time there were no "buts."

She was a 40-footer with a canopy, the side-curtains being lowered against the rain so that Large could not see her crew or cargo. Two soldiers were then revealed at the rear end as she passed, the man furthest away facing him so that he could have studied the features had he not been concentrating on whether his plan would suit this particular target.

"I wasn't interested in looking at a bloke I was possibly going to kill; just a bloke as far as I was concerned, hard luck."

He was, however, interested in how many more there might be inside. The launch with its canopy looked very like a four-ton army truck and Large convinced himself that there were plenty of soldiers on board, sitting on side benches with weapons between their knees; but that contingency was allowed for.

She was turning to starboard when at last Large beckoned his men. They leapt up and forward while he stood up behind them.

As the launch steadied on her new course Large fired once to start them off before looking quickly and anxiously up- and down-river for other boats appearing through the mist, which could mean disaster if not detected at once. Three shots followed on the instant and there was no question of missing an 8-foot wide target at 45 yards range.

A curt, angry expletive brought Large's attention to Scholey who was struggling with his rifle; that extraneous abortion which they had put out of their minds but which now failed to repeat after the first round. He did not honk now but applied himself with reflex dexterity to the stoppage drill. Meanwhile, Walsh and Millikin hammered the enemy's stern just above the waterline as fast as was consistent with aiming every shot, about one a second, and the timber splintered visibly. To Large's surprise the two soldiers were still there, so he shot them—to allow any return fire would be absurd and there was no sentimentality in his nature—after which he put ten rounds rapid into the hull before looking up to scan the river again and, turning right around, the land approaches. All was well, and back on target he emptied his magazine just as Walsh and Millikin had expended their allotted twenty rounds after no more than half a minute's firing.

Scholey had mastered his weapon and was still thumping away, but Large saw little reason for prolonging the action and much for leaving it behind. More than 60 rounds had hit the boat, which was dead in the water and twisting slowly to starboard; even more significantly, she had taken a list that way, only a slight one but it proved that bullets had pierced the bottom and so far there had been insufficient time for much water to enter. As Scholey watched her, considering whether to deliver a coup de grâce, smoke began to billow through the screens and men emerged to jump over the side.

"Stop!" They did so and all changed magazines, including Scholey who had fired only nine rounds; then Walsh and Millikin turned, ran, and turned again. Large and Scholey followed, but halfway up the slope Scholey was alarmed to see Large judder to a halt and dash back whence they had come, if anything faster than before. He followed, frankly terrified because the only possible explanation was that Large had seen an enemy in the trees and now they were going to have to swim which he could not do; so when Large reached the ditch and retrieved his precious water-bag, carefully emptying it and stuffing it inside his shirt with the comment, "The bastards aren't going to get that,'' Scholey discharged the most stinging broadside of double-shotted insults that young trooper ever aimed at old sergeant.

All together again they looked back for the last time. The boat's list had increased to the point where something fell off unaided, smoke mushroomed black and oily, and even as they turned away a huge match seemed to be struck beneath the canopy and flared brilliantly.

The patrol veered to their right onto the narrow jungle-covered spur which separated the rubber from the swamp, and headed up it as fast as they could move with the immediate aim of getting clear across the enemy's cut-off track or tracks before he could patrol them; and because the ground was clear of undergrowth that was very fast indeed.

High speed was, of course, not only a matter of footwork. Awareness and weapon reaction had to match it as nearly as possible, and those were Large's specialties. Even among the SAS—who all had to be good and strove endlessly to become better, trying to ensure that perhaps just one deadly encounter would go their way by a hair's breadth—Large was in the top ten because he made it his hobby as well.

Concerned only with the enemy, Large suddenly found that the computer in his brain had taken charge and that he was stock-still, looking at something approaching fast on the ground three yards in front through the steel ring of his rifle-sight, and doing so before whatever jungle creature it was had detected him; only just but it was the difference that mattered. Then it reacted.

"Jesus!"

It swung upwards with a movement so quick that it was hard to follow though the rifle did, and stood motionless but for its flickering tongue five feet from the ground which was rising so that its head was above Large's. Bronze, unblinking, hypnotic eyes, whose function was to petrify and induce a helpless acceptance of death and nearly did so, stared down into his from a body transformed by alarm from a nondescript mud-coloured snake into perhaps the most terrifying killer in the animal kingdom. There is nothing else like a king cobra, except a common cobra, and Large was in no doubt that he was confronted by a king-size specimen though he had never seen one before.

Behind the eyes were cheek-like bulges housing venom-sacs of ample capacity to allow the snake to chew its victim and so inject enough neurotoxin to kill a big man like Large in half an hour. The head formed a flat top to the hood, which was yellow and not so well curved as an Indian cobra's but made up for that by its size; Large estimated a foot wide by fifteen inches high— "All right, I may have been a bit shocked but I don't normally exaggerate." A slender four-inch-wide column curved gracefully to the ground where it coiled tightly to form a steadying base, a striking spring, and a reserve length for increasing the effective range; the whole forming a highly efficient psychological and lethal weapon-system with its target acquired, poised and rigid like—a candlestick.

In the very centre of the hood was a black circle, the foresight of Large's rifle which he never could have raised had he not been faster than the animal in the first place for the slightest movement now would surely trigger a strike. He very nearly fired instinctively, but first the reasoning part of his surprise-encounter drill demanded to be used; what if the enemy heard the shot? Worse, his three men would certainly hear it and not being able to see the cause—in fact, Scholey could and his rifle too was levelled at what looked like a "dirty great yellow dinner-plate" just above and to the left of Large's head while his thoughts whirred similarly—would immediately break into head-on contact procedure, leap into the bush, put down saturating fire which really would give the show away, and even retire to a rendezvous in the wrong direction, back near the river.

Whether all that would be more dangerous than the snake's strike depended on the latter's speed, of which he had no experience. Large judged the distance and supposed he might just have a chance of avoiding the strike by jumping sideways. He resolved to spring with his left leg should that be necessary; but an appreciable time, perhaps half a second, having already elapsed without its moving and Large giving it no new cause to do so, the tableau remained frozen for a further prolonged but indeterminable period.

At last, the snake—whose fearsome panoply was donned solely in consequence of its own initial terror—retracted its hood to the stowed position, shrank visibly in diameter, and coiled itself down neatly behind a log that lay between them.

Large walked carefully round the end of the log and hissed to Scholey, "Snake!," meaning a significant one or he would not have bothered. Scholey followed him, and passed the word to Millikin who also made the detour but delayed saying anything, perhaps because he had not seen the drama, until Walsh stepped over the log at precisely the wrong spot; whereupon the latter performed that inelegant ballet which comes naturally to people who think they may be treading on poisonous snakes they cannot see and growled, ''Thanks very much.''

They found a cut-off track, crossed it warily, and then made for home at a great rate. The acrid smell of burning fuel borne on the southerly wind kept up with them for the first 1,000 yards, indicating hearteningly that the fire had taken hold well. At sundown they reversed their priorities, turned through a right angle, and taking scrupulous care not to leave tracks or make noise with one man on guard behind against an enemy follow-up, found a good thick basha-site. As they pitched camp the enemy reacted at last by firing mortars well to the west of them, and Walsh commented with relief:

''That's fine, they think we've gone that way.''

But the crafty old sergeant replied: ''You know why they're mortaring *there*? Because that's what they want you to think; they've probably got men searching *here*.''

''Ah.''

Nevertheless, he also told them to cook a double-size meal because they were as safe in deep jungle as they could ever hope to be and tomorrow they had far to go at full speed; morale was a factor too, his own included. Millikin sent his signal. Then they rested, satisfied in mind and body.

The story might have been allowed to end there but it had the bit between its teeth and seemed determined that the last line, as in all good fiction, should be a crunch one. Having lightened their loads by burying all but a day's rations, they headed east across their incoming route into country which ''Old Joe'' Lock had told him offered good going and did. They crossed the Achan to Poeri track without incident and, keeping well clear of where the enemy platoon had been, hit the border ridge south of their entry-point. But the original landing-point was still the closest so they pressed on, maintaining their speed. Millikin now showed signs of distress. He was not yet at his peak after his operation and seemed to be dehydrated from not drinking enough water, an easy omission when time is short and sweat profuse. His load was the heaviest too, but despite his wasting strength he refused to be relieved of the radio, panting ''you bums couldn't use it.''

Late in the afternoon Large felt sure he was near the landing-point, but navigation was imprecise among these low hills with no dominant feature. Being concerned not to make Millikin walk any further than necessary, Large halted off the line of march. He instructed Millikin to signal for a helicopter to home onto their Sarbe and indicate their course and distance to the landing-point. But Flight Lieutenant Danger was keen to do better than that, and arriving within half an hour made to winch them out there and then. The wire proving too short, his crew extended it with parachute strops and two body-belts. Scholey inserted himself into one of these while the bergens were secured to the other. Up they went together, and at 120 feet from the ground when the winch reached the limits of its travel with a slight jar, the belt with the bergens fell off.

"It was pot-luck I'd chosen the right strop," Scholey said jauntily, later; but he was far from merry at the time, as Large, watching him swinging below the chopper with no hope of getting in and wide-eyed with horror, could see even from the ground.

That really is the end of the story. The landing-point was just a couple of hundred yards along their original line and soon they were on their way; by chopper to Lundu, Pioneer to Kuching, Land Rover to headquarters, and red carpet into the Brigadier's office. Large eventually received a Mention in Despatches and gave an oak-leaf to each of the others because he regarded it as shared between them all. It excited little comment in the Regiment because few knew what had been achieved and Large was not the one to tell them in other than the baldest outline, even officially; nor was there much more within the patrol itself and that was unimpassioned:

Walsh says, "Lofty's quite a brave bloke; don't know why he didn't get more than an MID, the system I suppose."

Scholey more or less agrees. "You don't expect to get medals just for doing the job you're paid for, but it's nice when they come, in spite of different commanders having different ideas of what makes a brave deed."

Large says, "I'd have done it free of charge, I enjoyed it; anyone would have done the same if they'd had my luck."

Millikin says nothing because he died young as he knew he would, in a car crash near Hereford.

That, then, was a typical patrol; typical not least in being different from every other and thereby fully extending the initiative as well as the skill of the SAS for which its members had been recruited and trained, and warranting such a force in the Army's order of battle. There were other engagements and all patrols continued unflagging to amass the information that would permit effective infantry "Claret" operations. The enemy kept quiet about his reverses and General Lea was encouraged to increase the pressure.

The end of "D" Squadron's tour thus also ended the phase in which the SAS had the cross-border field to themselves. How had they done? "Pretty small beer," says Farrar-Hockley referring to the strikes, unarguably in terms of scale, and his is the objective view from the top. But so is Moerdani's, and he said that Large's exploit hurt much more than the loss of just one launch because the main Indonesian supply line suddenly became insecure and in need of urgent, widespread and unwelcome troop redeployment to guard it. Such can be the effects of pinpricks if stuck in the right places; and it would be surprising if those inflicted by the SAS did not combine with the defensive efforts of all the British security forces to deter the enemy's aggression, for it is a fact that Mongkus was the enemy's last major incursion into the First Division in 1965. The SAS sought to do no more than play their part anyway, having no illusions that they could win wars on their own.

CHAPTER 11

"GET BACK IN!"

"A" Squadron's Fourth Tour, May to September 1965

"A" Squadron returned to Borneo for a tour from which de la Billière, the Squadron commander, could be trusted to extract the last drop of interest. In Indonesia none dare oppose the communists while Soekarno had struck up a warm and ominous relationship with China. Plenty of Indonesian troops were available in Borneo and the Mongkus attempt was but a fortnight old.

The danger was compounded by Malaysia beginning to split at the seams and it was her viability which was at issue. The great gamble depended on whether Malays and Chinese could live peacefully together without the British, and stress built up to the point where Lee Kwan Yew felt it necessary to state that Singapore would not secede which, because it was said at all, was startling. In Sabah and Sarawak racial rivalry included the indigenous peoples, not all of whom lived primitively in the jungle, and the mainly Chinese communists posed a sinister and powerful threat. Altogether, Indonesia could not be greatly encouraged.

General Lea on the other hand was remarkably unmoved. He regarded the local politicians with whom he consorted as "the chummiest chaps in the world, but . . ."; though whatever his reservations he bore them with composure. The British still ran the Borneo territories in all essentials as colonies, to the locals' heartfelt relief so long as the threat lasted, and after 300 years of empire they were really very good. United by common class, language, and upbringing which imbued dedication to the welfare of subject peoples, the "old boy net" of administrators, policemen, merchants, planters, bankers, lawyers or soldiers need waste no time on preliminaries but went straight to the heart of a problem and decided a course of action. Air Chief

Marshal Sir John Grandy, who had relieved Admiral Begg as commander-in-chief at Singapore, was very much on the net and Lea worked in close harmony with him.

The Sarawak Commissioner of Police, Roy Henry, was another such stalwart; happily since the twin threats of invasion and revolution had to countered mainly by the Army and Police respectively and, the tasks overlapping, collaboration uninhibited by demarcation lines or jealous restrictive practises was vital. Henry's policy with the clandestine communists was to keep watchful tabs on them through his Special Branch, but not to clamp down unless they began active operations for fear of driving them further underground and losing touch. In some cases, however, facts came to light which could be tackled at once; such as at Lundu where the Army might help the Police by obstructing the flow of revolutionaries from across the border. Pooled evidence from both forces now revealed that the elusive camp at Batu Hitam was not an army garrison but a CCO staging-post, sited expressly so as not to be found and presenting a challenge to, obviously, the SAS.

Lea had every reason to keep the Indonesian Army and CCO well apart and authorized two infantry "Claret" operations in late May and early June in which 32 enemy soldiers were killed without loss, then paused to observe the effects. The SAS were not involved except as providers of information.

"A" Squadron operated exclusively from the First Division where the threat and the prospect of action were greatest; though it should be remembered that even there they were not the only SAS unit and that other teams operated along the entire frontier.

de la Billière had no other officers, an unthinkable shortcoming elsewhere in the Army but it scarcely mattered to him and not at all to the Troop Sergeants. Three, however, were in the pipeline. de la Billière had acquired them at Selection time with characteristic forcefulness, first by picking out the most promising candidates for their character and intelligence (if they could not get over the hills they would fail anyway) and telling them, "You want to join 'A' Squadron, don't you?" which, put like that, seemed a good idea though they had not considered it before. Then he went to work on the Commanding Officer with wearing insistence to give him these ardent volunteers. Mike Wilkes, Malcolm McGillivray and John Foley were finishing their jungle training and would join their Troops, 1, 2 and 3 respectively, in July.

4 Troop was still commanded by Sergeant Maurice Tudor who was first across, to Segoemen in the south, and had a most unhappy time. He and his patrol were set down on the wrong landing-point without knowing it, and unwittingly passing through friendly troop positions were shelled by their own side's artillery. They pressed on nevertheless and brought back much useful information.

The Squadron Sergeant-Major, Lawrence Smith, doubled as second in command and trebled as operations officer, there being nobody else; but in spite of all those duties he was told, asked, or decided (his "rapport" with his Squadron commander sometimes making it hard to determine precisely how decisions originated) to lead the first patrol to that high priority objective Batu Hitam. He took Corporal Bill Condie's team, which included Steve Callan (not and no relation to the unsavoury individual who achieved notoriety in Angola and was never in the SAS) and George "Geordie" Shipley, who will now assume responsibility for representing "A" Squadron as Large and Co. have done for "D." Seniority and experience came no nearer to solving the mystery, however; a local spoke willingly of life in the area, how an unwelcome Indonesian patrol came once a fortnight and demanded to be fed free, but there was positively no camp and that rang true.

After four days the radio broke down, so they had to climb to the border landing-point at the summit of a 5,000-foot peak in the Pueh Range where they shivered uncontrollably in their sweat-soaked clothes. But seeing their helicopter also toiling upwards, they keenly anticipated the hot showers and other delights of Kuching. The aircraft settled delicately like a dragonfly on the tiny plateau with its slender tail extending into limitless space; but instead of the doorway being clear for them to step inside, it was filled by no less a personage than de la Billière, to their distinct unease when he handed out a new radio and a pack of rations. He indicated the great green yonder to the westward with an imperious gesture, reminiscent of an old-time general from his horse, and commanded:

"Get back in."

Rapport or no, Smith was open-mouthed and speechless, at least until the aircraft had lifted a few feet, tipped itself over the edge and slid gracefully down the mountainside leaving him with explosive thoughts that fought against loyalty to produce an incoherent muttering, which in after years he articulated as:

"It rather saddened us."

A suspicion remains, however, that they were also just a little gratified at having an officer who was such an arch-fiend that he could get away with that sort of thing. They set off with a fierce determination to find the unmentionable camp.

But this was Batu Hitam and not to be found. "It just wasn't there, it couldn't have been," grumbled Smith after a further week during which they found much else; including, it pained them to report, a previous SAS patrol's basha-site clearly identified by two ration tins. Then they climbed back to their mountain-top as disconsolate as they had left it, except that this time they would surely be allowed out. The helicopter indeed came and without a passenger, but so did a low cloud. The pilot homed unerringly to their Sarbe and hovered so that his wheels projected through the mist at head height, but he himself could not see the ground nor talk to the men so had no choice but to go away. Shipley put the rice on to boil; the pilot returned for another try; whereupon Shipley threw the meal away and packed up hastily; whereupon . . . Three times the indomitable airman stretched the rules to help the soldiers until it was quite dark, after which they spent a particularly cheerless night through being hungry as well as cold. The pilot was back again in the morning before they imagined he could see to fly, so that they were not ready and had to bundle themselves inside clutching their belongings like a disorganized family going on holiday. They were gratefully impressed none the less, and said so.

KOEMBA AND BACK

The search for Batu Hitam continued concurrently with other patrols to many places. Second in priority came the Koemba where Sergeant Malcolm Allen went to explore west of Large's ambush but found only swamp, though he got near enough to hear the launches. The area was next visited by Condie and his musketeers, Trooper Kilgour replacing the Sergeant-Major. "And that," they recall with feeling, "was the time we were chased out."

Condie's watch on the Koemba was to be at Large's place because it had the only known approach. He and de la Billière discussed the wisdom of that, but, using the same involuted reasoning as Large, hoped that the enemy would not think the SAS so foolish as to go there twice. Their route was similar too, accepting the swamp for their final approach now that they knew its limits.

They took five days to reach the cut-off track. Each night the enemy mortared the area they were heading for so that the ever-lurking fear that they were being tracked without knowing it could be a reality; but they heard launches too, which suggested unconcerned routine. ''Geordie'' Shipley sensed the track before reaching it and halted the patrol. It was wide and well maintained, with a carpet of leaves and no footprints. After a pause during which photographs were taken, Condie motioned Shipley to cross. The latter looked right, left, right again, and just glimpsed a whitish blur of movement which with a little imagination could have been a local's T-shirt but just as easily a bird taking wing.

A Chinese Parliament ensued to discuss what Shipley had seen, or just did not see, but Shipley was not to be coerced into elaborating the bald truth that he could not even be certain that it was anything at all. Condie's decision was a hard one. To be caught on the wrong side of the track could be disastrous, and if Shipley's vision had been of a local, the man's instant disappearance must mean that he had seen and would probably report them; but the evidence was far too ephemeral for Condie's robust determination, reinforced as that was by the SAS ethic and now by the ''Get back in'' code as well.

They crossed without incident, pressed on into the swamp for 1,500 yards, basha'd down on an island and contemplated the morrow without enthusiasm. Nothing happened, but that they slowly realized was ominous it itself; no launches had plied the river during the afternoon and after dark the accustomed mortars failed to fire, suggesting that troops might have deployed against them. Then, already on edge, they were startled into rigidity by a stamping and snorting not far away which sounded less like a stag in rut than a native simulating one, probably to induce them to move and so reveal their position. It was a rotten night, without the rest that would have strengthened them for great exertions to come. At first light they moved west towards the spur and river.

Condie's navigation was good, dry land appeared, and before advancing to their goal they stopped for breakfast with a less than heartening brew and food to individual choice. A shot cracked, no great distance to the south, and was answered immediately by another to the north. All moisture left their mouths and could not be replaced by tea because that tasted like cyanide, while Condie's biscuit and Shipley's sardine became as ashes and had to be spewed out, but they were already half conditioned to discovery and mentally prepared for four more shots to the east from, and it was useless to pretend otherwise, their night camp.

So this was it; they were penned in by soldiers who knew of their presence and were actively hunting them, except to the west where the river ran; but even as they considered how best to exploit that gap they heard a launch, of whose idling engine they had been subconsciously aware, steering towards them at full throttle, grounding with a gravelly crunch, and disembarking its crew at the double; soldiers certainly, no need to see them.

One of Lieutenant-Colonel Woodhouse's more advanced discussion exercises was called to mind—"What would you do now?" The patrol's plight thus began to seem almost normal, and since there was only one thing to do anyway, they quietly shouldered their bergens and headed northeast between two sources of shooting. But scarcely had Shipley moved into his leading position on the new course than he shrank down into the swamp. An enemy patrol crossed their path some fifteen yards ahead; one that had not fired a shot; clever.

The position seemed hopeless, but Condie subjected his mind to pure objectivity. Escape was the aim, to be pursued like all aims with skill and vigour believing it to be attainable, and reason suggested that not all the factors were unfavourable. The jungle was the best place in the world to get lost and they were probably better trained than the enemy in its lore: hiding, moving, awareness, reaction, shooting. Every target they saw must be an enemy whereas the Indonesians could never be sure; and best of all, the enemy clearly had no walkie-talkies and had to reveal their positions by signal-shots. Having to move was a snag, but the men would be much quieter, less bulky and more agile without their bergens so Condie ordered those to be submerged and abandoned. But there was still that bloody track, where if they arrived by a miracle the enemy would certainly be waiting with machine-guns sited to fire along its length. It hardly seemed worth the effort even to start, but such frying-pan into fire reasoning was subjective and must be ruthlessly suppressed in favour of using all their energies to surviving *now*.

The patrol's progress was desperately slow with every muscle under conscious control lest an involuntary movement should swish the water or rustle leaves. Adrenaline coursed and could not be dissipated by exertion, but the enemy played the game by firing signal-shots just when they were most needed so that the pattern of his patrols—four at least—became clear. For five tremulous hours they moved thus, their course varying as the shots dictated between northwest and east like a sailing ship clawing off a storm-swept lee shore, until the seeming miracle occurred and no more shots came from the north.

Now for the track. Shipley did not expose even half an eye to see if it was clear, but stopped and beckoned the others; they bunched and leapt across as one man, offering a target too fleeting even for Large. Quite easy, really! Then they froze to listen for evidence that they had been seen. There was none, and light in heart and burden they motored away.

They expended most of their little remaining nervous energy evading an alert enemy through his forward platoons and on the border itself; even the landing-point could be as dangerous as anywhere, especially if natural relief and relaxation were not firmly suppressed, though prodding for mines with "parangs" helped to concentrate the attention. While de la Billière listened to their story he could see they were drained, and sensing their brooding tension he told Condie:

"Take them into Kuching and get drunk."

They continued to niggle his mind, however, as he resumed his interrupted consideration of how the Squadron should be employed.

The enemy's much improved defence of the Koemba paid tribute to Large's success and confirmed that the river remained an attractive target for the coming but seemingly delayed "Claret" offensive. de la Billière was concerned both to speed things up and to ensure that the SAS were fully involved. They certainly should be, for only they knew the way and could offer the infantry valuable help as decoys or agitators; but much SAS experience showed that pressure would probably be needed, and he was only a major.

The omens were favourable nevertheless. Brigadier Cheyne wanted nothing better than to get his forces moving, provided that could be done within the constraints of secrecy and minimal casualties. General Lea was no less keen despite his heavy responsibility for balancing military necessity against the risk of political disaster, especially as the enemy had just perpetrated a mischief that cried aloud for condign retribution. This incident had been a small-scale affair but heavy with portent; two parties of Indonesian troops had penetrated to the road between Kuching and Serian and there joined with local Chinese communist guerillas to attack a police station and loyal Chinese families with a brutality rare in this campaign. It was clearly aimed at intimidating the Chinese community into supporting the communists against the government, and they were duly terrified. The government too was alarmed, for this could well be the start of that junction between Indonesian Army and CCO which was feared as the greatest, perhaps uncontrollable, threat.

What de la Billière now needed was an ally, and as though sent by fate Lieutenant-Colonel Nick Neill and his 2/2nd Goorkhas arrived to take over the Lundu front. Neill was a fighter, dedicated like all Gurkha officers to his soldiers. He called them his hatchet-men for, despite their charm, humour, kindliness and romantic origins, fighting was their first love. They had joined the British Army to find it, and under officers like Neill they did. He believed singlemindedly that the function of an infantry battalion being to fight the Queen's enemies, its commander should use his utmost endeavour to get at them, leaving to his seniors the task of restraining him should their hearts grow faint.

Neill and de la Billière therefore formed a pressure group which Cheyne found difficult to resist; not that he tried very hard, for what commander is not inspired by subordinates with unlimited enthusiasm? Other battalions, just as efficient, keen and well led, had to wait for their chances merely because their COs lacked (if that is the right word) Neill's damnable persistence, enhanced by de la Billière's, which would obtain the lion's share of the hunting for the 2/2nd. Now, however, Cheyne kept them chafing for the statutory month while they familiarized themselves minutely with their area and demonstrated that they were at the peak of their form. But he did allow reconnaissance for planning purposes and the first patrol with SAS guides was even now being organized.

In pondering these matters de la Billière did not forget Condie's patrol, for he had seen that look on men's faces before when 3 Troop had returned from Shi'b Taym. Having then been through hell himself and being obsessed with his own guilt, he had lavished praise and sympathy on them, led them an easy life, and found to his astonishment that they became even more sorry for themselves and their restoration to fighting fitness was delayed for an unnecessarily long time. He learnt the lesson that old-fashioned "bull" if administered perceptively could be a far more effective and therefore kinder therapy. The four musketeers had scarcely consumed one of the many bottles of whisky needed to fulfil their orders faithfully when a messenger brought an immediate summons that starkly evoked memories of being abandoned on a mountain-top and deep foreboding. Sure enough:

"I've had a re-think. It'd be much better for you chaps if you went straight back in again; the Gurkhas want to be taken to the Koemba tomorrow so go and get ready."

Saddened again, they did so; but as Condie says:

"He was so professional you had to take it from him; in the ops room 24 hours a day (General Lea once told him to take a night off but he wouldn't), knew everything the moment it happened and took instant action, and when you were in the jungle you *knew* that."

They knew it because de la Billière encouraged off-duty patrols to wander into the operations room to see it done, which was good professional morale-building. Professionalism was certainly his aim, but humanity obstinately followed closely and sometimes overtook. Despite his outward disregard for his men's feelings, inwardly he could now hardly bear to send them back into danger while he himself was safe. He resolved to take the first opportunity of going on patrol himself, suppressing what he knew to be true—because he just had to go—that he was far more use to the men in base.

ACROSS THE BEMBAN

Major John Edwardes's Cross-Border Scouts had meanwhile continued to harass the enemy, with growing success because Edwardes either led them himself or sent his attached SAS to do so. This his orders forbade, but he was no pirate; the task could not be achieved otherwise and his apparently swashbuckling disregard for authority really stemmed from duty and demanded high moral courage. But now the order was partially revoked for the important task of finding and disrupting the CCO trail, which led obscurely back into Kalimantan from Batu Hitam, itself undiscovered but being searched for by others; only he himself was still restrained as being too well briefed in current Intelligence. Realizing that this time he could not hope to evade the eye of authority, he stayed behind to control operations from the longhouse he had built for his scouts at a lonely part of the coast and known as The Island.

de la Billière allotted half of 2 Troop to Edwardes, although only three men joined at the start of the tour: "Rover" Slater, Jimmy Green, and their leader Corporal Rob Roberts, a man of

great stature in body and spirit, like Don Large. A gentle giant
except with the enemy, Roberts was highly motivated, expert in
most skills, and blessed with the divine gift of leadership to
which men responded not just willingly but eagerly. The Ibans
and Land Dyaks learned to worship him in a week, which was
all the time he was allowed before leading his first foray; and if
it is thought imprudent, even irresponsible, to send a lowly corporal with two troopers and eighteen peradventurous headhunters to find and possibly attack a camp beyond a major river
10,000 yards inside enemy territory, events would prove such
doubts to be misplaced. The camp was the first CCO staging-
post back from Batu Hitam, and Edwardes had good Intelligence reasons for supposing it to be somewhere on Gunong
Kalimantan at the main bend of the River Bemban.

Roberts crossed the river north of the objective, apparently
undetected; the natives may have had their weak points, but it
was reassuring that they would miss no signs of any followers.
Two days later, after a slow and cautious approach, he established an operating base on the mountain's lower slopes and
began the search. Two armed Chinese were seen almost at once
and raised hopes of soon finding the camp; but, as at Batu Hitam, the CCO proved themselves clever at hiding and for the
next two days not even the scouts spotted any human indications. Then came the first significant discovery; a track, cleared
of jungle for ten feet on either side and so wide that a Land
Rover could have driven down it.

It ran northwest-wards towards the mountain and must surely
lead to the camp, but no; they followed it by looping and it just
went up and over, on and on. After dark, Roberts, Slater and
four scouts walked down it the other way. Their persistence
seemed at last to be rewarded when they came to the river with
a well-built log bridge and the dim outlines of huts on the far
side where they had no reason to expect a village. Then they
saw what they had previously missed in the darkness, a telephone wire suspended above the track and across the bridge.
This must be the camp. Right; in the morning they would "take
it out."

Before first light they were back with the whole team, crossing the bridge stealthily, surrounding their objective like malig-
nant ghosts and waiting, tautly patient, until the sky lightened.
Soon the inhabitants rose to go about their business, chatting
unconcernedly but causing Border Scout Ansang to start involuntarily and whisper (in rough translation from the Land Dyak):

"My goodness it's a small world! That's my uncle Gaya."

With Roberts's approval, Ansang shed his military kit and went forward unarmed for a family reunion with his uncle, Auntie Gawani and several cousins. He learnt much of great interest. No, this was not a camp but a new village built within the last few months as jungle dwellers do when their old land is impoverished. The nearest army base was six miles upriver and, yes, Gaya knew of a Chinese camp on the mountain; he was strictly forbidden from going there, but strongly suspected that if you went up the track to where a dip followed a rise and turned right at the big fig-tree with the ripe fruit you could not miss it.

Roberts withdrew his men to the west bank, putting the river between them and their base, and considered. The patrol had been exposed not only to the family circle but to anyone with eyes to see; their footprints too were all over the track and would inevitably be noticed by the next traveller. Aggressive action must therefore be taken at once or not at all; but the camp's position being still uncertain, Roberts decided to cut the telephone wire and tempt the enemy into a trap.

Expecting the reaction to come from the CCO camp, Roberts took Slater and nine scouts into ambush 800 yards from the river in that direction, while the third SAS trooper, Jimmy Green, with Sergeant Nibau and the rest of the scouts covered the bridge. It was there, six hours later, that the enemy in fact came. The first five of a seven-man patrol, two of them Chinese, were on the bridge when Green sprang the ambush; the scouts responded to training and leadership with exemplary discipline and accuracy, hitting all five and knocking them into the water. Number six, who was on the far bank, managed to fire a few wild rounds but was then hit and also fell in. The last man was wounded too, but got away.

Three minutes after the first shot, Green's men were on their way north to the rendezvous, and Roberts acted similarly on hearing the racket. When all were together again, he ordained a rest and a brew because they had been at high tension without sustenance for a long time and no enemy follow-up seemed likely. He underestimated Indonesian determination however. The seven men had been only an advance party, another group was following a short distance behind and after a pause these came into action with a mortar whose bursts rolled slowly closer. Disquiet and itchy feet were evident among the scouts, but Roberts did not fancy his tea too hot and savoured it lingeringly, nicely calculating the enemy's progress and, like Sir Francis

Drake, the steadying effect of such apparent unconcern. Then they moved further north to the crossing place, checked it minutely by daylight, crossed in darkness, and made their way home in the morning with all convenient speed.

Edwardes was delighted and said so warmly, disdaining the rather chilly SAS convention whereby the best is only to be expected and is therefore unremarked. But the camp on Gunong Kalimantan had still to be found, so he set about planning a larger operation with stronger SAS backing, accepting the time taken in training and rehearsal which would allow the enemy to simmer down.

SPOILS OF WAR

To stir the enemy up again, there now arrived Captain Malcolm McGillivray, a lean, taut young man from the Black Watch with a restless urge to go always much further. He had coerced his reluctant Regiment into sparing him for the SAS; first, by taking Selection without authority and passing easily, that degree of exertion being habitual to him; and then, it is said, by eating nothing but porridge with such dour persistence that his brother officers could not endure it and weakly let him go. Now 2 Troop Commander, he brought with him to the Island Troopers Franks, Henry and "Taff" Bilbao; and to complete the SAS component for the Mount Kalimantan operation came those three musketeers Condie, Callan and Shipley, getting back in yet again as their inexorable destiny dictated.

Air reconnaissance produced excellent photographs of a clearing with huts high up on the mountain, to Roberts's surprise because he thought he had searched that position thoroughly. A full-size replica was built which the team of ten SAS and 21 scouts attacked repeatedly until McGillivray was satisfied. They set out on 9 July 1965, and even as they neared the first rise, a huge monitor lizard lifted his venerable grey head and regarded them benevolently. The scouts were delighted at this good omen; and so were the SAS, patronizingly, there being no ladder aslant the track.

In five days they had crossed the River Bemban and reached the mountain's lower slopes. On the sixth day they split into patrols and began the search, full of confidence in their Intelligence and the lizard which soon seemed justified when excited scouts returned with news of bootprints and the smell of cooking. They reported in the language of their own conventions, which was logical enough to them but not immediately comprehensible to another culture.

"How far was it?" McGillivray asked; a simple enough question he would have thought, but the reply reminded him of his old schoolmaster setting a problem in mental arithmetic:

"Half as long as it took me to get there and back."

"Oh very well! Let 'x' equal . . ."

Then the scent went cold; the tracks faded and the appetizing odour had no apparent source. The team worked their way south to the big track that Roberts had ambushed but the camp eluded them, nor were there any outlying signs as would be expected around a place with a resident community unless the latter were unusually clever. That might indeed have been the case; McGillivray had spent many hours memorizing features and key angles which now fitted the actual terrain in every detail, except the one that mattered. He was always accompanied by "Rover" Slater, nominally the signaller but who saw his role more as a familiar spirit charged with stimulating his master with astringent goading. Whatever McGillivray proposed, Slater disputed, and when weary and frustrated they stood in a glade of virgin jungle and McGillivray sighed:

"Everything checks, it *must* be here," he was granted no solace but only further torment:

"Well it obviously isn't, is it?—Sir."

The lot of a junior SAS officer is never easy, but if he subordinates pride to accomplishing the task he will get by. The relationship shared by McGillivray and Slater ensured that every avenue was explored, the jungle offering plenty of avenues. McGillivray even contributed his exceptional ability at treeclimbing, which he had acquired as a boy in Kenya up coconut palms; only the tallest would serve and although their soaring trunks were branchless for a hundred feet, he shinned lithely to the tops, where the views were magnificent but the camp formed no part of them.

They never did find it and failure was hard to bear. But the track was undoubtedly the main CCO trail to Batu Hitam, and a successful ambush on it would be a good second best. Early on the 16th, McGillivray took Slater, Sergeant Nibau and a bright English-speaking Iban called Percy to a place he had previously earmarked some 2,000 yards northwest from the river. A big log spanned a steep-sided gully which flattened out on the near, north, side into an unobstructed semicircle, across which one could shoot from perfect cover at anyone on the log whence there would be no escape. "A beastly way to hit them, but effective," and that was the point.

As though to confirm that assessment, four heavily-laden locals crossed the log where they were wholly exposed and vulnerable. McGillivray sent Nibau and Percy to fetch Roberts and the team, retaining only the constant Slater who, for the moment, could find nothing to disparage. Then, from the left, came a patrol of soldiers. McGillivray gripped his rifle. Slater thought, "Crikey, he's going to start shooting" and gripped it too, just to make sure but unnecessarily; there were eleven men in the enemy patrol and at five-yards range shooting would not have been a good idea. They looked to be Indonesian. One soldier had a light machine-gun, the rest rifles. They moved fast and purposefully.

McGillivray met the team at a lying-up place and immediate rendezvous 200 yards to the rear. Then he took Roberts and fifteen men forward to keep the first watch. He placed each man individually, in three groups with different functions though forming one continuous line at from five to twenty yards back from the track depending on the cover. In the commanding position abreast the log were Roberts, Franks, Nibau and three scouts; they were the killers. Condie, Callan and Shipley, each with a scout, formed the right-hand flank group; their tasks were to spot the enemy early and report him by pulling the cord which stretched along the whole line, then to pick off any enemy trying to escape and, finally, to give warning of any counterattack. Acting similarly on the left were Henry, Bilbao and their scouts. All was ready by one o'clock in the afternoon and the tense hunter/hunted syndrome set in.

Not expecting the enemy patrol to return until the evening, McGillivray went back to ensure that the rendezvous was organized to accept the withdrawal after a contact, a crucial moment when each man must be checked by name and the enemy prevented from joining in. He did not like his first position and had the bergens moved to a better one. Slater griped that this was most improper because the ambush party might miss it even if told of the change; but McGillivray planned to relieve the watch before anything was likely to happen and all would then be fully briefed.

At two o'clock drenching rain fell, its hissing noise together with that of the wind lashing the tree-tops, smothering all other sounds. Then, at three-thirty, the enemy returned. They came so fast with heads down, weapons slung and clearly intent only to be home and dry that Shipley, out on his limb in thick undergrowth with little more than a peephole view of the track, almost missed seeing the blur of the leading man; but he pulled his cord and then again, five times in all, as rapidly as he could jerk his arm. Condie received the signal, amplified it to Roberts who alerted his group just in time. The five soldiers were scarcely on the log than they were off it again, dead or wounded.

"Stop!," ordered Roberts; but after a pause quite long enough for the message to register, Bilbao fired two rounds on the left flank and earned his chief's incisive displeasure. He was, however, only doing his precise duty, having spotted one of the enemy trying to crawl away.

Then something much more drastic happened on the right. Even as the ambush was sprung, Shipley became aware of a second enemy group, who now reacted violently. Deploying off the track on the near side, they put down a hail of fire with their machine-gun and rifles up the line of the ambush, in preparation it seemed for the classic manoeuvre of "rolling it up from the flank." He was, literally, the flank, and waiting to be "rolled up" seemed to him to serve no useful purpose even if he were still alive when it happened, which seemed unlikely. Branches snapped, foliage flew, saplings shattered, bullets whined, thudded and cracked, but he himself could see nothing beyond a few feet and was so enclosed that he could not even swing his rifle.

Condie was not so immediately threatened, but was quick to see the danger to his juniors and shouted, "Fall back on me."

Shipley and Callan began to do so, joining each other with their scouts. Then they saw that lower ground to the rear would be "dead" from the firing and there they dashed, missing Condie who crept forward into the barrage to check that they were safe. Condie was what the SAS call "a hard man." Shipley and Callan continued to the rendezvous because it was standard drill to retire immediately after an ambush; arriving, they were greatly agitated to find nothing and nobody there.

McGillivray, mortified and furious, listened to the action in which standard operating procedure strictly forbade him from joining. Slater prodded him about the old rendezvous so, in a desperate need to do something, he took two scouts part of the way there and told them to guide the ambush party to the right place. Then he met the first of the retiring scouts, excited and running pretty fast but by no means panicky, who shouted, he thought, that their revered "Rob" was hurt. That decided McGillivray to go forward, standard operating procedure or not,

which earned him a blast of invective from his far from incapacitated corporal that rocked him backwards with its virulence,
but observing the other's rifle levelled squarely at his chest, he
accepted the rebuke meekly.

Firing continued on the right, but the enemy was plainly deterred from advancing through the thick cover. McGillivray then
discussed the position with Roberts who told him that under the
log were at least two bodies which had not yet been searched.
Two scouts, Ibans, stood near, strangely expectant, and when
McGillivray told them to collect the weapons and any papers
they leapt forward exultingly; but only when they drew their
"parangs," which would be useless for that purpose, did he
realize helplessly what he had done. Then he visited every man's
position in the ambush to see for himself that none was left
behind wounded, a selfless act which in Shoot-and-Scoot days
might have been thought unprofessional, but not now.

McGillivray collected the scouts, who had done their duty by
retrieving the enemies' rifles and exceeded it by taking their
heads as well. Back at the rendezvous the scenes of triumph and
jubilation took the British unawares and astonished them; these
people were not generally thought to have taken more than the
occasional head since the Japanese left twenty years before, but
there was no doubt now that the urge persisted very, very
strongly. Attached to its body, a head is the abode and window
of intelligence and personality, sometimes attractive, always interesting; sever it, and the mask of those attributes instantly
becomes revolting and terrifying, even though the amputation
is made with the skill and precision of a surgeon. Put it in a
plastic bag, moreover, and distortion of the features makes it
unendurably loathsome; so that the SAS, tough and hard though
they liked to think themselves, turned away and considered what
they had seen.

Could such expertise have derived from folklore alone? Practise, surely, must have played a part. Those plastic bags too, new
and of exactly the right size; for what other purpose might they
have been brought? And in the face of such tribal fervour was it
not inconceivable to tell the Ibans to throw the bloody things
away? Even dangerous? McGillivray's turn of mind slanted towards the sinister, and he wondered whether his own head might
have been forfeit if he had tried to thwart their passion. He knew
that was absurd for they were his friends and colleagues in shared
fun and hardship; nevertheless, he thought it.

But, as Shipley observed, the heads were relevant only to the Ibans, whose motivation for a worthy cause was thereby strengthened, and to the enemy, whose morale was likely to be affected more negatively. No actual harm was done to anyone, but it might be should such welcome ammunition be passed to hostile propagandists. The best policy was for no one to know. It happened therefore that a certain officer not so far up the line of command and by no means noted for absence of mind was able to say with the ring of absolute candour:

"Cutting off heads and putting them in plastic bags is not an incident I readily recall."

"CLARET"

In July 1965 General Lea at last authorized an intensified series of "Claret" strikes to make absolutely clear to the Indonesians that their proper place was behind their own frontier; quite a distance behind it, in fact, so that they would find crossing less and less easy, though there was never any intention of occupying Kalimantan. The main SAS commitment being to help the infantry, they were even willing to forego their own excitement if necessary, but very much hoped they would not have to. That their prime motivation was adventure for adventure's sake and not "seeking the bubble reputation" was well illustrated by these cross-border operations since very few people, even in the SAS, would know what they achieved.

The first operation would not be until August. Failure was unacceptable so there must be no skimping of reconnaissance, planning and training. Some of 22 SAS joined infantry recce parties; others were held back by de la Billière to train for a joint operation he had devised with Neill of the 2/2nd Goorkhas. Neill had named the operation "Kingdom Come," "because that's where we're going to send the Indos, or wherever it is that Muslims go."

The few remaining cross-border patrols concentrated on discovering tactical details of particular interest to the Gurkhas. Sergeant-Major Lawrence Smith did so in the Sentimo area in preparation for "Kingdom Come"; he found a large army camp on the Poeteh tributary south of Berjongkong. Sergeant Malcolm Allen of 1 Troop made two trips to the vicinity of Sawah, the centre of communications for Bemban and the cultivated area around Batu Hitam, but the open country offered little scope for "Claret." Even for a four-man patrol it was hazardous enough;

Allen climbed a lone tree for a view of the wide "ladang" whereupon three locals sat down under it for a rest and a chat, but he remained undiscovered like King Charles before him because man is essentially an earthbound creature who does not naturally lift his eyes to the heights.

Two more of de la Billière's young officers arrived and cut their jungle teeth. Captain John Foley of the Royal Green Jackets took after his forbear Thomas, one of Nelson's captains who was renowned within that gallant band for keeping an excellent table as well as being a thorough planner, innovative tactician and indomitable fighter who would certainly have been welcome in the SAS. Foley took command of 3 Troop and went first to Berjongkong, where he saw a great deal of military activity from very close range but skilfully avoided becoming involved in it.

1 Troop was taken over by Captain Mike Wilkes whose first objective was the route between Poeri and the important enemy forward base at Kaik. It seemed from the map to offer ideal conditions for company-size forces to ambush both track and river after a short, hilly, jungle-covered approach. More detail was needed which Wilkes provided: there were no fewer than three tracks, which might have been confusing had it not been for a telephone wire that revealed the military priority of one, and the trees continued right down to the 40-foot wide river. Reporting all this, Wilkes was told to come straight out, which surprised him as being an apparent reversal of de la Billière's normal form. It saddened him too as he wanted to set his own ambush. He argued, not having been long enough in "A" Squadron to know better.

Surprised again but now satisfied, Wilkes had no sooner returned than he was told to get back in and tap the wire. This was not a standard drill and two days were spent improvising the gear and practising with it; an ordinary portable tape-recorder was to be connected to the line by tapping-wires with the smallest terminals available, which nevertheless stood out starkly as alien in the jungle environment. "Gipsy" Smith's moss technique might have helped, but Wilkes hit on the idea of stripping the bark from a sapling and wrapping it round the wires to camouflage them as creepers. Two claymore mines were sited to cover the tapping-point to forestall any suspicious enemy from reacting aggressively.

All conversations were recorded over five days, at the end of which Wilkes felt he knew the main personalities quite well without understanding a word they said: the routine signallers; the soft-spoken man who courted his listener's attention; the one who snapped too readily and alienated his; and the commander whose advent on the line was heralded by a respectful silence and the timbre of whose voice demanded attention and obedience.

Nobody used the track for four days. Did that indicate suspicion, possibly caused by extraneous noises fed unwittingly into the line? Perhaps, though talk continued normally without noticeable tension. On the fifth day, however, there came a patrol of eight paratroopers, very smart, well-equipped and extremely alert. They stopped, apparently for a breather, right opposite the observation post, and noticed at once that something was not as it should be. As good jungle soldiers, they did not advertise their unease, but the equally uneasy watchers were in no doubt that they felt it by their hastening on without finishing their cigarettes. Just as hastily the SAS unrigged their gear and decamped, not a moment too soon because the enemy paras acted as smartly as they looked by advancing up the flank in a cut-off movement and engaging with their mortar.

The tapes were safely delivered but Wilkes never kenw what they contained, to his disappointment. The original aim of finding a good "Claret" objective for the Gurkhas had also been achieved. Neill was delighted and made a plan which he code-named "Blood Alley," not being a man to mince his words and knowing that soldiers must be sent into action with a simple and explicit aim; in this case to kill.

By August the 2/2nd Goorkhas had worked off their probation period and shown their fitness, so there was no further need to resist Neill's importunity. Other battalions would also deal the enemy stinging blows across the Sabah and Sarawak frontiers, but because the 2/2nd worked closely with 22 SAS—with whom this book is concerned—their operations must serve to illustrate all.

A month to the day after the 2/2nd's arrival on the Lundu front, Neill launched Operation "Guitar Boogie." The objective of the Support Company under its temporary commander Captain Surendraman Gurung was the River Sentimo below Babang Baba, the approach to which was now well mapped by the SAS after much patrolling in the area; but even so the going was difficult, this time because the swamp was low and the water so muddy that the only means of drinking was by catching rain,

and little fell. That was typical of the unexpected hazards for
which adventurers must always be ready, in addition to those
they anticipate. It is sometimes said that Gurkhas are not invariably doggedly persistent when the project is routine or the
end indeterminate, but all things were possible now that action
beckoned. Thirsty but undetected they reached the river and
killed eight soldiers in a longboat; no more, in fact, than Letts
had done with four men further up the river, but the comparison
is far from odious, eight were all there were.

Neill was pleased on several counts. First, he could now reassure his seniors that company-size raids to the full 10,000-
yard limit could achieve success without casualties; that is, of
course, if undertaken by the 2/2nd Goorkhas, he could not vouch
for anyone else. Secondly, he was pleased with Support Company for withholding fire until the range was at its least and
thereby killing the greatest possible number, that being their aim
as he emphasized again and again. Brutal it might sound, brutal
indeed it was, but aggressors who renounce gentle behaviour
are discouraged by nothing less. Once they put their hands up,
well and good, but until then the 2/2nd would kill every enemy
soldier they could find, and they would search diligently. Thirdly,
Neill was pleased with the SAS:

"Of all British soldiers I rate them highest. I planned my first
operations entirely on their information and found that everything they said was true; I couldn't have done it without them."

That was indeed praise even with the qualification "British,"
Gurkhas to a Gurkha officer not being comparable with anyone.

"KINGDOM COME"–"BLOOD ALLEY"

In August 1965 Soekarno fell ill and was expected to die. The
Indonesian communists saw their chance and stepped up their
preparations for seizing power with a purge of right-wing politicians and a crescendo of abuse at their enemies. Malaysia too
seemed more than usually uncertain of her corporate destiny.
Tunku Abdul Rahman expelled Singapore from the federation,
fearing that the thrusting Chinese would dominate the easygoing
Malays in their own country, and Southeast Asia wondered anxiously whether Malaysia would first fall apart and then be taken
over piecemeal. Voices were raised urging Britain's immediate
withdrawal, but she remained resolute amid the confusion. Operation "Kingdom Come" was launched; though Southeast Asia
knew nothing of that.

It was the largest cross-border operation ever mounted, with no fewer than six major ambushes by the 2/2nd Goorkhas on or near the rivers Koemba and Sentimo, while 1 and 3 Troops SAS went a little further to provoke the enemy into movement. It was also nearly the greatest wash-out. Rain, torrential even for Borneo, fell unremittingly for five days and flooded some normally dry places to a depth of ten feet. SAS and Gurkhas floundered, waded and swam, with high fortitude but sodden misery and a growing conviction that the task was truly impossible, as it proved to be for four of the Gurkha teams and all the SAS.

de la Billière was there as he had promised himself, with 1 Troop, supported by Squadron Headquarters in the person of his trusted companion of much campaigning, signaller "Geordie" Low. Low possessed the same gift for establishing communication as Millikin, and he also made good his leader's physical disabilities of colour-blindness and partial deafness with intuitive understanding. But even Low could not raise 3 Troop, so that de la Billière's horizon was limited to a few watery yards; all he could command was 1 Troop, which Mike Wilkes was fully competent to do by himself without a heavyweight treading on his toes, and the only decision needed was miserably to throw in the saturated towel.

Worse still—no, the thought was ungenerous in those who fail where others succeed so that SAS confined their emotion to ruefulness—two of the Gurkha forces accomplished their missions brilliantly. Major Lauderdale with 100 men reached the River Koemba near Poeri with unfaltering determination, necessarily discounting concealment and employing any method that served including building bridges; but boldness and the weather enlisted fortune on his side so that concealment was, in fact, preserved and a boat-load of ten soldiers killed.

Support Company went to the River Sentimo again under its appointed commander, Captain Bullock. There was so much fresh water this time—waist- or shoulder-deep depending on whether one was a Briton or a Gurkha—that the river-bank's position had to be determined by probing with the feet. Only eight men at a time could stand there and Bullock changed them round every 90 minutes, except for himself. On the first day a boat was paddled into the ambush by a local whose eyes met Bullock's, and who then paddled distinctly faster out of it; on the second day a python of impressive length, girth and aspect swam sinuously between the already immobile men on a level with their eyes and scared them into complete rigidity.

By the third day Bullock was numb from the waist down, but his resolution was unimpaired, and justified. A boat came by with four soldiers, who could only have recognized the channel as a path between two lines of trees because water lay everywhere; they could scarcely have been aware of their peril before they were all killed.

Lauderdale and Bullock had saved "Kingdom Come" from failure, but the enemy had not been hit as hard as intended and two more operations therefore followed quickly. One was "Blood Alley" between Poeri and Kaik, where Wilkes had paved the way and Condie had later taken Major Geoff Ashley of "C" Company, 2/2nd Goorkhas for a personal view. Ashley was a bold officer, as would be expected in the 2/2nd where the other sort did not last long, with a rare talent for imposing his will on the enemy. Having placed his main force of 45 in ambush on the track, he himself took ten men forward to the river. It was a bold move because he would be very uncomfortably placed should the enemy come first along the track in strength and force the Gurkhas to retire after a fight, but it also showed flair because the enemy actually came in the order he expected. First, six men in a boat, who were all killed, and then, triggered by the noise, a large body racing down the track and probably hoping to catch that by now ubiquitous menace—a small SAS patrol.

Ashley's sergeant, Lalsing Thapa, let the first fifteen into the trap and his men killed them all. It was then that Ashley's foresight proved masterly; the remaining enemy reformed quickly and came in bravely for a "roll-up" counter-attack, but the flank group of Gurkhas was waiting for precisely that in precisely the right place and exacted another six lives. In all, 27 young Indonesians died. That was more like it; a pity, of course, but Confrontation had only to be called off for the killing to stop. In the meantime, no track or river was safe from the risk of such casualties, which were quite unacceptable, tactically and morally. The Indonesians began the process of withdrawing their forward bases behind natural obstacles such as rivers, and as for raiding into Sarawak the question just did not arise.

"JACK SPRAT"–"HELL FIRE"

After "Kingdom Come," "Hell Fire"; at least that was Neill's progressive intention for the Indonesians, but the fire turned out to be mutual and the hell too, very nearly. Bullock had barely time to dry out before being sent back in the with 65 men of his Support Company, who were beginning to know the Sentimo area well; and similarly with de la Billière and Wilkes's 1 Troop, accompanied this time by 4 Troop (still commanded by Sergeant Maurice Tudor), for this was to be another joint venture.

Gurkha and SAS plans were but loosely coordinated, the latter even choosing their own codename "Jack Sprat" with more subtle but no less deadly overtones of meaning. The Gurkhas were to ambush the Poeteh tributary, the enemy's supply route between Babang Baba and the camp south of Berjongkong which Sergeant-Major Lawrence Smith had discovered on his last patrol. The mission promised to be interesting, so Smith himself went along as guide. Troop movement could be expected on either the river or its accompanying track. To encourage it, the two SAS troops would stir up trouble along the main River Sentimo and its continuation the Ayer Hitam.

The SAS went in three days before the Gurkhas and established themselves in ambush on the Ayer Hitam above Babang Baba. de la Billière and 4 Troop positioned themselves on the south bank and 1 Troop on the north, though not of course opposite each other. This was when Wilkes found Letts's loop in the river and was shaken by the devastating effects of SLR bullets. No enemy came by for three days so de la Billière sent patrols up- and down-stream to look for signs of activity. Corporal Wally Poxon investigated towards Babang Baba and after being alerted, most providentially, by the throb of a diesel generator found a large army camp with dozens of men stripped to the waist building defences.

This, de la Billière realized, must be the enemy's response to the 2/2nd's previous assaults, and that the place to catch enemy boat traffic now was even further downriver beyond the camp. He took 4 Troop there accordingly, accepting the risk of being on the wrong side of all those soldiers because of his men's ability to lose themselves in the jungle. They marched in a wide detour around the "Guitar Boogie" and "Kingdom Come" ambush sites as well as the camp, crossed another tributary and hit the river again further than anyone had been before where the enemy would least expect trouble.

The rainstorms had ceased, the river-bank gave good cover among dried-out mangroves, and Tudor had the whole Troop in ambush by one o'clock on 1 September. de la Billière and Low guarded the bergens at the immediate rendezvous 50 yards behind and seized the opportunity to catch up with events elsewhere; but although 1 Troop was only 5,000 yards away, they could not be raised, and de la Billière again felt guilty for being in the wrong place in order to satisfy his personal compulsion. Base responded however, and signals were tapped out and received, coded and decoded, though there was still a backlog when at one forty-five the ambush sprang into murderous life.

Two longboats out of a possible four (the following ones being but fleetingly seen) were allowed into the killing zone; their eight-man crews were smartly dressed and looked out keenly, though for all the good that did them they might have taken their last few minutes of life easily. The killing was accomplished coolly and professionally, and after two minutes' firing the stillness of death lay on the water. The leading boat had sunk and not a ripple emanated from its occupants. The second had grounded within two yards of the nearest trooper, and its crew lay in its bottom without a twitch or a groan.

The first men to return from the ambush burst into the rendezvous before de la Billière and Low had collected their codes, maps and signals. They all left hurriedly nevertheless, prudently because the crews of the rear enemy boats again justified the Indonesians' reputation as worthy opponents by landing and advancing rapidly. A mortar opened fire from the direction of the big camp before long, and signal-shots then indicated a large-scale follow-up. A lengthy journey to the border lay ahead, made longer by the need to give the camp a very wide berth. But by nightfall it became clear that the enemy assumed the Troop to be taking the direct route and had lost the trail.

4 Troop reached the border in three days without incident, unlike earlier Indonesian raids deep into Malaysia when heavy retribution was usually exacted on the way out. That was not only because the British had more helicopters with which to position cut-off groups, but largely because the Indonesian soldiers, despite their undoubted courage, were not trained to anything approaching the standard needed to pioneer a diversionary route through unknown jungle and had to plod back on the well-worn track by which they had come. On this occasion, however, they were also otherwise engaged, as will be apparent.

Maurice Tudor received a Mention in Despatches for this action as a culmination to his many and invariably successful operations. He had commanded his Troop as a sergeant for three years and de la Billière saw no need to replace him by an officer. Rather, Tudor was to become an officer in his own right and the first ranker ever to command a Squadron, an honour that is not bestowed lightly in the SAS since the Regiment's quality depends more on that of its Squadron commanders than any other single factor.

Meanwhile, the Gurkhas had arrived on the Poeteh, guided by Lawrence Smith, who underwent the split mental condition common to the SAS in those circumstances: delighted to be surrounded by large numbers of brave and competent soldiers, but appalled by the clashing of mess-tins, the thwacking of kukris and the tramp, tramp, tramp of the boys marching. Also present was a gunner officer from New Zealand, Captain Masters, forward observation officer for the guns that were now being lifted by helicopter to remote spots whence they could best support cross-border operations from friendly territory. The technique had been pioneered during this campaign and would make possible the advance on Port Stanley in the Falklands.

Bullock put 40 men in ambush on the Poeteh and its track, with 25 in a secure base to the rear where Smith also stayed:

"Once you've taken them in you're better off out of the way and let the Company commander get on with it; which he did. Young chap, quite good really."

Smith was ready to take action should the need arise; though what he might have done, but could not, was to keep in touch with the SAS in the field. Thus Bullock did not learn of Tudor's action, which would certainly have interested him greatly, and neither he nor Wilkes knew that they were rather too close to each other for comfort.

Collaboration between Gurkhas and SAS may have been loose, but apparently it worked, for the day after the latter's engagement a company of Indonesians hurried down the track from Berjongkong and straight into the ambush. The Gurkhas were outnumbered by three to one, but that only became evident after the first 25 enemy had walked into the trap and lost twelve men. Then it was no longer an ambush but a battle. The main body came storming in from the flank, perhaps expecting the usual SAS patrol, but not in any way dismayed by the formidable force they actually met. The ferocity of the Indonesians was hardly surprising after their recent losses, even without their knowing that they had picked the right outfit on whom to wreak revenge, if they could.

Bullock was quick to see that withdrawal was imperative and urgent. His machine-guns were well sited to cover this, but as each group fell back on his orders to a check-point just behind the ambush, so the enemy was equally quick to realize that they had left, following into a hail of fire with unheeding courage and to the admiration of the Gurkhas. The mêlée around the check-point surged in to five feet at one moment and seemed dangerously confused, but Gurkha discipline held and Bullock was able with great skill to withdraw his force to the secure base with only three men unaccounted for.

The missing men were the Company Sergeant-Major, the signaller, and Masters the gunner, whose absence was critical at just this moment when gunfire was essential to check the still-advancing enemy and enable a clean break to be made. But, and here lies the justification for touching on this exciting encounter which would otherwise be out of context, Smith came to the rescue.[1] Inactive, unseeing, but with the sharp ears of long experience, he formed in his mind an amazingly accurate picture of the developing situation:

"You note the volume of fire and where it comes from; mortar there—burst there; that's a rifle, rifle, rifle, rifle; light machine-gun, one of ours . . ."

Realizing that the Gurkhas were retiring with the enemy after them, Smith alerted the guns on the border, worked out a fire-plan which he presented to Bullock on his arrival and, with the latter's ardent approval, put into immediate effect. Smith had never been a gunner, but the SAS pride themselves on being able to fill any breach; had a tank surprisingly materialized among the trees, he would equally confidently have driven it into battle.

Smith's first sighting round startled the jungle very close to where Wilkes and 1 Troop still lay in ambush on the Ayer Hitam. That was the alarming climax to an hour's anxious listening to the savage din of a major battle not far behind them, and seemingly coming closer to judge by the occasional mortar-bombs which also exploded nearby. Enough being enough, Wilkes withdrew the Troop some distance and tried to find out what was going on from his Squadron commander, who was, of course, miles away and out of touch. Then he asked base, who told him about Tudor's ambush for the first time, advising him that the river-banks were probably being searched. Later, at the evening call, Wilkes was ordered to move and did so. It was not a happy time.

Smith found the range and the effect was telling, the enemy

---

[1]The full story is told in *A Pride of Gurkhas*; see Bibliography.

halting and keeping his distance. The Indonesians tried engaging with mortars, but whenever one fired, Smith gave that a salvo too. Bullock waited 90 minutes for the three missing men; that is to say, his Company did, but he himself went back with two Gurkhas to find them. They ran into a large party of enemy, which was surely inevitable, and killed several instead of all three being killed themselves, which was surely not. Culpably foolhardy? Sublimely brave? No one can say who was not there, but such acts by a commander for his men will make his unit invincible.

The final withdrawal went smoothly with one night-stop; shell-bursts controlled by Smith brought up the rear and in the last stages heavy mortar-bombs too, discouraging the enemy and earning Bullock's generous thanks: "Without his help we would have been faced with a running battle back to the border." And that could hardly have been accomplished without more casualties. He thanked the gunners too for an impeccable performance, in person because the gun position was also the border landing-point.

There too was the Gurkha signaller with a riveting story of how he had shot one of a group of enemy surrounding him at such close range that the body fell on top of him, and of how after a discreet, death-feigning pause he had crawled out, evaded the enemy, who were everywhere, and walked the five miles back without map or compass. But Master's story capped even that and it was not yet ended. Arriving later in the day with his strength nearly gone, he told how he and the Sergeant-Major had been similarly isolated in the battle of the check-point; how the Gurkha had been shot in the leg and completely immobilized; how he himself had fought back to earn a respite; and how when the main battle flared up and distracted the enemy, he had hoisted his companion onto his shoulder and staggered with him out of the combat area and for an incredible 6,000 yards further. That was his absolute limit so he had laid down his burden and come back alone for help, utterly exhausted but ready to turn straight round as he knew he would have to do if the man was to be found.

And so it was; Bullock led the search party, which Smith—who can doubt it?—joined and further endeared himself to the Gurkhas by finding a winching-point, homing-in the helicopter in a thunderstorm and supervising the lifting of the Sergeant-Major whose life and limb were saved, but only just for gangrene had begun.

A serious casualty meant inescapable publicity so it was put out that the battle had been in Sarawak. Thus the only people in the know apart from the participants and a very few on the British side were the local Indonesian commanders. They should have told Djakarta, but probably did not so as to leave their high command with the comfortable impression that aggressive operations into Malaysia were continuing splendidly. Unwillingly therefore, the British abetted the enemy's propaganda on which his Confrontation largely depended; but that was unavoidable because the military security of Malaysia came first.

At the Kuching base the masculine environment permitted that delicious sensuous pleasure, the discarding of sweaty clothes. de la Billière stretched luxuriously on his verandah with nothing on his mind but the next operation, a wholly congenial preoccupation, and nothing on his body but his Army issue briefs, tropical cellular. Immediately below him several cars drew up at the front door, but without disturbing his absorbed tranquility, until a tingling at the back of his neck caused him to turn in alarm and behold with awe the Brigadier West Brigade Bill Cheyne, the Director of Borneo Operations Major-General George Lea, the British High Commissioner for Malaysia Lord Anthony Head (later to become Colonel Commandant of the SAS Regiment) and full supporting cast of staff officers.

"We've come," they said, "to be briefed."

"FIND BATU HITAM"

September 1965; and now the Gurkhas were on their own, the SAS having told them all they knew and helped them all they could. The operation de la Billière had been mulling over was quite different in nature, and also in the manner of its initiation; without giving him any opportunity of dreaming up his own ideas or exerting his usual pressure, Brigadier Cheyne had told him, straight, to go and find Batu Hitam camp. Nevertheless, the job was a proper SAS function; communist subversion in the Lundu district had increased and the continuous stream of revolutionaries from across the border must be stopped.

A colourful article entitled "Picnicking in the Lion's Den" by one such individual shows how simple it was for a small team to evade detection by the skilful use of jungle and acceptance of hardship. This group lay-up by day and moved on tracks at night "when the enemy patrols were very passive which is an English characteristic," and avoided Land Dyak villages which were "despicably primitive and pro-English." Arriving near their destination, they were looked after by local Chinese communists, hatching plots and disseminating their message of hope, or vicious doctrine, depending on the viewpoint. Life was still hazardous; a Gurkha patrol once came within ten yards of their hideout. It was very clear from the article that the organization depended greatly on the system of camps in Kalimantan for training, assembly and jumping off.

Batu Hitam, the camp that never was, presented a challenge that "A" Squadron was delighted to pick up. Intelligence knew it existed but not where, nor whether it was moved from time to time as a further impediment to finding it. Taking a line from Gunong Kalimantan where the trail was well marked, across the Pueh Range to Lundu, the final staging-camp must surely lie somewhere in the six miles separating the rivers Bemban and Sempayang. de la Billière determined that such an area needed the whole Squadron, less 2 Troop who were still with the Cross-Border Scouts. He would go too, of course; if his recent exercises in commanding from the field had fallen a mite short of expectations, there would be more advantage to be gained this time and every reason for developing the techniques until they worked. "When will he ever learn?" muttered Condie darkly, but no attention was paid to him.

Planning and rehearsal were conducted normally, that is to say painstakingly, with particular emphasis on communications and the function of base in relaying messages between outstations when an addressee could not be raised directly by the sender. Also high in priority was snatching prisoners as a promising means of finding the camp, an exercise that was not easy to accomplish neatly and safely because it was necessarily done with both arms at the critical moment before the rest of the enemy group could be engaged. Sergeant Malcolm Allen was appointed 1 Troop snatcher and practised the art on his fellows with such assiduity that they never knew when he would jump and began jumping involuntarily themselves.

The whole force crossed the high Pueh mountains on 10 September and then separated for three troop areas. The scope and daring of the enterprise deserve to be recognized; a dozen four-man patrols, carefully coordinated for optimum coverage and to avoid muddle, would search for up to three weeks in a confined area that was fully garrisoned by the enemy and, for Borneo, thickly populated. It was not just a matter of each patrol combing its area, but of constant change in the light of discoveries so as to localize the goal and finally reach it. Should one patrol be compromised, the others would be set back or even endangered. Being in the jungle himself, de la Billière could meet troop and patrol commanders to hear their news at first hand and take decisions far more realistically than by relying on cryptic signals. His HQ comprised four men, including his Sergeant-Major, which was both prudent and allowed him to patrol on his own account.

Maurice Tudor and 4 Troop were given the southern area between the Sempayang and its tributary the Batang Ayer, in the centre of which was Batu Hitam village though that was no longer regarded as anything but the roughest guide to its namesake camp. Almost universal cultivation made searching extremely difficult at the best of times as previous patrols had found, and September was the worst of times because the season required the locals to be out in force on the "ladangs." Experienced though he was, Tudor could do no more than inspect the area through binoculars from the jungle fringe, which revealed nothing significant. No prisoner was snatched because none of the likely tracks had enough cover and locals were everywhere.

3 Troop were in the centre bordering the Batang Ayer. The initial task of the Troop commander, Foley, was to snatch a prisoner and the best place to do that was on the Sawah to Bemban track, first discovered by Graham-Wigan of "B" Squadron back in January and regarded as a most promising objective ever since. Foley planned to use the whole Troop, but first went forward himself with Troopers Jackson and Blackburn to find a good spot. While they were there, a platoon of 30 soldiers toiled up the ridge and rested at the top, as people do after a climb when they apprehend no danger. Yet there were two curious circumstances which might or might not have been significant; they carried no packs and were seen before they were heard, so silent was their approach.

The same platoon returned in the afternoon, but now made no effort to conceal their presence. They rested as before, rattled their weapons to check them, talked, smoked and relieved themselves in the bushes just as any group of soldiers would do; but there was something intangibly abnormal in the atmosphere and the watchers caught the tension, as well they might with three of them against 30. There was no question of snatching one of this lot, but it could easily happen the other way round, and adrenaline served its vital functions of intensifying perception, strength, and speed of reaction for fighting, flying or both.

One man stooped to pick up his rifle, quite casually it seemed, but was it? Then he and a companion strolled over to another pair and after a few words all four lined up and entered the jungle where the patrol hid breathlessly some eight yards in. The man opposite Foley could not have seen him because his eyes were on the ground; but he did see something that made him tense, stretch out his hand as a warning, raise his weapon, and sign his death-warrant. Foley shot him three times, Jackson and Blackburn followed suit against their nearest targets upon the instant, and all three turned and ran so quickly that Foley's man was still falling.

With impressive speed the enemy reacted with saturating fire from every weapon he had, but Foley and Jackson were untouched as they sped towards the troop rendezvous. Blackburn was going well too when they caught a glimpse of him to their left, but he took a diverging course and was soon lost to view; why? It made no sense, but only the man in a spot knows what he sees and feels; like James Condon in whose case no one would ever know. The enemy followed up hard, and Foley, re-united with his Troop, had no option but to retire after waiting for Blackburn as long as he dared.

This was not the sort of operation in which the main concern now became to reach the border safely: firstly, a man was missing, and secondly, de la Billière had no intention of calling off the search for Batu Hitam until it was found or time ran out. The enemy being present in strength, he signalled for a company of the 2/2nd Goorkhas to help search the contact area in case Blackburn was lying there wounded. Neill willingly sent one and Lawrence Smith went back to the border to lead it in. With 100 men behind him—he had worked on them and they swished now, rather than tramped—he became, first, uneasy, then anxious, and finally the most wretched sergeant-major in the British Army; for he, a founder-member and father-figure of the reborn SAS with Woodhouse's standard of excellence to live up to and twelve years jungle experience, was lost.

Even Smith's own dictum on which a generation of troopers had been raised—"You're never lost in the jungle even though you don't know where you are"—returned to smite him, because now it mattered very much that he should know precisely where he was so as to meet his Squadron commander at a specified time and place. He had taken the usual meticulous care with his navigation, but no stream, ridge or other landmark confirmed his calculations. Smith's ears glowed a radiant scarlet, proclaiming his shame to the following horde, though being themselves of dusky pigmentation they might, with luck, not recognize the symptom. Unable to contain his distress, he halted the column as though for a rest and went forward alone with feigned composure and a fervent but faithless prayer. Directly in his track and not 200 yards on, de la Billière awaited him, but so deep had been his chagrin that, rapport or no and despite his near-bursting relief, he concealed the truth with an effort both then and afterwards.

The Gurkhas went right up to the Bemban track hoping for a scrap, but the enemy was not there. Neither was Blackburn, and de la Billière's heart sank. There must, of course, be no question of assuming the worst without positive evidence, but all he could think to do was institute the usual helicopter search and ask the artillery to fire a gun at intervals as a guide to the border and safety.

Then he prised Foley and 3 Troop away and told them to search the Batang Ayer basin as originally planned. There they found signs of an extremely interesting camp, around which were heavily used tracks and four tall trees with climbing-spikes and seats at the tops, while from within it came sounds of domestic activity and small arms practise; but before they could reach viewing distance, signal-shots announced the arrival of a large enemy search force—not surprisingly considering all the British activity—so there was again no choice but to move on.

To the north, 1 Troop was allotted the River Bemban and its hinterland east of Bemban village, outside which Wilkes set up a snatch ambush and Allen awaited his chance; but Foley's contact not far to the south persuaded de la Billière that the enemy would now be snatch-resistant, so he told Wilkes to proceed with the search and Allen was unfulfilled.

The Troop split into patrols and searched in ever-increasing circles, without misadventure though Shipley suffered a heart palpitation which he thought momentarily might be fatal. He was Condie's lead scout as usual, very experienced after three Borneo tours and mentally prepared, he believed, for anything; but having sidled round the spreading buttresses of a great tree in undisturbed primary forest, he found himself without any transition fully exposed on a hillside completely cleared of undergrowth, gazing up at a massive fortress which reminded him of Durham Castle. He sprang back with irresistible momentum into Condie and Callan, who had bunched when they should not have done. All three then collapsed in a huddle, not at all in the best tradition of the Special Air Service.

The fort was empty, as they found after a more circumspect approach. When at last they entered, with eyes wary for booby-traps, they were much impressed by the formidable complex of protected sentry-posts, machine-gun dug-outs and mortar-pits, cleverly sited to observe all helicopter activity over the border and to confound the most skilful jungle warriors, themselves. It was, however, an entirely military outpost and not the communist camp they sought; nevertheless, 1 Troop's fifteen-day search was so thorough that de la Billière felt able to discount the possibility of Batu Hitam camp being in their area.

Blackburn diverged from Foley and Jackson because that way allowed him to place the greatest distance between himself and the enemy in the shortest possible time, which he badly needed to do, so heavy and accurate was the fire. Nevertheless, he fell, but being conscious of no wound realized that his belt had slipped to his ankles and thrown him, so he kicked it off and sped on into the shielding forest. After covering 300 yards at full speed, he stopped to catch his breath and listen; he was certainly being followed, but now adopted caution as his policy, moving silently and covering his tracks until nightfall when jungle noises supplanted warlike ones. Then he had leisure to assess his chances, and they were poor. Just recovered from sickness on his first operation of any kind, in an environment very different from the Royal Electrical and Mechanical Engineers' workshop to which he was accustomed, he had 9,000 yards of alerted hostility before him and worldly goods that were only too quickly mustered: Armalite with nine rounds, map, escape compass, which he found to be rusted solid, jack-knife, field dressing, matches, and one small packet of nuts and raisins.

There would certainly be much goodwill from the Regiment, but that did not seem of any practical help when, at first light, signal shots came from every side including the direction of the Troop rendezvous. So, he was on his own; but he was fit, his load was light, lack of food would not weaken him for several days and life-giving water was abundant. Success was at least possible given singleminded determination, and having assimilated the SAS ethic well, Blackburn called that into play. He covered 2,000 yards before darkness halted him again; not far, but his progress was silent and trackless.

On day three he came to the upper reaches of the Batang Ayer, where locals working in "ladangs" forced him to retrace his steps and cross the river elsewhere. Being without a useable compass, he then followed the trend of the headwaters further to the southeast. He heard a helicopter, which was heartening even though he could do nothing about it. For the next two days he made steady progress up the gentle slopes of the main ridge foothills. He heard de la Billière's gun for the first time but could not pinpoint its position for innumerable echoes and neither did he trust it, not being a standard operating procedure.

He felt hunger now but suppressed it, knowing that food was the least important of his needs; a new pair of boots would have been far more welcome for his were splitting and that was serious. Nevertheless, he noticed a place where pigs had eaten some sort of fruit and tried one which they had discarded, like the Prodigal Son; presumably it nourished him a little—orangutans maintain their great frames on nothing else—but when he searched around and found only a few nuts, which tasted horrible, he realized that his remaining energy was much better expended in making distance in the right direction.

On day six he tackled the steep climb to the 4,500-foot border ridge with greater caution than ever, for here the enemy would be expecting him. Sure enough, on crossing over near Gunong Tempurong, he again heard signal-shots to north and south. Pressing on eastwards, he shied away from established landing-points as dangerous, hoping for a natural clearing where he might use his matches to light a smoky fire and attract the helicopter; but there was none, and he resigned himself to yet more nights in the wild and to walking further again than he had already come.

Yet, in the cool sweet air of freedom, day seven was wonderfully different. His march was downhill all the way, beginning in steep "ulu" but soon on a track which there was nothing to stop him using; then came "ladangs" being tilled by people to whom he could wave openly, and he rested that night in the luxury of a friendly village. Day eight was better still; marching with flip-flop bootsoles but swinging stride in company with a local Border Scout returning from leave, he attained the golden road to Sematan, and thumbed a lift.

"Not bad," they said in the Squadron, "not bad at all"; especially de la Billière, who found that waiting for people to turn up became increasingly trying with experience. The whole operation was far from bad either, indeed it was unique; 50 men, commanded effectively from the jungle, had roamed for nineteen days over a strongly garrisoned enemy area with only one setback, and the standard of jungle and other skills that enabled them to do so can only have been of the highest. Never before had so much detailed information been gleaned; all there was to be had, near enough. Except Batu Hitam camp.

The failure would normally have been transformed into a tooth-gritting challenge, but as things were it was excruciating because the tour was ended. And so "A" Squadron bowed out of Borneo and the story, with much honour but less acclaim, for such is the SAS way of life; particularly true was it of this tour when the Squadron deliberately played second fiddle to the Gurkhas in their major effort, forming an essential component of an undoubted tactical success which might yet prove strategically significant too. Then again, the information on which the Gurkhas entirely relied had been amassed as much by "B" and "D" Squadrons as by "A," but that too fitted the ethic; the aim must be achieved, but who achieves it is immaterial, or as nearly so as human pride can be subdued to a lofty principle.

It would be intriguing to follow the men from "A" and the other Squadrons into the future, and perhaps identify some of them with those rare moments when the dagger has momentarily flashed into public view from beneath the cloak; but that is not the SAS way, nor could they do their job were it possible. Sergeant-Major Lawrence Smith can, however, serve as an example; he may at times have been a handful to control, but de la Billière was in no doubt that his initiative and decisive leadership were exceptional and recommended him for a Military Cross, which he received. The MC is an officer's award and he, a Warrant Officer Second Class, earned it by doing a commissioned officer's job on active service for a long time with "Skill, courage and devotion to duty far above the norm." After completing his time in the SAS, he went on to confirm that assessment of him by rising to command no less than a battalion in the Sultan of Oman's armed forces, until the war there was won in 1975. Then, like so many of his fellows, he found it impossible to lead a civilian life and became difficult to trace for the purpose of hearing his reminiscences of Borneo. "Ah yes," enquiries would elicit, "I think he's doing something in the

Middle East''; and although that will certainly evoke suspicion that the ''something'' was underhand in the worse traditions of modern spy fiction, and although a very few ex-SAS have let enthusiasm overtake discretion to some extent, the proud fact is that many of Britain's allies around the world are given vital help by these men in the best traditions of the Regiment, both as to skill and honour.

Lawrence Smith died prematurely in 1978, in his bed; but his memory endures as one of the Regiment's greats, who restarted the Regiment in 1950 and built it into what it is today. The officers may think they did that and the sergeants likewise, but both know that both are right: ''The gentlemen hauling and drawing with the mariners and the mariners with the gentlemen, showing themselves to be one company'' (after Francis Drake).

Even as ''A'' Squadron packed up and ''B'' settled in, the Indonesian communists judged their moment to have come and, having fomented riots and feverish excitement in the capital, they initiated what they believed to be the inevitable march of history; and muffed it. Before breakfast on the first of October, a group of dissident officers seized six generals and tortured them to death most horribly. That was evidently a standard operating procedure designed to discourage all enemies of the people; but who were the people, and who their enemies? By teatime, loyal troops under Generals Suharto and Nasution had utterly crushed the revolt and then the ''parang'' was in the other hand.

CHAPTER 12

SQUADRON OPS

"B" Squadron's Second Tour, October 1965 to February 1966

Coherent news from Djakarta was slow in coming and took further time to evaluate, so that Lieutenant-Colonel Neill of the 2/2nd Goorkhas was able to squeeze in another "Claret" operation. He called it "Flat Banjo," which was not a mealy-mouthed euphemism because banjo, verb transitive, means in the trade precisely what Major Joy and "B" Company did to seven soldiers in a speedboat at Large's place on the Koemba: killed them all and sank the boat.

There followed what the SAS called a "be kind to Indos" period, to give the latter a chance to indicate whether the coup and counter-coup would cause them to modify their aggressive policies. Developments certainly seemed encouraging, for chaos reigned. The Djakarta mob burnt down the communist headquarters with even greater verve than it had applied to the British Embassy; the army significantly did not intervene, though its commander in central Java lagged behind events in the capital and declared for the communists, while in Sulawesi Island the communists attacked the army. The economy was in such ruins that it could hardly be said to exist. Soekarno was rumoured to be in protective custody while still nominally presiding over the government. General Suharto began to emerge as the key figure, but his attitude to Confrontation was not yet known.

The pause gives an opportunity to recall that the 2/2nd Goorkhas and 22 SAS were not the only marauders across the length of the Kalimantan border. Many battalions qualified for the honour and had achieved some notable successes; while the Australian and New Zealand SAS performed just as effectively as the British, according to impartial observers of whom 22 SAS was not one.

The para-SAS companies had been hard at work too, though mostly restricted to border surveillance in wild areas. In September, however, the Guards Independent Parachute Company under Major L. G. S. Head were allowed across the Sabah border to act offensively. Sergeants McGill and Mitchell with two patrols ambushed 40 enemy, killed five of their scouts and escaped unscathed. This professional performance and others were to result in the formation of "G" Squadron in 1966. That would be a welcome addition to 22 SAS whose services were increasingly in demand, but which they felt unable to achieve by normal recruiting having exhausted the potential market when raising "B." Standards would on no account be lowered, but since volunteer guardsmen came forward with the enthusiastic backing of their own establishment—an agreeable change from precedent—sufficient numbers passed Selection.

"B" Squadron now returned to a very different scene from the one they had left in February. Where they had ventured uneasily with blank maps, British soldiers now roamed at will for several days' march into Kalimantan. That, while admirable, was also challenging as "B"'s first patrol led by their Sergeant-Major, Ball, discovered; not only was there a long way to anything of interest, but crossing a wide river beyond which the enemy had withdrawn was particularly daunting lest it flood without warning and cut off retreat at a critical moment.

On, on, to Batu Hitam; which "B" had looked for first and would now certainly find, all others having failed. 6 Troop tried the Batang Ayer, which "A" had thought most promising but proved not to be; and Intelligence opinion reverted to the "ladang" area around Batu Hitam village itself, where patrolling was very difficult and the locals had become impatient with SAS patrols popping out of the jungle fringe and asking where the camp was.

Major Terry Hardy had relieved Johnny Watts in command. Originally a Sapper, who enjoyed bomb disposal as far as it went but needed more excitement, and physically so hard that he had passed Selection without preparation, Hardy favoured the direct approach. To resolve the Batu Hitam enigma, he advocated marching through the "ladang" with a force large enough to defend itself, investigating each of the several likely localities until he found the right one and then destroying it. That would be a great change from anything the SAS had so far done in Borneo, but the risk of casualties among civilians as well as SAS personnel was high, which was anathema to the General's policy. Hardy's thinking was, however, implemented to some extent in his ensuing operations.

"Being kind to Indos" brought no reciprocal gesture and it was they who ended the respite by sending an incursion to the Katibas basin in the Third Division of Sarawak. Whether that conformed to General Suharto's policy or stemmed rather from local enthusiasm, General Lea took no chances and again let slip his dogs of war; if the enemy could be taught beyond all doubt that Malaysia was inviolate, he ought logically to conclude that Confrontation was a distracting and unnecessary addition to his many grievous problems. In the First Division area 2/10th Gurkha Rifles fought two successful actions, including the famous one in which Lance Corporal Rambahadur Limbu earned the only Victoria Cross of the campaign. The 2/2nd, not to be outdone—and it was hard to outdo them—fought four, and "B" Squadron 22 SAS fought one; not the usual small aggressive patrol, but nearly the whole Squadron under Hardy himself, a rare departure for the SAS.

"PRETEND YOU DIDN'T HEAR"

Hardy took 6, 7 and 8 Troops to John Edwardes's "Island" to pick up 9 Troop (already there except for its commander Captain Alec Saunt and one patrol who were searching with undimmed zeal for Batu Hitam) and nineteen Cross-Border Scouts under the redoubtable Sergeant Nibau. All practised together, particularly with claymore mines, which Hardy planned to use on the flanks of his ambush. The objective was the Bemban to Sawah track, which "B" Squadron had yearned to exploit ever since they first discovered it, and the aim was to inflict as many casualties as possible. Major John Slim, who came to give the final briefing, wagged his finger at the scouts and warned them, just for a laugh, which he got:

"I don't want to hear of you lot taking any heads."

The approach down the spur from the Pueh Range took three days. Nibau and his Ibans used their jungle skills to the utmost, so the chances were good that the patrol went unobserved. On the fourth morning the battle was set in array on the crest of the spur as Hardy had planned, so many patrols having been there that he knew exactly what he would find. The wide, well-trodden, north/south track led down to Bemban on the right and

Sawah to the left, and was intersected by a smaller ridge-track which was handy for approaching and withdrawing. The junction resembled a roundabout rather than a crossroads with the central clearing 40 yards across (a helicopter landing-point without a doubt). The ambush extended for 25 yards beyond this area on either side; the flanks were dropped back at right angles behind claymores pointing outwards to guard against a "roll-up." On the right was 7 Troop, Captain "Duke" Pirie, augmented by a patrol from 9 Troop and nine scouts. 8 Troop on the left, similarly reinforced, was commanded by Sergeant Bigglestone, who had been promoted since the last tour when he had shown his worth. Captain Andy Styles and 6 Troop protected the rear.

Just behind 6 Troop was Squadron headquarters of eight men, one of whose tasks was to check every man through on retirement when urgency, noise and confusion might make it extremely difficult. Hardy, however, was not there but in the centre of the front, supported by Jim Penny (now a Lance Corporal) and Jeb Aitcheson; they were both armed with silenced submachine-guns to deal with any small enemy groups without compromising the ambush for bigger game later.

Two locals came by carrying bananas and it seemed, eerily, that 100 eyes intent upon them from only a few feet away must surely excite an extra-sensory response; but they passed on oblivious. The next travellers, however, a man and a boy, did indeed receive a message though it was wholly carnal: somebody in the rear, who could not know that his moment was ill-chosen, farted. The sound rumbled comfortably rather than blared, but its frequency spectrum was so manifestly human that the pair halted involuntarily right in front of Hardy, turned their heads and—obviously—thought furiously. Penny reacted too, lifting the muzzle of his weapon very gently and his eyes to Hardy's, with a grimace intended to convey a strong recommendation to mercy.

A slow head-shake relieved Penny profoundly as Hardy thought rapidly. Killing locals was not allowed, thank God, so that was not the issue. These might be detained but would then be missed at their destination and a search by their fellows could compromise the whole force. Let them go and they could report only their suspicions. The man muttered to the boy and no interpreter was needed to understand him:

"Keep moving; pretend you didn't hear."

They walked on, pictures of innocence, but having passed

over the brow and out of Hardy's sight they paused again while the man blazed a tree with knifecuts; and the tree he chose was the one behind which the left-hand man of the ambush, Sergeant Jimmy Hughes, was hiding.

Word came back to Hardy, who realized that an enemy reaction was now likely. The Indonesians would probably send up a platoon to investigate what was, after all, no more than a bad smell. That would suit the aim of the operation very well. Even if he deployed a company, "B" Squadron was in a commanding position with probably superior firepower and certainly superior training. The enemy might, of course, send a battalion or cut off the Squadron silently from behind, but to take counsel of those remote possibilities, when he probably though he was dealing with a four-man patrol, smacked of overdoing prudence to the point of timidity.

The waiting was trying nevertheless, and hours must elapse before the enemy could appear; but the men were in good heart for this their first major operation, the largest to be mounted by the SAS in Borneo. Hughes on the left and Bigglestone next to him were very experienced and knew that the first contact might well be theirs; but then came someone who was not experienced at all, Trooper John White, Billy's brother.

Billy White had been buried in Singapore, but John had accompanied the family to a memorial service at Hereford and had been so impressed by the SAS itself that he joined. The Regiment had hesitated to accept him at first, fearing he might be motivated by revenge, but that was nonsense; he was merely picking up his dead brother's sword and continuing the good fight. Now he lay cocooned in shrubbery with just a peephole view of the track in front and a cord knotted to a twig that dangled above his nose. He was feeling lonely because although he knew his Troop commander to be five yards on his left and a veteran trooper, Jake Vaughan, the same short distance to his right, he could see neither. More isolating still, they were both quite at home in circumstances very strange to him; he read his book, but desultorily for it failed to grip him.

He dozed a bit too, every other man being allowed to, until three-thirty in the afternoon, "When all of a sudden I heard these heavy feet running; crash! What the hell's that?" Hughes and Bigglestone were in no doubt that it was the enemy beginning his attack, and their experienced ears told them much of how he planned to do it. Having approached silently, speed was now his policy; though not in one charging phalanx but in dashes with one half covering the other forward. His force was spread on both sides of the Sawah track for a classic "roll-up."

The first enemy to break cover stepped onto the track opposite Hughes, obviously not yet expecting trouble and going hard for the ambush centre. Having already appreciated that this was an assault and not a group in transit, which should be allowed into the ambush, Hughes shot the man dead. Instantly, others appeared to his right and left and 8 Troop was in action, firing fiercely at very close range; John White saw figures flashing by his peephole and let fly, for the first time in earnest. The enemy retaliated commendably quickly though his shots were mostly high, except for one which hit the ground in front of White. Dirt blasted into his face and, worse, eyes. He was blinded, permanently, he thought in a moment of real dread and what a time and place for that to happen; but copious tears washed out some of the grit, admitting first a glimmer of blessed light and then allowing him to shoot again, blearily.

On the nearside of the track, five of the enemy charged towards the flank patrol, but Hardy had sited his claymores well and one was detonated. The result was shocking even to the watchers who expected it; hats, limbs, bodies flew and then lay grotesquely still, "a right mess." The remaining two claymores pointing down the track were fired blind and produced screams and groans, evidently from a follow-up force which must have been halted in its tracks for it never appeared.

A stunned lull ensued and Hardy realized that mortar-bombs were flying right over his own head and landing not far to his rear, he hoped not among 6 Troop. Alerted, he spotted the weapon's next discharge at the far edge of the clearing, where its field of fire was unimpeded but its crew of two were just visible. Penny and Aitcheson killed one with their submachine-guns and the other made off without the mortar.

"Stop!" ordered Hardy, so as to hear whether the enemy was still engaging. He was not. Eleven visible bodies were reported with no SAS casualties, and Hardy spent little time deciding that immediate and fast withdrawal was the right course of action. He might have waited for more of the enemy to come up. Indeed, Styles with 6 Troop in the rear was fretting at missing the action and urged Hardy, "Come on, let's sort 'em out." But the enemy had already been hit hard 10,000 yards inside his own territory, the point was made and the law of diminishing returns would surely operate from now on. What purpose would be served by risking casualties which were particularly undesirable in the "Claret" concept? Much better now to concentrate on avoiding any.

The drill whereby each Troop's withdrawal was covered by another and every man was checked by name had been carefully rehearsed, for the good reason that when a static formation suddenly becomes fluid and a running man first seen five yards away may be anybody, trigger-fingers become tautly sensitive. Now, the enemy had been neutralized, but not everyone knew that. On the left wing of 6 Troop, where they had listened to the noise in front and mortar-bombs bursting nearby without being at all sure who was winning, they were particularly alert for an enemy break-in.

8 Troop's turn came to go, by curving into the centre-line and back along the ridge-track; and how Vaughan and White failed to hear either the order or the movement, while Hughes and Bigglestone outside them did and conformed, can only be explained as one of those things that happen in the jungle.

"Suddenly everything was deadly quiet," says White, "and Jake said, 'Christ! They've all gone.' And I said, 'What do we do Jake?' And he said, 'Get to hell out.' So we went roaring back, not across the front but straight towards the check-point at an angle. It was quite an experience. 'Turn your hat inside out,' Jake said (to show the recognition band, which was red), and then started shouting, 'Jake Vaughan, John White' at the top of his voice; and there were a couple of guys ready to open fire, but one of them said, 'Hold it! I can see the band.' And then we were through and bounding away up the road."

The two guys in question blasted the jungle hip-high behind Vaughan and White preparatory to retiring themselves. They were 6 Troop Sergeant, Dick Cooper, and another newcomer, Ken Elgenia, who had passed Selection with White and was now considerably sobered by having nearly shot his friend. The recognition procedure had worked but, hell, it needed to in the fleeting moment between detection and action which was all the jungle allowed. It could easily go wrong: a hat-band was only effective if the man still had his hat; and British names shouted by British voices might well be drowned by the noise of battle.

Later, when he had time to reflect further, Elgenia became uneasily aware that he had a problem which was all his own. His name was not British (though he himself was) but French Canadian. No one outside Canada had ever heard of it; neither could they pronounce it—Eljeeny—which in any case sounded like a first cousin to Ali Baba or the equivalent in whatever country he happened to be campaigning. Worse still, he and White had joined the Squadron after the tour started and were by no means intimate with all its members, what with the constant coming and going of patrols. It worried him a little.

The passage back was exhausting, uphill all the way at full speed with one night-stop, but Hardy's assumptions proved right and if the enemy did try to intercept he was far too slow. Intelligence indicated about 20 enemy killed, and although John Slim would have liked more, he pronounced the operation a success. General Lea expressed no judgement either way, but was probably well satisfied, for at the end of November when at least 120 Indonesians had died over the First Division border for the loss of one Gurkha soldier, he thought that was enough for the time being and imposed another "be kind to Indos" break.

Lea found himself strangely undecided, nevertheless. Sound military doctrine teaches that one does not give a half-beaten foe time to recover, but harries him until he gives in. The Indonesians showed no sign of doing that, probably because their government, such as it was, had no idea that its frontier troops were indeed being beaten and "Claret" secrecy prevented the truth being told. On the other hand, the border seemed secure, and Lea was confident in his troops' ability to deal with any incursion. There were the usual restraining counsels too, with which for the first time he surprised himself by instinctively agreeing. He enjoyed his command hugely, gratefully aware that no general could ask for a better one and that most would never put their long years of preparation to such a worthy task with such splendid troops; but now he found himself wishing, quite simply, that he could call a halt to "young men killing each other."

The revelation of the British military mind may seem unconventional, but, in truth, our armed forces are a peace-loving pressure-group in the most literal sense. Now, the issue was when and how much to relax the pressure, though one such easement happened by routine. Nick Neill and his hatchet-men, those purveyors of death and scourges of the border the 2/2nd Goorkhas, reached the end of their tour and left. An honest pacifist would surely expect their going to result in blessed peace descending upon a strife-torn Borneo; but for some inapprehensible reason the reverse occurred.

* * *

Not at once, though, for December was an uneventful month in which the enemy licked his wounds and no doubt wondered where he was going to be hit next. Even in Djakarta all seemed calm, but below the surface turmoil seethed. The generals tried to topple Soekarno, whose great personal charisma and political skill could not be quickly overriden. He would not ban the communist party, but an ominous groundswell of resentment against it heaved among the people and that Suharto exploited; not only did he turn a blind eye to anti-red excesses, but when the communist leader Aidit was captured, he was quickly shot and it was rumoured that thousands of his followers were being locked up.

In the wilds of Borneo, however, the communists were still able to infiltrate Malaysia. Lea drew a clear distinction between them, who would never give up even when Confrontation ended, and the Indonesian Army who presumably would. The search for Batu Hitam and the CCO trail was therefore pressed ahead with vigour; and with high hopes too after Saunt's patrol saw fourteen armed Chinese heading westwards on a track which came over the mountains in a direct line from Lundu and could not but lead to the camp nearby. Yet, when he took his whole Troop in for a final shoot-out that the communists would remember as a "Bad Day at Black Rock," there was still no camp, and nobody used the track. The anticlimax was overwhelming. A little further, but how far it was.

Styles and twenty men tried the area west of the Bemban where Roberts and McGillivray had so nearly succeeded; then again with Charlesworth and a company of 42 Commando Royal Marines; followed later by Howell lower down the river. None of them found anything; "B" Squadron's tour would end in February, and laugh as they might that the CCO, like the Irish, changed the question when somebody looked like solving it, their mood was quite grim and very determined.

1966 came, bringing reasonable hope to the Borneo peoples that the New Year would be a happy one. No major raids crossed the border either way, but SAS patrolling continued so as to check that the enemy was as quiescent as he seemed. Pirie took his Troop to the Koemba and found the river traffic to be much curtailed; no longer did large diesel launches bring up stores and troops. He had been authorized to remind the enemy that he was never safe, so a pathetic two-man boat had to be the target.

"APA NAMA?"

In the light of hindsight it might have been better if more patrols had acted similarly. Towards the end of January 1966, Intelligence warned of an imminent incursion from a place called Sentas across the border from Tebedu. Brigadier Cheyne was for once able to order a pre-emptive strike in the manner originally envisaged for all "Claret" operations. He selected Hardy's "B" Squadron, and thereby greatly disgruntled the 2/7th Gurkhas whose area it was.

No patrol had ever visited Sentas, surprisingly because Tebedu had always been one of the enemy's favourite targets. There was no time now for preliminary reconnaissance except from the air, which showed the village to be dilapidated and deserted by its inhabitants. Believing that the village had been converted into an armed camp, the British employed artillery fire against it, a rare expedient but practicable in this case because the longhouse roof could be seen from the border ridge and accuracy was assured. But bombardment alone could not ensure that the place was unusable, so the SAS went in.

A total of 44 men were mustered from 6, 7 and 8 Troops. 9 Troop was engaged on a mission which it should hardly be necessary to specify, so numbers were made up by eight New Zealand and Australian SAS, a few Cross-Border Scouts, and a Royal Artillery forward observation officer whose guns waited ready behind the border ridge. Accompanying the force to the River Sekayan was a platoon of the Argyll and Sutherland Highlanders, whose task was to hold the crossing, the enemy camp being, inevitably, on the far bank.

The final approach had to be in darkness to achieve surprise, so Hardy struck the river 1,200 yards upstream from the objective on the third evening and waited for nightfall. Then bergens were left with the Argylls, faces blackened (Fijians and Ibans excused), a strong swimmer wearing flippers took a rope across the Sekayan to enable the rest of the group to pull themselves over, more swimming than wading. A main communication track bordered the far bank, with a telephone wire looped along it which was quickly cut. Then 6 Troop, whose turn it was to lead, set off for Sentas with Sergeant Dick Cooper in command and Hardy well up in front. Charlesworth's 8 Troop followed, and Pirie's 7 Troop brought up the rear.

It rained, making the night dark but the track was easy to follow. Some 300 yards short of the village, a log bridge over a steep-sided tributary reached the end of its useful life just as the men were crossing and fell with a hideous crash into the muddy stream. No one was hurt and the noise could have been mistaken for a dead tree falling. The place was ideal as a defensive position through which to withdraw and Pirie made a note of it.

The plan was to surround Sentas silently by night and attack at dawn, but two small features revealed by air photographs had to be taken into account before the village could be reached. Situated on knolls to the right of the track, the first feature was a collection of huts interpreted as a pepper farm, and the second a heavy anti-aircraft machine-gun. The latter would on no account be disturbed until the morning when it would receive special attention; but Hardy thought that the farmer and his family should be gently persuaded to stay quietly where they were and resist any temptation to influence events.

Log steps led up to the pepper farm and 6 Troop deployed for its preliminary task, of hearts and minds or gunboat diplomacy as circumstances demanded, keenly alert for the unexpected. Among the men who advanced up the steps and spread out around the edge of the little plateau were Mason and a scout leading, Cooper, Lou Lumby and "Ginge" Ferguson with silent weapons, Ken Elgenia, Bob Bennett, an Australian, two Maoris, and Fred Marafono, who noticed a telephone wire as he climbed and thought it significant, but said nothing assuming that Hardy had seen it too. All being ready, the latter moved towards the largest of several huts with his weapon in one hand and a bag of sweets in the other, an imaginative provision for winning the farmer's heart through his children's stomachs but which is now a rather sensitive recollection for his only return was a bullet past the ear.

Lumby and Ferguson supported Hardy with their silent weapons while he retired quickly behind a small hut near the entrance which he had thought was the cookhouse but now proved to be a reinforced sentry-post, though unmanned. Mason meanwhile had spotted a washing-line and crept forward to retrieve a shirt from it which was unmistakably military and confirmed that this was no pepper farm but an armed camp, perhaps the one they were looking for.

The SAS certainly got the better of the fire-fight which ensued, for none of them was hit while many of the enemy were, to judge by cries of distress and the cessation of firing from individuals who had revealed their positions by gunflashes. It was frightening when the big machine-gun opened fire from the next knoll but its aim was high, either because it could not depress sufficiently having been positioned for air defence or because its gunner was afraid of endangering his friends.

Then Elgenia had what nobody denied was a good idea and hurled a phosphorus grenade at the main hut to see it alight and illuminate the enemy. He maintains that it did so, but others say that it hit the sentry-post roof and bounced back among some of the SAS before exploding and they have painful evidence to authenticate their version. Cooper, in particular, was drenched in blazing phosphorus which set his hat and clothes alight and burnt him severely. Others suffered in lesser degrees, including Elgenia himself. But much more seriously, their tactical advantage was reversed at a stroke, from being still able to exploit the enemy's surprise and quite possibly carry the position, to being picked out individually in a glare of light.

Retirement was inevitable and imperative, but it was not done precipitately; standard operating procedure and conditioned instinct both affirmed that to run away from an alerted enemy would invite casualties because he could shoot accurately and unimpeded, and now that several men carried illuminated bull's eyes it would have been suicidal. The five or six men in the phosphorus patch therefore got down again into firing position, one inadvertently in "the big shit-pit that was there and stunk pretty bad," and emptied two magazines each into the huts with forceful deliberation. Enemy fire which had been heavy slackened, and then the word was "Go!" All reached the river track safely.

Nevertheless, the enemy could not but know that he had won the second round and quickly prepared to exploit his luck. First with grenades; "I don't know if you've heard a grenade coming through trees?" asks Elgenia; and in case you haven't, it goes swish, smack, thud as it hits foliage and branches. Hardy shouted, "Grenade!" and dived off the track; Charlesworth, with whom he was discussing the next move, disappeared in the other direction and the missile exploded where they had been. It was also of phosphorus and two more men received searing doses. Further grenades came down and Hardy saw that he had now lost the initiative as well as the position; he ordered retirement, at least to behind the tributary barrier which Pirie of 7 Troop in the rear, hearing the firing, was already preparing for defence.

Elgenia, however, missed hearing the order to withdraw, as White had done on the Bemban track, but instead of just staying put he began a series of adventures which were logically comprehensible but not credible. Assuming that the setback was only temporary and that the Squadron would at once return to the attack, he went straight back up the steps. Half blinded by the flashes, in visibility that was negligible anyway, he felt someone jostle him and try to snatch his rifle; he pushed the man away rather roughly, thinking him to be a panicky Border Scout, and carried on to the top where he settled himself into a comfortable firing position, changed his magazine and waited for battle to recommence. Screams came from the main hut, confirming that the enemy had suffered casualties.

People moved close to him and at first he assumed them to be friends in line with his fixed idea, but very soon a prickly sixth sense demanded an intellectually painful and physically terrifying reappraisal. They did not speak, which would have clinched the matter at once, but made small sounds and moved in a way that was indefinably but distinctly not European. Elgenia was unusually sensitive to such influences, and becoming convinced that they were enemies, squarely faced his predicament.

He got up slowly, walked quietly down the steps and the enemy followed; not, presumably, because they knew who he was or they would have shot him. They may have thought him to be their leader in some definite purpose, his delicate perception sensing a confidence in their movements that was not at all like those who move through the jungle wary of what they might find. He reached the main track and turned left. So did they. He would dearly have liked to run, but it was too dark and the enemy might have cottoned on. Elgenia walked the 200 yards to the tributary; not as to a sanctuary, however, but an even greater hazard, for he fearfully remembered his concern for his name of which he was as proud as the next man but wished now was any other. Firing broke out behind him and he wrote himself off the strength of the Regiment; but it was not directed at him.

"Apa nama?"

The urgently shouted words meant nothing to Elgenia, though the voice was British. The man who shouted them used Malay because there might still be a Border Scout on the wrong side of the gully and everyone in the Squadron would, he thought, understand such a common phrase; but Elgenia was too newly joined even for that. Had the question been in English—"What's your name?"—he might have answered straight, "Eljeeny";

but confused as to what was wanted of him, he said, "John? John White?" not to gain admittance by false pretences but to make contact with his friend who would recognize his voice.

In close quarters fighting enemies often talk to each other to demand or accept surrender and particularly to mislead, learning simple phrases from the other's language for the purpose. Calling a typical enemy name was an old dodge to get through his outer defences and the SAS were not to be fooled that way. Elgenia, halting, heard a muttered conversation between several men, though not the words or he would have joined in.

"Says he's John White; OK?"

"Hold it; John White's been through, hasn't he?"

"Yes, saw him myself."

"Fire!"

Seconds only were available for decision as several shadowy figures appeared behind Elgenia, who was certainly not John White and now seemed to be one of the group. He stood at the very epicentre of a claymore mine whose blast was shattering. After it, nobody remained in view. John White himself, by now well to the rear, could not do for Ken Elgenia what the latter had done for him.

Deterred no doubt by the claymore and the gunfire, which Lieutenant Norris the gunner brought down on the camp on Hardy's orders, the enemy did not press forward immediately. The tally of men was checked and four were missing. Three of them, Lumby, Ferguson and an Australian had been seen by other members of 6 Troop to rush down into the river ablaze with phosphorus. It seemed quite possible that by the time they regained the track the enemy sallying from the camp had cut them off. The recent burst of firing lent weight to that theory and, if so, their plight, though grim, was not necessarily hopeless; the river could be crossed in many places and their training and experience fitted them to extract themselves and survive.

But nobody could offer an explanation for Elgenia's absence. Unless? Unless . . . The possibility that was the unthinkable truth began to seethe in Hardy's mind and in that of the man who had fired the claymore, and it was dreadful. If it was so, there could be no doubt that Elgenia was dead, killed by his friends.

Now, however, the river must be recrossed before it rose too far with the rain and the enemy could be reinforced from the adjacent camp upstream. As the Squadron moved back westwards, Norris brought the barrage along behind it at a brisk pace, so that those behind cried "Forward!" most earnestly as they raced just ahead of the bursts. The crossing was difficult to the point of danger, but all came safely over. This position was the emergency rendezvous, so Hardy stayed there until ten o'clock the next morning, oppressed with a sense of failure and hopelessness for the missing men that weighed ever more heavily with the dragging hours. Then the rope was cut and the force marched quickly back in the same day.

As Hardy had surmised, by the time Lumby and his two companions had washed off their phosphorus in the river and started back towards the check-point the enemy had reached the track, seen them and engaged. That was unexpected and literally a close shave, a bullet passing through Lumby's shirt; but then they reacted aggressively in SAS fashion, silenced the enemy momentarily and vanished. Moving east past Sentas itself, they confirmed that it was decayed and apparently deserted. A boat lay at the landing stage as though awaiting them, and into it they loaded their belts and weapons, guiding it slowly across the stream by swimming alongside. It was fortunate that they drifted with the current and away from the big machine-gun, which was still firing from its knoll.

Landing safely on the north bank they started to make their way westwards to the rendezvous; but coming across a newly-built longhouse, which could have belonged to an ordinary civilian community but in that position might equally well have been a base for a border screen of local scouts, they turned sharply right before anybody saw them, headed straight for the border and reached it even before the Squadron. It was a good escape and evasion exercise, which proved once again that all those qualities and skills the SAS are at such pains to acquire are essential if their sort of adventurous operations are to be attempted.

Hardy was nevertheless still thoroughly depressed when he reported to Brigadier Cheyne, who had to use all his ebullience and experience to reassure him. The operation had not achieved all its aims, but it was by no means a failure. The enemy had certainly taken casualties in the fire-fight and his camp had been thoroughly wrecked by the guns. Whether he would persist with his incursion, only events would show, but the attack should indicate to him that the British knew of his plan and he might very well not. The 2/7th Gurkhas naturally thought they could have done much better, for it had been essentially an infantry rather than a specialized SAS type of operation, but the claim was a bold one in the face of such a complete reversal of expectations in utter darkness. Time spent on reconnaissance is never wasted, says the adage, and lack of information was certainly critical at Sentas; but what if no time is available? Do nothing?

Even as regards Elgenia, Cheyne refused to despair. "I know the SAS," he said, and truly because Blackburn's solo walk was a recent and vivid memory. "They don't die easily and if he's alive he'll turn up"; and the infantry having withdrawn from the border after passing "B" Squadron through, he ordered them straight up again. It was a nice, even charming, gesture which Hardy wanly appreciated, but no more than a gesture because a man cannot stand in front of a claymore and survive.

Yet claymores were no nearer perfect than anything else. It had been known in practise for the charge of shot to emerge unevenly or in a mass, and even for antiwar protestors in America to sabotage weapons during manufacture, but whatever the reason Elgenia was not touched by a single pellet.

"When this flash went off I didn't know what it was, but I knew I hadn't been shot . . . there was hotness all round my body and I was lifted up in slow motion. Next thing I remember I was in the river; no weapon. The bank had been worn away by floods so I got under it. I heard shouting above me, John White's name. It might have been another head-call, but I couldn't answer. Then a lot of mortar fire came down, enemy I think; but it was our own artillery that came screaming in like express trains and one of the buggers landed in the water near me. That really set me up."

Keeping under the overhang, Elgenia let himself be carried downstream until he came to a natural ford of rocks with white water rushing over and between them. He could have leapt across had he dared, but there was no question of that because the machine-gun was firing along its length. He remembered his recent training.

"First get away from the scene of action as soon as possible—done—and then evaluate the situation. Aim? To get back to base. What have I got? No weapon, right; belt with bloody heavy and useless ammunition, sodden field dressing, water-bottles and emergency rations I can do without, and I'm not going to get across that torrent with it on so get rid of it. Ah! Make sure map and compass in shirt pocket."

Battered by sluicing rapids against rocks to which he had

nevertheless to cling for dear life, fearful for dear life of raising his head for the gunner to see, he went under many times as he wrenched himself from boulder to boulder and took in what seemed like choking lung-fulls of water. But he reached the far bank before his strength ran out, as he had coolly calculated he would. Pulling himself out under a leafy branch that swept the surface, Elgenia crawled into thick jungle and obscurity.

Exhausted, bleeding and bruised in a hundred places, seared with livid phosphorus burns, an arm and a leg torn from his shredded clothes, his map and compass gone, Elgenia counted his assets again. None. So what?

In the morning he took an approximate course from the sun which, on the equator, would bear east until noon. Having been somewhat punch-drunk the night before, he was clear-headed now and moved with the alertness and caution of an SAS soldier, slowly and with painstaking care to leave no tracks. The primary jungle was admirable for his needs, but offered no glimpse of the distant scene so he climbed a tree to spot the border-ridge, which was high and stood out well. He covered about one of the three and a half miles and the night passed quietly.

On the second day the primary forest changed to "belukar," which made walking more difficult and hotter for lack of shade, but there were often old fruit-trees in such places and he considered whether to spend time looking for them. Imbued with the SAS doctrine that no man is given up until hope had finally gone, he expected the border to be manned for him when he reached it, he being the only man in the Squadron unaware that it was a claymore which had hit him and that he *had*, very nearly, been given up. But nourishment would be prudent just in case he had to walk to the nearest friendly village and, luckier than Blackburn, he found a bunch of delicious small bananas. Then the "belukar" reverted to primary forest with low spurs between small streams up which he headed, sure of his direction.

Suddenly he saw a vision, and as suddenly he crouched down and no longer saw it. The image was retained only just long enough to fix it in his mind as a figure in green squatting on its haunches, like a woodland character from *A Midsummer Night's Dream* except that it was smarming its hair with oily cream and a rifle lay on the ground beside it. Then it faded and Elgenia began to doubt whether he had seen anything at all; peering for hour after hour into the jungle, keyed up to see things, he quite often imagined that he had. He must be sure whether this was a ghost or a man, for if the latter there would be others, constituting an emergency.

Elgenia raised his head sufficiently to see the figure's outline through the leaves, but it was just a shapeless green mass as motionless as the trees beside it and equally part of the landscape. How to be certain? Inspired, he made a low whooping noise that might have come from bird or beast, and ever so slightly the head turned, then froze again. Elgenia chuckled inwardly as he read the other's deepest thoughts, which asked in their turn, with mortal fear, "How now, spirit, whither wander you?"; though lest the noise came not from a spirit but a mortal foe the man dared not make the least move towards his weapon.

Feeling a warm glow of power and command of the situation, Elgenia regretted only his lack of a knife with which to resolve it unobtrusively. Instead, he crawled noiselessly away until it was safe to rise, then walked deliberately in the wrong direction taking care to make distinct footprints and bruise the occasional leaf. Finally, he retraced his steps for half the distance, this time undetectably, and resumed his journey to his own country another way.

He was, however, far from powerful as well he knew, with his presence revealed to the enemy and the border still too far to reach that day. He was climbing the foothills, though, and the country became typical "ulu" with rushing streams and densely canopied jungle giving sparse cover on the ground. Of overriding importance now was to pass the night unobserved. He debated whether to lie up under one of the few bushes whence he could move away from danger in any direction; but that might mean exchanging one prying enemy for another, so he searched for a hiding place where nobody would think of looking for him and lighted upon that classic resort of jungle fugitives, a pig-hole. Whether his was muddier, smellier or infested with more leeches, biting insects and bluebottles than Lillico's or Thomson's must be disputed between them, but it was all of those to an extreme degree. The resolution needed to lie there for eleven hours must surely have included an element of something more than just his own desire to survive. It did; his duty to the Regiment.

With no temptation to lie abed in the morning, he struck out for the border ridge with the usual care but also confidence. He was not a little pleased with his unaided navigation when he recognized features he had noted on the way in, which led him to the track then made by the Squadron and across the border-ridge itself. Approaching the landing-point rendezvous, he was so sure that friendly troops would be there that he decided to march boldly rather than present a furtive mien which might trigger a nervous finger. Even so, he saw the two Argylls a moment before they saw him, and all three leapt for cover to avoid any misunderstanding and conduct their mutual introductions with due form and deliberation.

"SAS; don't shoot," shouted Elgenia.

"Come out with your hands up . . . Now."

"Jesus!"

The latter invocation was not part of the drill, but what else could they say? Even when Elgenia had left the river he would have presented the convincing image of a broken-down scare-crow. Now, when fouled from matted hair to ragged boots with nauseous slime, he was hardly recognizable as human, far less as the British soldier with unimpaired vigour and morale which he actually was.

Not a hero, though, needless to say.

"Oh they were glad to see me back, obviously, because I was part of the Regiment; they cared more than they said. *I* was concerned for the Regiment too; I'd been an embarrassment to Major Hardy and I felt a bloody idiot coming back without a weapon."

The Regiment, however, thought he had really done quite well; at any rate his name in it was made—Algy.

Ten days later, Charlesworth took 30 men—including Elgenia, for his intimate knowledge of the country—to assess the effect of the raid on Sentas and its garrison, but they were frustrated by the river being flooded and impassable. Then, even as they were patrolling, the enemy showed that he had not been deterred from launching his incursion, by doing so from the next camp downriver, the SAS detecting many signs of it but being unable to intervene. It comprised about 70 men with CCO involvement, and nearly reached the Serian road before being checked and finally checkmated by helicopter-borne 2/7th Gurkhas in a series of bishop's and knight's moves that had by now been developed to a high skill. Few of the raiders returned to Kalimantan. The Gurkhas' achievement was most satisfying to them and they did not mind being given the opportunity at all; though the SAS did, a bit.

Now it was "B" Squadron's turn to leave Borneo as "A"

had done, wishing they could have had just one more try. But the moving finger had writ and they had to go; so after a final head-call, to ensure that nobody was still out looking for Batu Hitam, they went.

CHAPTER 13

ENVOI

Not only did "B" Squadron go, but nobody from 22 SAS came out to relieve them, the field being left to the Australian and New Zealand SAS. The Aden war was nearing its climax with the SAS heavily committed in souk and alleyway as well as desert, while in Borneo General Lea had reasons for hoping that Indonesia might be having second thoughts about Confrontation. Common sense certainly dictated that she should; if her chaotic economy were not reconstituted soon the communists might well take advantage of public disorder and rise again, and since she could not conceivably reconstitute it herself she must solicit aid from the west, which would not be given until she stopped behaving irresponsibly.

Confrontation would, in any case, get Indonesia absolutely nowhere so long as the British stayed in Malaysia, though it was hard to determine whether that message was beginning to sink in. However, there now began a gruesome and appalling massacre of communists by the hundred thousand, a savage expression of the loathing invariably engendered by those misguided people, which signalled the removal of a major malign influence.

Concurrently, Lea became aware of peace-feelers, surreptitious and tentative at first, but discernible. Despite incursions continuing—perhaps initiated by Indonesian blood-brothers of Nick Neill, or so as to save face and negotiate from strength—he ordered a halt to offensive operations as he had long wished to do. Cross-border reconnaissance to obtain warning of incursions continued, but the work was very hard with scant success because, as now became incontestably manifest, it was the deterrent effect of "Claret" more than the British defences that had preserved Malaysian Borneo for many months.

That was in March 1966. In April a second incursion came in towards Serian, one of the CCO's strongest areas; but the Army and Police were well up to their jobs and there was no real danger. At the same time, peace noises became less muted and the Indonesian attitude almost conciliatory. Economic help was sought, and Britain was the first to offer it—the two countries, as may be recalled with a wrench of the mind, never having been other than at "peace" with each other. Signs of change were evident in the field too; an SAS patrol watching an Indonesian base-camp found that the troops had left, to the delight of the villagers who invited the Australians inside to heal the sick and be entertained, a happy and fulfilling consummation for all the SAS Regiments.

May, however, brought yet another incursion, near Bareo, and truly it was an anxious time for commanders and men on the border, though they always succeeded in containing the raids; but General Lea with his ear to the ground did not re-start "Claret," and in an act of sublime courage announced that the troops would be home for Christmas. Later in the month Indonesia made a direct approach to Malaysia and a meeting was staged: the result became known as the "Bangkok Accord," although it did not resolve all the differences or stop incursions which persisted even during the talking. Leisurely face-saving negotiations continued in June, still accompanied by incursions, and it even began to seem that a serious attempt might be made to infiltrate Brunei and leave a force there after the peace. But at last direct visits were exchanged between the antagonists, and an Indonesian mission was established in Kuala Lumpur; it was led by none other than Colonel Moerdani, whose life had been spared by Large and was now put to good use. On 11 August 1966 peace was declared.

Victory was total. Not the sort in which the enemy is smashed to smithereens and then ground to pulp, but the better kind that all wars ought to aim for, whereby one's objectives are limited to those that are truly vital, the force used is adequate to ensure success but not excessive, de-escalation is pursued whenever possible, and propaganda is based on truth and never strident; so that when the day is won the least physical and mental damage has been caused and friendship can be renewed with the fewest hard feelings. The vital achievement was Malaysia's complete independence of Indonesia—even to the extent of retaining British bases or not as she chose (which she did). Friendship revived almost overnight. That was greatly helped by a change of government, for Soekarno had at last been toppled by Suharto, and although the latter had been as keen as anyone to crush Malaysia when the going seemed good he could now put the blame on the old reprobate.

General Lea assesses Confrontation as a serious attempt to dominate the tip of Asia and the islands—Maphilindo—in line with Indonesia's ancient empire. "Tactically, she tried to do it by armed subversion and infiltration to establish cells of terrorists and saboteurs, while strategically she built up considerable forces and threatened to use them. Such activity amounts not merely to an internal security problem: it is Aggression. It was beaten by reacting promptly and very firmly, by matching their strategic threat with Navy, Army and Air Force, and by inflicting disproportionate casualties until Indonesia was convinced that her aim of crushing Malaysia was unattainable.

"Success therefore was first and foremost a military one. It has been argued that the new regime in Djakarta coupled with the parlous Indonesian economy brought about the Bangkok Accord; those were certainly important factors, but the significance of our *military* contribution can best be judged by asking what would have happened if we had not given it. There can be no doubt that Borneo certainly and Malaya possibly would now be under the complete control of the Indonesians.

"Many voices were raised in favour of what was called a political solution, believing there could be no valid military one. This was dangerous muddled thinking because it posed a political solution as an alternative to a military, whereas in fact the two were complimentary. Peace follows war. When one side seeks a solution by force it has to be convinced by force that it can't succeed, and only then does a political settlement become possible. But side by side with military action it is very important to remove the economic, political or sociological causes of discontent on which subversion flourishes; though, again, in order to do so you must provide a basis of security so that the police, administrators and ordinary people can go about their business without fear."

Military action, however, can vary greatly depending on who takes it, the British approach being encapsulated in Lea's tribute to his men: "Morale was so high you could positively feel it. Partly from pride in a high degree of professional skill and achievement, but also from a sense of purpose. To ensure that the ordinary village dweller could choose his own way of life, poor and primitive though that might be, without living in fear of having his throat cut was a job supremely worth doing.''

What then was the butcher's bill, those ''disproportionate casualties'' that proved so decisive? British and Commonwealth troops, 114 killed and 181 wounded; Malaysian civilians, 36 killed, 53 wounded and 4 captured; Indonesian troops, 590 killed and 222 wounded for certain—so the number must be increased by those who could not be counted, especially across the border, but probably not greatly as the narrative indicates, and 771 captured of whom none was tortured or murdered. For Lea they were too many; but as the price of a nation's very existence against a huge adversary they were so slight as to be scarcely credible. Even the British offensive operations saved enemy lives, for he could not then mount his own incursions, which usually cost him far dearer than ''Claret'' strikes.

When Denis Healey rose in the House of Commons to set the seal on Borneo and close the file, he spoke both as the Secretary of State for Defence who had presided over the triumph and a deeply read scholar: ''When the House thinks of the tragedy that could have fallen on a whole corner of a continent if we had not been able to hold the situation and bring it to a successful termination, it will appreciate that in the history books it will be recorded as one of the most efficient uses of military force in the history of the world.''

''D'' Squadron had returned to Borneo in July but were not invited to the peace celebrations in Kuching. They and other units were not even allowed to stay in the capital so that the victory would seem to have been Malaysian with just the occasional help from Britain. In fact, the Malay Regiment from the mainland only hit the headlines twice: once when they were trounced at Kalabakan in 1963 and now when they strutted like conquerors among those they treated as inferior rustic colonials, provoking disturbances until confined to barracks.

The Malaysians' desire to run their own country was understandable but their method ungracious, and the SAS, banished to the Island, ''got a bit uptight'' as one of them reported. ''But then we said to hell with it if that's the way they want it . . .'' and went about their business tidying up a few loose ends. Jonathan Mackay-Lewis watched a house on the Serian Road for a CCO suspect, a Chinese girl, until locals started to cut down the ferns where he and his patrol were hiding. They stood up, smiled politely and withdrew, de-escalating the confrontation. Mostly, however, the Squadron led what they called a lotus-eating existence by which they meant filling their time constructively with hard training in jungle-craft, boatwork and, predictably, demolition.

They left Borneo along with all the British forces well before Christmas, relinquishing the Haunted House to which the ghost then returned; she was certainly there in 1978, when our driver was visibly uneasy at visiting the place and covered his tracks afterwards with wraith-repellent herbs in his windows. The Ibans, Land Dyaks, Muruts, Kelabits, Punans and the rest were turned over to the Malays under whom they prospered, if not exceedingly then rather better than they would have done under the Indonesians, or the communists.

THE FRONTIERSMEN

Can we ever fully understand men such as the SAS with their love of danger and compulsive yearning to attempt the impossible? Yet what is strange in laying hold of our brief span of life and living it to the full? In welcoming stress as a spur and overcoming its anxiety by achievement? In performing a service vital to humanity and enjoying it? Is it not far stranger to imagine that we can escape anxiety by avoiding stress or by taking pills, or that accepting our needs from others and working as little as possible for inflated wages will give us any satisfaction at all?

The SAS strive to attain skills and an endurance of hardship unlimited in degree for good practical reasons. The frontier, of its nature, is harsh, hostile and lonely; just reaching it and living there is daunting enough even before any task is attempted. Then, the SAS must be better fighters than their enemy without knowing in advance how good he will be, and only by keeping a jump ahead will they be able to surprise him by doing something he thinks impossible. The SAS go always a little further not just for the challenge but because they have to, and although a large unit can carry some individual weakness if the leaven is good, every man in a tiny SAS patrol must possess all the qualities.

The relentless pursuit of excellence is only possible for men who want to do it above all else, the least reservation reducing the standard. When Alf Tasker said, "If you're fighting for your life with a fifty-fifty chance you've *got* to *enjoy* it," he surely meant that if your heart is not really in it the odds against you will shorten. One SAS wife describes their dedication—to adventure, the Regiment and the nation—as "radiant," a particularly revealing insight, since it contains no hint of jealousy; perhaps she knows she is secure in accepting the old warrior-lover's confession, "I could not love thee, dear, so much, lov'd I not honour more." Such motivation is rare; though an enemy may well possess it, too, however evil we believe his cause to be, and we are lucky to have the SAS in our service to do vitally important and dangerous things that we cannot do for ourselves.

What of the risks though? The SAS do not want to die young any more than we do, and, by means of painstaking professionalism, they have every chance of merely fading away after many years as old soldiers should. The sad loss of James Condon, "Buddha" Bexton and Billy White must be seen against the corollary that all the others in their patrols ought logically to have gone the same way, and that those three with Lillico and Thomson were all the SAS casualties by enemy action in a major campaign lasting over three years.

The frontier on which the SAS operate is, firstly, the dividing line between civilization and barbarism, and to think that it has little significance for us because our peaceful life is an immutable natural order is dangerous. Wherever there is civilization, some barbarian will batter at its gates to plunder and enslave it, and we can only enjoy it if some of us are prepared to go out there and keep him at bay. It behoves us therefore to value our armed forces when times are quiet or the frontier is as far away as Borneo or the Falklands, aware that without them it could come closer and our friends be abandoned, to our shame as well as our disadvantage.

There is no law on the frontier. That is its second essence: no friendly policemen are on call and disputes are settled by bullets not judges, so that those who go there have no choice but to use force. Like so many cherished principles, the sanctity of human life is found in practice to depend on circumstances. Killing is sometimes justifiable even where law holds sway, and on the frontier it may be the only means of life and achievement. Its morality lies in ensuring that it is done in the name of civilization and that there is no less drastic alternative, which the British soldier does, with intelligence and deep concern. The mental effort and self-discipline he needs to master—or forego—the use of force in circumstances where most brains would seize solid with terror was well illustrated in Borneo, and to dismiss him as an unthinking man of violence is either naïve or wicked.

Our soldiers, sailors and airmen serve the community to a degree equalled by few, since they willingly put their lives at risk to do so. More important still is their contribution to civilization itself, which is simply stated: it could not exist without them; and easily understood by those who have not shut their minds to understanding it. What may be harder to grasp is that they, understanding it well and accepting their awesome responsibility, are themselves highly civilized, deserving our support, our thanks, and—why not?—our hearts.

GLOSSARY

MILITARY

Armalite	5.56mm calibre light automatic rifle.
Basha	Hut or makeshift shelter.
Belt	Carried essential short-term equipment.
Bergen	Main pack.
Claymore mine	Dished canister firing 900 steel shot in a cone.
L-P	Landing-point for helicopters.
LUP	Lying-up position.
OP	Observation post.
Panji or punji	Concealed sharpened bamboo stakes capable of inflicting serious wounds.
RPD	Ruchnoy Pulemyot Degtyaryov. Soviet 7.62mm calibre weapon, commonly called Degtyaryov light machine-gun.
RTU	Returned to unit.
RV	Rendezvous.
Sarbe	Radio search and rescue beacon for homing aircraft.
SLR	7.62mm calibre high velocity self-loading rifle.
SOP	Standard Operating Procedure.

BORNEO

"Amok"	Run in frenzied thirst for blood.
"Batu"	Rock, stone.
"Belukar"	Overgrown "ladang" with thick undergrowth, secondary jungle.
Border tribes:	
Iban or Sea Dyak	Sarawak, warrior race.

Kelabit	Sarawak, highlands centred on Ba Kelalan.
Land Dyak	Sarawak, 1st Division.
Murut	Sabah.
Punan	Sarawak, nomadic.
"Bukit"	Hill.
CCO	Clandestine Communist Organization.
Divisions	Administrative areas of Sarawak instituted by Rajah Brooke.
"Gunong"	Mountain.
"Jarit"	Murut delicacy of uncooked pork with salt and rice buried in split bamboo for a month.
"Kris"	Dagger with sinuous blade.
"Ladang"	Cleared jungle under cultivation.
"Padi"	Rice, wet or dry depending on how grown.
"Parang"	Jungle slashing knife, machete; often decorated with human hair.
RPKAD	Resemen Para Kommando Angaton Darat—Indonesian Para Commando Regiment; an élite unit.
"Tapai," "Tuak," "Borak"	Raw wine made from fermented rice or tapioca.
TNKU	Tentara Nasional Kalimantan Utara—North Kalimantan National Army. A Brunei-based guerrilla organization opposing Malaysia; launched Brunei Revolt in December 1962.

BIBLIOGRAPHY

BOOKS

Carver, M. *War Since 1945*. Weidenfeld and Nicolson, London, 1980

Geraghty, T. *Who Dares Wins: The Story of the Special Air Service, 1950-1980*. Arms and Armour Press, London, 1980

——*This is the SAS*. Arms and Armour Press, London, 1982

James, H. D. and Sheil-Small, D. *The Undeclared War: The Story of the Indonesian Confrontation 1962-1966*. Leo Cooper, London, 1971

——*A Pride of Gurkhas: 2nd King Edward VII's Own Goorkhas (The Sirmoor Rifles) 1948-1971*. Leo Cooper, London, 1975

Mackie, J. A. C. *Konfrontasi*. Oxford University Press, 1974

Mackinnon, J. *Borneo*. Time-Life International, 1975

Pocock, T. *Fighting General: The Public and Private Campaigns of General Sir Walter Walker*. Collins, London, 1973

Warner, P. *The Special Air Service*. William Kimber, London, 1971

ARTICLES

Bramill, Lieutenant-Colonel E. W. N. "Reflections on Borneo." *The Infantryman*, November 1967

Collins, Lieutenant-Colonel P. E. (Commander Army Aviation Borneo) "The Front was Everywhere." RUSI *Journal*, May 1967

Eley, Wing Commander D. L. "Helicopters in Malaysia." *RAF Quarterly*, 1966

Ferry, Major J. P. "Full Employment." *Journal of the Royal Artillery*, 1965

Fillingham, Lieutenant-Colonel J. A. I. "Operations in Sarawak." (⅔oth Gurkha Rifles) *British Army Review*, 1965

Foxley-Norris, Air Vice-Marshal C. N. "Air Aspects of Operations Against Confrontation." *Brassey's Annual*, 1967

Lyon, Lieutenant-Colonel R. "Borneo Reflections." *Royal Artillery Journal*, 1966

Mars & Minerva Journal of the Special Air Service Regiment

Mayman, Major I. "Company Operations in Borneo." (Tenth Gurkha Rifles) *British Army Review*, 1964

Millman, Major H. C. "Sarawak and Confrontation." *Army Quarterly*, 1966

Riggall, Major J. S. "Light Aircraft Operations in Borneo." *Royal Corps of Transport Review*, 1966

Stirling, Colonel D. "Memorandum on the Origins of The Special Air Service" and other articles; *unpublished*

The Times "The Malaysian Campaign." 12th, 13th, 14th August 1964

Walker, General Sir W. "How Borneo was Won." *The Round Table*, January 1969; and other articles

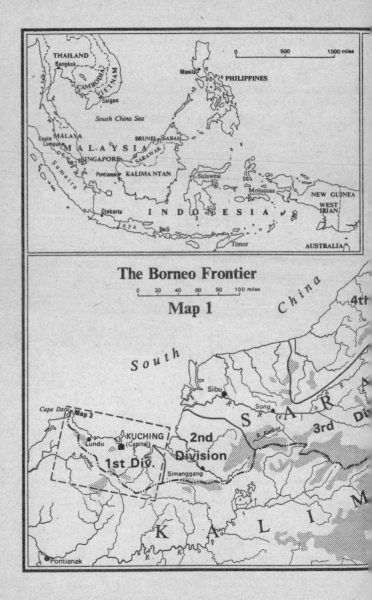

The Borneo Frontier

0   20   40   60   80   100 miles

Map 1

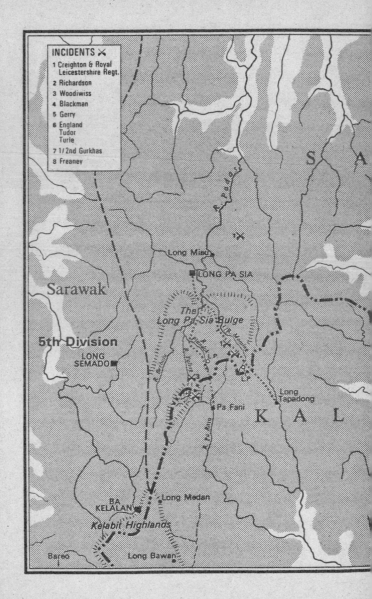

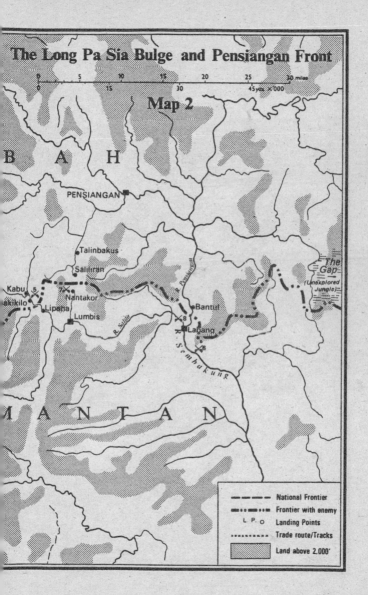

The Long Pa Sia Bulge and Pensiangan Front

Map 2

B A H

PENSIANGAN

Talinbakus

Salinran

Kabu

skikilo

Nantakor

Lipaha

Lumbis

Bantul

Labang

R. Semhukung

M A N T A N

The Gap
(Unexplored
Jungle)

– – – – National Frontier
▪▪▪▪ Frontier with enemy
L P ○ Landing Points
•••••• Trade route/Tracks
▨ Land above 2,000'

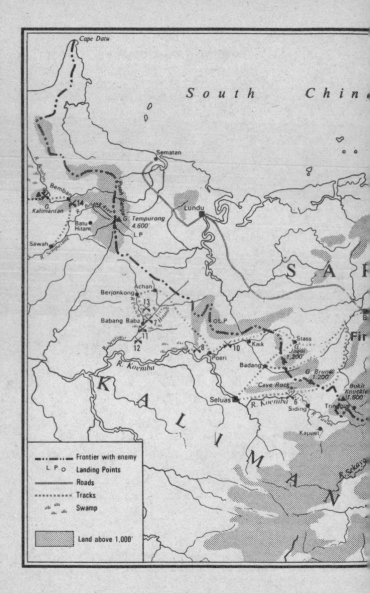

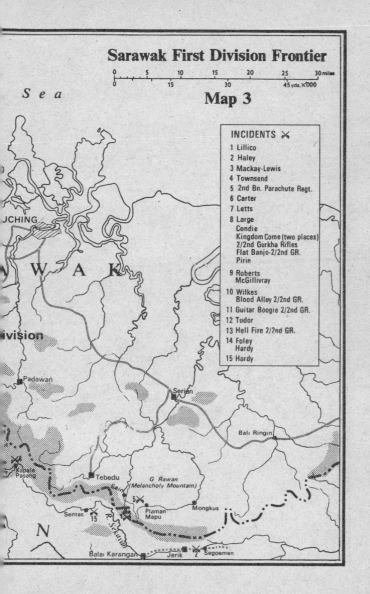

Sarawak First Division Frontier

Map 3

Scale: 0 5 10 15 20 25 30 miles
0 15 30 45 yds. ×'000

Sea

JCHING

WAK

ivision

Padawan

Serian

Bali Ringin

Kapala
Pasang

Tebedu

Sain

G Rawan
(Melancholy Mountain)

Sentas

Plaman Mapu

Mongkus

R. Seluman

N

Balai Karangan

Jerik

Segoemen

INCIDENTS

1 Lillico
2 Haley
3 Mackay-Lewis
4 Townsend
5 2nd Bn. Parachute Regt.
6 Carter
7 Letts
8 Large
    Condie
    Kingdom Come (two places)
    2/2nd Gurkha Rifles
    Flat Banjo-2/2nd GR.
    Pirie
9 Roberts
    McGillivray
10 Wilkes
    Blood Alley 2/2nd GR.
11 Guitar Boogie 2/2nd GR.
12 Tudor
13 Hell Fire 2/2nd GR.
14 Foley
    Hardy
15 Hardy

INDEX